THE CORINTHIAN LETTERS OF PAUL

THE CORINTHIAN LETTERS OF PAUL

An Exposition of I and II Corinthians

by
G. CAMPBELL MORGAN, D.D.

WIPF & STOCK · Eugene, Oregon

Wipf and Stock Publishers
199 W 8th Ave, Suite 3
Eugene, OR 97401

The Corinthian Letters of Paul
An Exposition on I and II Corinthians
By Morgan, G. Campbell
Copyright©1946 by Morgan, G. Campbell
ISBN 13: 978-1-60899-288-1
Publication date 3/26/2010
Previously published by Fleming H. Revell Co, 1946

G. Campbell Morgan Reprint Series

Foreword

If it is true that the measure of a person's greatness is their influence, not only on his own time but on future generations, G. Campbell Morgan must be regarded as a great person. His greatness is seen not only in the wide impact of his ministry on both sides of the Atlantic, but in the fact that his books are still read and studied sixty-five years after his death. Named one of the ten greatest preachers of the twentieth-century by the contributing board of *Preaching* magazine, Morgan made the Bible a new and living book not only to the congregations who listened to him, but the vast multitude of persons who read his books.

Fox sixty-seven years Morgan preached and taught the Scriptures and served churches in England and the United States. What is remarkable is that his commentaries and expositions of the Bible still speak to persons of a new millennium. There have been many changes in the world since he faithfully preached and taught the Scriptures, but the wide appeal of his books testify to the timelessness of his message.

Although he held pastorates in the Congregational and Presbyterian denominations, he had an ecumenical appeal to persons of all denominations and traditions. The mystic Thomas á Kempis once wrote, "He to whom the eternal word speaks is delivered from many opinions." In one of his sermons, he referred to the words of Amos that there would be a famine for hearing the word of God (Amos 8:11). The timeless work of G. Campbell Morgan addresses that hunger, as his books enable his readers to get beyond opinions to the living Word.

Wipf and Stock Publishers have rendered a great gift to the religious world in reprinting dozens of Morgan's books. This growing collection makes his books more available, so that readers have an option other than searching the internet for used, and often expensive, copies. Among this collection is the classic *The Great Physician* and commentaries on the Gospel of Matthew and John. Persons seeking a living faith and a meaningful encounter with God would profit from reading any of these Morgan books.

Near the end of his ministry, in a sermon entitled "But One Thing," Morgan commented on how Portugal changed the words of a coin after Christopher Columbus discovered America. No longer did the inscription say, *Ne Plus Ultra* (nothing more beyond) but *Plus Ultra* (more beyond). It is the hope of the G. Campbell Morgan Trust that the reprinting of these books will bring readers to the "more beyond," and an even deeper encounter with the Word in Scripture.

THE MORGAN TRUST
Richard L. Morgan
Howard C. Morgan
John C. Morgan

CONTENTS

I CORINTHIANS
- i. 1–8 9
- i. 9 18
- i. 10–17 23
- i. 18–31 29
- ii. 1–16 40
- iii 52
- iv 67
- v 79
- vi. 1–11 85
- vi. 12–20 90
- vii. 1–24 95
- vii. 25–40 100
- viii 105
- ix 110
- x. 1–13 120
- x. 14–xi. 1 127
- xi. 2–16 132
- xi. 17–34 138
- xii. 1–3 144
- xii. 4–7 149
- xii. 8–31 152
- xiii 161
- xiv 167
- xv. 1–34 182
- xv. 35–57 194
- xv. 58–xvi 204

II CORINTHIANS
- i. 1–11 225
- i. 12–ii. 11 229
- ii. 12–iv. 6 234
- iv. 7–v 238
- vi, vii 244
- vii, ix 250
- x 255
- xi–xii. 13 260
- xii. 14–xiii 271

I CORINTHIANS

INTRODUCTION i. 1-8	A. CORRECTIVE. *The Carnalities* i. 10-xi	B. CONSTRUCTIVE. *The Spiritualities* xii-xv. 57	CONCLUSION xvi

I. The Writers 1
i. Paul
ii. Sosthenes
	I. Divisions .... i. 10-iv
	  i. The Wisdom of Words and the Word of
	    the Cross .... i. 10-ii
	    a. The Contrast .... i. 10-25
	    b. The Application .... i. 26-ii, 5
	    c. The Wisdom .... ii. 6-16
		I. The Unifying Spirit .... xii. 1-31
		  i. The Creation of Unity 1-3
		    a. The Contrast 2
		    b. The Principle Implied 3a
		    c. The Power "In the Holy Spirit" 3b
			I. Concerning the
			   Collection 1-4
			II. Paul the
			   Worker 5-9

II. The Readers 2-8
i. Defined 2
ii. Saluted 3
   Grace and Peace
iii. Described 4-8
  a. As to Character 4
  b. As to Equipment 5-8
	ii. Causative Carnality Corrected ..... iii, iv
	    a. The Cause of the Schisms .... iii. 1-4
	    b. The Correction .... iii. 5-23
	    c. The Appeal iv
		ii. The Administration of Unity 4-7
		  iii. The Realization of Unity 8-31
		    a. Gifts of the Spirit 8-11
		    b. Ministrations of the Lord 12-27
		    c. Workings of God 28-30
		      Cf. xii. 31 & xiv. 1
			III. Timothy the
			   Worker 10, 11
			IV. Apollos the
			   Worker 12

	II. Derelictions .... v, vi
	  i. Discipline v
	  ii. Disputes .... vi. 1-11
	  iii. Desecration .... vi. 12-20
		II. The Unfailing Law .... xiii, xiv
		  i. The Law xiii
		    a. Values 1-3
		    b. Virtues 4-7
		    c. Victories 8-13
			V. Injunctions to
			   Workers 13, 14
			VI. Inter-relation of
			   Workers 15-18

FUNDAMENTAL
AFFIRMATION i. 9
	III. Difficulties .... vii-xi
	  i. Concerning Marriage vii
	    a. The General Question 1-9
	    b. As to the Married 10-24
	    c. Unmarried Daughters 25-40
		ii. The Law at Work xiv
		    a. General Instruction 1-3
		    b. Argument 4-25
		    c. Corinthian Application 26-40
			VII. Salutations 19-24
			  i. Of others
			  ii. Of Paul

i. God is faithful
ii. Ye were called
   into
iii. The Fellowship of
   His Son
	ii. Concerning Things Sacrificed to Idols viii-xi. 1
	    a. The Principles Stated viii
	    b. The Principles Illustrated .... ix-x. 13
	      1. The Limits of Liberty ix
	      2. The Abuse of Liberty .... x. 1-13
	    c. The Principles Applied .... x. 14-xi. 1
	      1. Definite Prohibition .... x. 14-22
	      2. Final Instructions .... x. 23-xi. 1
		III. The Ultimate Triumph .... xv. 1-57
		  i. The Gospel of Christ's Resurrection 1-11
		  ii. The Importance of Christ's Resurrection 12-34
		  iii. Intellectual Difficulties 35-50
		  iv. The Assurance and Challenge 51-57	

	iii. Concerning Women .... xi. 2-16
	    a. The Apostolic Praise 2
	    b. The Relation Between Man and Woman 3-12
	    c. The Appeal 13-15
	    d. The Dismissal 16
		THE FINAL APPEAL .... xv. 58	

	iv. Concerning the Lord's Supper ...... xi. 17-34a
	    a. Apostolic Praise Withheld 17a
	    b. The Corinthian Disorder 17b-22
	    c. Institution of the Supper 23-27
	    d. Responsibilities for Preparation 28-34
	  v. Conclusion 34b		

I CORINTHIANS
 INTRODUCTION   i. 1–8

  I. *The Writers*   1
   i. Paul
   ii. Sosthenes

  II. *The Readers*   2–8
   i. Defined   2
    a. Primarily   2a
    b. Ultimately   2b

   ii. Saluted   3
   Grace and Peace

   iii. Described   4–8
    a. As to Character   4
    b. As to Equipment   5–8
     1. " Enriched "   5, 6
     2. The Purpose   7, 8

   The Church at Corinth
   " All That Call "

I CORINTHIANS i. 1–8

PAUL's two letters to the Corinthians are among the most remarkable of his writings. We shall attempt a survey of them somewhat carefully.

To begin, then, with the first, and taking the first two verses in chapter one,

"Paul, called to be an apostle of Jesus Christ, through the will of God, and Sosthenes our brother, unto the Church of God which is at Corinth, even them that are sanctified in Christ Jesus, called to be saints, with all that call upon the name of our Lord Jesus Christ in every place, their Lord and ours."

There are one or two preliminary and simple things to observe. This letter was written in answer to one that Paul had received from Corinth. That is self-evident. At the beginning of chapter seven Paul wrote, "Now concerning the things whereof ye wrote." He did not get down very quickly to the business of answering the particular questions raised in that letter, because there were other things that he wanted to say, that needed to be said to that church. He dealt first with some facts in their condition, of which he was aware. We know how he had found out, and how the facts had come to his knowledge. In the tenth verse we read,

"Now I beseech you, brethren, through the name of our Lord Jesus Christ, that ye all speak the same thing, and that there be no divisions among you; but that ye be perfected together in the same mind and in the same judgment. For it hath been signified unto me concerning you, my brethren, by them which are of the household of Chloe, that there are contentions among you."

We do not know anything more about Chloe than that she was a householder in Corinth, a member of the church, and was in communication with Paul. She had written and told him about certain conditions in the church. So before coming to the questions they had raised, he dealt with conditions that he knew were existing.

We note first the structure of the letter; the first part, chapters one to eleven; and the second part, from chapter twelve to sixteen. These sections are quite distinct, while intimately related.

At the beginning of chapter twelve we read, " Now concerning spiritual gifts, brethren." This is the reading of both Authorized and Revised Versions. Notice that the word "gifts" is printed in italics. That always means that there is no equivalent word in the Greek; but it has been supplied, because it was thought to be necessary by the translators, to give the sense. Mostly, these additions of words are very useful in elucidating the subject. But sometimes they are hindrances. At this point I maintain that this word "gifts" is a distinct hindrance. It takes our thought off the principal idea in the mind of the apostle. If we go on in that twelfth chapter to the fourth verse we read, " Now there are diversities of gifts," which word is correct there. To translate literally the Greek word *pneumatika* is to read *spirituals*, " Now concerning the spirituals." We could substitute another word which exactly conveys the meaning, the spiritualities. With what, then, had Paul been dealing up to that point? Something, I venture to say, with which he was very glad to be done. At verse thirty-four in chapter eleven we read,

"If any man is hungry, let him eat at home; that your coming together be not unto judgment."

He had been dealing with something wrong in their habits. But he went on,

"And the rest will I set in order whensoever I come.
Now concerning the spiritualities . . ."

He was tired of the subject. The information he had received from the household of Chloe, and the inquiries he had received in their letter to him, to which he made reference in chapter seven, show he had to deal with these things of disorder that ought not to have been there, that needed to be corrected. At last when he had done all that, quite evidently there were other things of which he did not approve—" The rest will I set in order whensoever I come. Now concerning the spiritualities . . ."

What had he been dealing with then, in the first part of the letter? He had been dealing with the carnalities, the things of the world, the things of the flesh, the things that had entered into, and spoiled the witness and testimony to the people in Corinth. But now (as though he said, "Let me get away from these things, and deal with the higher, better, corrective things") "Now concerning the spiritualities . . ." That is the clear dividing line of the letter.

The whole letter can be taken in that way: the first part dealing with the carnalities, correcting; and the second, with the spiritualities, constructing. He was dealing with people who had certain responsibilities in the fulfilment of which they were failing, and the reasons are all found in those first eleven chapters. There is much positive teaching in them of course. Then he turned from them to the spiritualities, and we shall find a most remarkable balance between the corrective carnalities and the constructive spiritualities.

What were the carnalities? Divisions, derelictions from duty, difficulties in life, all caused by carnality. Those are the three movements in the first eleven chapters. When he turned to the spiritualities, he put, first, the unifying Spirit; secondly, the unfailing law of love; and, thirdly, the Gospel of the resurrection triumph. Those three spiritualities will correct all the carnalities. That is to summarize ahead.

Dealing first with the opening statement, we are introduced to the writers of the letter, and to the readers.

Who are the writers? Paul and Sosthenes. "Paul, called to be an apostle." Those two little words "to be" are printed in italics, which means they are not there in the Greek. Paul is not saying he is called to be an apostle, but that he is one. He is declaring his office and his vocation. This is more emphatic.

Go on to the next verse, "Unto the church of God which is at Corinth, even them that are sanctified in Christ Jesus, called to be saints." Here again the words "to be" are not there in the Greek. "Called saints." They are not called to be saints. They are saints. There is a tremendous importance in this. Paul was the apostle called; that tells his position. They were saints called; that is their definition. That is what these people were to whom he wrote.

Paul here insists upon his authority, "called an apostle of Jesus Christ, through the will of God." It is remarkable how constantly he did this. He did not do this in writing to the Thessalonians, or to the Philippians, or to Philemon. Reasons could be given for that omission in each case; but in every other letter he wrote, Corinthians, Ephesians, Colossians, and all the rest, we find that little note, whether at the beginning, or before the letter is ended, insisting upon his authority. There is no doubt—to use human language—that Paul almost had to fight for his position. He was, as he told people, "one born out of due time." He was not in regular orders, according to the view of certain people; but he said, I am "called an apostle of Jesus Christ through the will of God." Whatever he is going to write to these people, whether corrective or constructive, he reminds them who he is. There were some questioning that fact, but he insists upon it at the very beginning. "Paul, called an apostle by the will of God."

Then, interestingly, he introduces Sosthenes. He says, "Sosthenes our brother." The Greek there is "the brother," as though there were something peculiarly brotherly about Sosthenes. His name appears again in Acts xviii. 17, when he was beaten. We do not know whether that was the same man. At any rate, here he is mentioned, and Paul links him up with him in all he is going to say. He is "the brother." He has some very severe things to say; but he has linked up with him a man of brotherly heart. He is going to say wonderful things about the spiritualities, and Sosthenes is with him. I have no doubt he talked with him about the letter, and consulted with him. Here are the two associated in the writing of the letter.

Now, notice the readers—"The church of God which is at Corinth." We, in this period of the Christian era, with our New Testament, are familiar with its meaning. But supposing in the transmission of this letter to the church at Corinth, the bearer of it, arriving in the city, had lost it. And supposing a citizen of Corinth had found it. Of course they did not write letters then as we do, beginning, "My dear Sir," and ending, "I am, yours sincerely." They always put the names of writers and readers first. As this person unrolled the parchment, he would read, Paul, oh, yes, I have heard something about him. He was here at one time. "Called an apostle, a messenger of Jesus Christ." Oh, yes, I have heard about them. At that time they did know in Corinth something about the message of Jesus Christ. "Unto the church of God which is at Corinth," the ecclesia of God. Some stranger, not being a member of that church, picking up the letter, would ask, What does that mean, "the ecclesia of God"? Every citizen of Corinth knew about the ecclesia of Corinth. In every Greek city the ecclesia was—to use a modern term which will help us—the town council. It was the governing body in the affairs of every Greek city, consisting of a company of men called out to take oversight of the city. No slave was allowed to hold office. The members were free citizens. This citizen who I am supposing has found this letter says, "What does this mean? This man is writing to the ecclesia of God. Here is something I never heard of."

I leave him in his perplexity. We know what Paul meant. There was in his mind as he wrote, not only the old Hebrew idea of the church, the synagogue, the assembly, "the church in the wilderness," as it is once translated in the Acts; but also the Greek idea of a company of people constituted a body set in authority, the ecclesia of God. That is what the church is. "I will give unto thee the keys of the kingdom of heaven; and whatsoever thou shalt bind on earth shall be bound in heaven; and whatsoever thou shalt loose on earth shall be loosed in heaven." Those were the words of our Lord, moral authority, binding and loosing, keys the insignia of the office of the scribes. Paul is writing to a people constituted an ecclesia, but it is the ecclesia of God, the church of God in Corinth.

One could stay to say much about Corinth. At that time it was one of the greatest cities in the Roman empire, characterized by wealth, luxuriousness and lust, by extreme cleverness and the arguments of its philosophers. The language they used then was supposed to be the highest form of the Greek language. There was a phrase of the time, "To speak as they do at Corinth," which meant they spoke with accuracy and beauty, and with artistic finish. Corinth was the centre of everything intellectual, on the level of their own philosophies; but it was rotten at heart, utterly corrupt, given over to every manner of lasciviousness.

Paul is writing to God's ecclesia in a city like that, "the church of God which is at Corinth." It is interesting to notice he does not say the church of Corinth. That is a most unscriptural idea. The Scripture is particular. The Church universal; in Corinth the local manifestation. So it is found through the New Testament. The Church is one, but it has many local habitations. Paul is writing to the church in Corinth.

But more, and in that next sentence we find ourselves. This letter is written not only to the church at Corinth, but to "all that call upon the name of our Lord Jesus Christ in every place, their Lord and ours." I cannot read that without believing that Paul felt there that this letter he was sending to Corinth would have a wider circulation. So he included all who form membership in the Church of God, in Corinth, in any place, in every place, where they call upon the name of the Lord, their Lord and ours. Who are these people? They are saints, separated ones.

A wonderful letter, written by Paul, who has associated Sosthenes the brother with himself, to a church, an ecclesia, a body set in moral authority; but far more than that, a body or community of people who have a message, an evangel, a Gospel for that very city, with all its heart-breaking lust and necessity and agony, conceit and pride and ruin. They are defined, the ecclesia of God. They are sanctified, separated in Christ Jesus. They are men and women who are living life in union with Him, and they are "called saints."

Remember the general application of this letter. Think of it, as we take our way through it, not merely as addressed to a city of long ago, today lost comparatively and in ruins, with all its splendour gone, but as addressed to a church there, and to all who in every place call upon the name of our Lord Jesus Christ. This letter is to us.

In this next paragraph (verses 3-8) there are three things to observe: first, the apostle's initial greeting of these Corinthian Christians (verse 3); then, the thanksgiving that he uttered concerning them (verse 4); and, finally, the equipment which they possessed, which was the ground of his thanksgiving (verses 5-8).

His greeting. He had named them the Church of God—them that are sanctified—and his greeting followed, "Grace to you and peace from God our Father and the Lord Jesus Christ." Thus he used two words, "grace" and "peace," which are "from God our Father and the Lord Jesus Christ," and said that grace and peace were given to them.

"Grace," the great New Testament word, is found in every section of every letter which Paul wrote. That statement can be verified. Whether Paul was arguing or rebuking or exhorting or comforting, the word grace is always appearing. It is the word of the other writers too, but it is supremely Paul's word.

What is grace? The whole conception of grace is included in this greeting. The word "grace" first refers to the whole realm of order and beauty. It was an intellectual word, an artistic word, beauty as against ugliness, health as against disease, order as against chaos, all the realm of that which is beautiful. That is its first meaning. Then, in the Greek language this word, in process of time, as is so often the case in our own language, gained new significances and meanings; and grace came to mean a desire on the part of God—for it is postulated of Him all through—to impart these things of order and beauty and life to others. That is grace, a giving. Until, finally, the ultimate meaning came in the New Testament, and in no other Greek literature. Grace became not merely the realm of order and beauty and loveliness, and the desire to impart to others; but also the activity that carries out the desire. That is the grace of God, the activity of God. Grace is ultimately the activity of God which puts at the disposal of sinning men and women all the things that give delight to Him. That is how Paul begins his salutation—"Grace."

"And peace." We cannot put grace and peace in the other order. That is a characteristic of the Bible. We must proceed in the Divine order. Nothing is out of place. There is a meaning also in the order of the names. If we read here, "the Lord Jesus Christ," be careful that we keep that order, and do not say, Jesus Christ the Lord. So here, "Grace to you and peace." Peace is the result of grace. It is the corollary of grace. It is the activity of God that produces peace for the child of God. Take the word "peace," again we are dealing with most familiar things. The Greek word is peace in a certain sense, not cessation of activity, or stagnation, not a stillness in which there is no movement at all. The Greek word is *eirene*. Irene is a transliteration of the word translated peace. Irene means always peace beyond conflict. It is not stagnation, but it is the ending of strife and conflict. That comes only through grace. "Grace and peace."

"From God our Father and the Lord Jesus Christ." "From"—notice the remarkable way in which these names are put into conjunction here. They are in conjunction in all the activities of grace, and peace that results. Grace has come from God our Father and the Lord Jesus Christ. Notice the apostolic definition: unity of substance and unity of action, "From God our Father and the Lord Jesus Christ." That is how Paul greeted these Christian people. He was not desiring that they might have grace and peace. He was recognizing that they were theirs. They belonged to them, this grace and peace, this double force or power, this corollary of peace operating through grace, grace producing peace. These things belong also to us, to Christian souls, to the Church of God, to "all that call upon the name of our Lord Jesus Christ in every place, their Lord and ours."

Having thus greeted them, we have next,

His thanksgiving. He is thinking of them in that way. "I thank my God always concerning you, for the grace of God which was given you in Christ Jesus." That is the reason for the thanksgiving. It is based upon the recognition of the fact he has already referred to, that grace and peace are from God and through Christ Jesus. Based upon the recognition of the grace that is theirs from the Father and from Jesus Christ, he thanks God for it. He does not now say anything about peace, but it is included. It is the grace for which he is thanking God, and the grace that was given them in Christ Jesus, that is, the manifestation and the activity of the Divine grace, in which our Lord Himself, being very God and very man, had fellowship and partnership. He was the channel through which grace reached men, and it is given to men in and through Him. Grace came to us through Him, through His death, the great value of which is cleansing and acceptance by God, through the virtue of His human life, as made dynamic by Himself, the life pure, which is communicated to us. And because He is the victorious Lord, victory comes to us through

Him; His death, His life, His presence; our death to sin, our life as possible of holiness before Him, and our victory through our relationship with Him. He is not thanking God for any particular aspect of their realization. He is thanking God for the definite fact of the possibility. He thanks God always concerning them for the grace of God which was given them in Christ Jesus, not the things manifested in them. There were a good many things he was not thankful for in those Corinthian Christians; but he was thankful for the possibilities that were theirs. However much we may fail, the possibilities are all ours in Christ Jesus, not for failure, but for success and realization.

The Equipment. In the next verses that immediately follow that thanksgiving he shows what these things of grace really are, and what they do. Verse five commences, "That in everything." Do not miss the force of "That." Everything that follows will interpret these things of grace. He has thanked God for the stupendous fact of grace at their disposal in Christ Jesus. Now he goes on to things that made him thankful when he realized that grace was theirs in Christ Jesus. What were the things? "That in everything ye were enriched in Him, in all utterance and all knowledge; even as the testimony of Christ was confirmed in you; so that ye come behind in no gift; waiting for the revelation of our Lord Jesus Christ; Who shall also confirm you unto the end, that ye may be unreprovable in the day of our Lord Jesus Christ."

What were the things, then, that made him glad and thankful? First, "Ye were enriched in Him." Second, "Ye come behind in no gift." Third, and the final thing, He "shall confirm you unto the end." There is the backward look. There is the immediate situation. There is the forward look. "Ye were enriched"—that is the backward look. "Ye come behind in no gift"—that is the present. He will "confirm you unto the end"—that is the onward look. All these things result from grace, and what wonderful things they are.

First, the backward look, "Ye were enriched." No word can be better than that. The Greek word is *ploutizo*, the word from which we derive our word plutocrat, which means an extremely wealthy person. That is the word here. We were made wealthy. That is what happened when grace came from God the Father and the Lord Jesus Christ.

In what way were they made wealthy? "In all utterance and all knowledge" two remarkable things. We may imagine that the apostle was thankful that they were enriched in some way that is personal, in spiritual things. No, this is relative. "Ye were enriched in all utterance." The Greek word is *logos*. They were enriched with a deposit, to be declared. They were wealthy people. They had a message. They had a word, a *logos*, an utterance, but it was not merely a word as wisdom for their possession. It was a word as wisdom which they were to utter. He talked about what grace had done for them, and he reminded them that whatever had come to them had come as a deposit for which they were responsible to other people.

And then, knowledge, experience, not experience merely, but intellectual understanding. What grace does is to make us plutocrats, wealthy in a message we have to deliver, and in understanding of that message. I wonder whether, very often, it is not true that we have the utterance, that we value the message, and yet do not give time to understand it. Hence the necessity for pondering these things of God, and trying to grasp their significance. Grace is at our disposal, not only giving the message, but illuminating the heart and mind and intellect that we may understand it. That is what happened to the Corinthian people. Paul did not write about the blessing of their lives, of the happiness of their own lives, and of their hope of heaven. He was looking at these people in Corinth, and he said through grace they had been made wealthy men and women in a sense that the wealthy ones of Corinth did not possess. The wealth of the church in Corinth lay in their message committed to them. He had enriched them in knowledge, had enlightened their minds that they might apprehend the meaning of their own message. That is the backward look.

He went straight on, "Even as the testimony of Christ was confirmed in you." Testimony simply means a witness. The witness of Christ was confirmed in them. Enriched with great wealth, with a message, and intellectual apprehension, and its value, through that the testimony, the witness of Christ is "confirmed in you." Through them Christ was to be revealed, manifested; the message of Christ was to be proclaimed, and not only proclaimed, but intelligently proclaimed, and demonstrated in their lives. Men will believe because of what they see in you of this very grace and this very peace that is yours in Christ Jesus.

Taking a backward look, we see the Church of God, and in the Holy Spirit's view, as revealed through the apostle, we see what Christ gains in His Church. He gains a witness, born of intelligent apprehension, and the possession of a great message concerning grace, God's activity, and that activity on behalf of men. We must never forget this, overwhelming as it is. The whole teaching of the New Testament is that God has gained, and does gain, something through His Church. It is a vehicle of vision, a medium of manifestation, a method by which He is able to do amongst men what, apart from that Church, He cannot do. In another of his letters Paul makes use of a remarkable expression concerning the Church, that it is "an inheritance of

God." God has an inheritance in the saints, Christ has an inheritance in the Church. Keep the city of Corinth in mind, dark, wealthy, depraved. God had an ecclesia there, a company there; and Paul was greeting them. He thanked God, not for their realization, but for the grace of God which was at their disposal in and through Jesus Christ. He tells them what the grace meant, that they were enriched; and there we have a clear revelation of what Christ has gained in His Church, that He had men and women in Corinth who were a testimony concerning Him and were confirming the arguments for the Gospel of grace. The final arguments for the Gospel of grace are to be found in Christian people.

He then looked at their present. "Ye come behind in no gift." They had all that was necessary. The great word there is gifts, *charisma,* the gifts of the Holy Spirit, the gifts of Christ through the Holy Spirit. They had everything they needed for the fulfilling of their function. They had utterance. They had knowledge. In their lives they had become the witnesses to the Christ. They had everything necessary for the carrying out of their true vocation there in the city of Corinth.

Then he glanced on, "waiting." The Greek verb there means fully expecting, being fully assured. Of what? Of the revelation, *apocalypsis,* manifestation of our Lord Jesus Christ, "Who shall also confirm you unto the end, that ye be unreprovable in the day of our Lord Jesus Christ." So this grace for which he thanks God has to do with their past when they became members of that Church of God; it has to do with their present enrichment, and it assures the great hope of the future.

THE FUNDAMENTAL AFFIRMATION   i. 9

   i. " God is faithful, through whom . . ."
  ii. " Ye were called into . . ."
 iii. " The fellowship of His Son "

    The Fact.

      " Jesus   The Manifestation.
       Christ   The Service.
      Our Lord " The Result.   (16a)

I CORINTHIANS i. 9

WE shall devote this study to a consideration of one verse, because it is altogether too important to be hurried over. It is really the fundamental affirmation of the whole letter. In the first eight verses of this chapter we have seen the superscription, the greeting, and the thanks-

THE CORINTHIAN LETTERS OF PAUL 19

giving, and also the Corinthians' equipment. Paul now writes, or dictates, this tremendous declaration, " God is faithful, through Whom ye were called into the fellowship of His Son Jesus Christ our Lord."

That statement could be left out without seeming to interfere with the movement of the letter. Yet it is supreme, and all the letter, from beginning to end, is based upon the declarations therein made by the apostle. All that he wrote afterwards, both in correction in the first eleven chapters, and then in construction (12–15), gathers its force from the stupendous facts contained in this great saying.

Go to the end of the letter, to the fifteenth chapter, and read the final verse therein, and see the connection. He is drawing the letter to a conclusion in that fifteenth chapter. He has something to say beyond it, about the collection for the saints, and greetings, and salutations, which are all in the sixteenth chapter. But the last verse of that fifteenth chapter reads, " Wherefore, my beloved brethren, be ye steadfast, unmovable, always abounding in the work of the Lord, forasmuch as ye know that your labour is not vain in the Lord." Some expositors seem to have some difficulty with that verse as to its placing. When the apostle said, " Wherefore," they have said he is referring to what has immediately preceded it, to the glorious day of resurrection, when death is swallowed up in victory. It is perfectly fair to say that this was in his mind when he said, " Wherefore . . . be ye steadfast, unmovable." But I do not think that exhausts it. I believe that statement included more than that wonderful resurrection chapter, that the " Wherefore " leans back finally upon the ninth verse of chapter one. Everything written between those two verses, of correction and construction, depends upon them. If we want to know the ultimate argument for what he asks in xv. 58, we shall find it in i. 9. " God is faithful, through Whom ye were called into the fellowship of His Son Jesus Christ our Lord. . . . Wherefore, my beloved brethren, be ye steadfast, unmovable, always abounding in the work of the Lord." We see at once the relationship between them, and the greatness of i. 9 lies within the compass of the appeal of xv. 58. He appeals to these Christians at Corinth, and to all who in every place call upon the name of the Lord, to be steadfast. God is faithful; be ye steadfast. What in? The work of the Lord. God has put you in fellowship with Jesus Christ, so be you steadfast, unmovable, abounding in the work of the Lord. Those two verses bound the letter, the fundamental affirmation and the final appeal.

Coming to this verse, i. 9, two facts are revealed. First, the fact as to God, " God is faithful "; second, that we are called into the fellowship of His Son, our Lord Jesus Christ. We will take these two facts, but consider them in the reverse order.

We begin, then, with the statement, "Ye were called into the fellowship of His Son Jesus Christ our Lord." We halt, first, with that word "fellowship." What a familiar word it is. How well we know it in its use, and we have certain spiritual apprehension as to its value. The three letters of John are all concerned with this matter of fellowship. In his first chapter he states it very strongly when he writes, "Our fellowship is with the Father, and with His Son Jesus Christ." That word "fellowship" is the same.

What is fellowship? The exceeding value of the word is revealed by a very simple fact that in our New Testament, in the Revised Version, there is a diversity of translation of the same word. The Greek word, *koinonia*, is the abstract noun. We have also the word *koinonos*, which is the common noun. What does this word mean? To state the different ways in which *koinonia* and *koinonos* are translated, there will be discovered something that belongs to all of them, the same quality in each. It is translated *fellowship, contribution, communion*, and once, in the sense of stewardship, *dispensation*. It is also translated *"to communicate."* The common noun *koinonos* is translated *partakers, partners, communion*.

What is this common quality that lies in the word? Sometimes we call it fellowship or contribution. The Old Version translates it once *distribution*, but the Revised translates it *fellowship, communion, dispensation, partakers, partners,* and *communion*. All these words are required in translation to carry over the idea, according to the context, of this Greek word, *koinonia* or *koinonos*. The simple idea is, that the root from which the words come is *koinos*, and the best translation of the meaning is found in the book of the Acts of the Apostles (ii. 44). There we are told that the early disciples after Pentecost had "all things common." That is the meaning of *koinonia*. That is the meaning of *koinonos*. That is to say, they were not privileged people, except as all were privileged. They had things in common, they shared. That is the true use of the word "shared." Do not be afraid of the simplicity of that. Lift it. "God is faithful." Who has called you "into the fellowship of His Son Jesus Christ our Lord." Daringly, I will adopt the suggestion I have taken from the Acts. God is faithful, Who has called you into the position of having all things in common with His Son Christ Jesus our Lord. We may be amazed, almost frightened, at the suggestion; but that is what it means, all things in common.

Now look at the fact—partners. First, "His Son Jesus Christ our Lord." The arrangement of the titles is valuable, and is of meaning in the New Testament. Notice what Paul says, "His Son," relating our Lord to God the Father. "His Son," in all the fulness of the meaning of that expression, the Son of God. Who is He? "Jesus," the One through Whom came the manifestation of God, and of the heart of God, and of the activity of God. "Christ," the anointed One, the One Who carried out the purposes of God, and is carrying out those purposes in the world. What else? "Our Lord," the One in complete authority. That is One of the partners in this fellowship.

"Ye," that covers the ground, and must be interpreted by the verses that have gone before, "the church of God, called saints, sanctified in Christ Jesus," who have received grace, and resultant peace, who are made wealthy or enriched with a logos, an utterance, and with intelligence, the understanding of the grace. "Ye," not only those in Corinth, but all in every place who call upon the name of our Lord, are in the company, "ye," He, "the Son of God, Christ Jesus the Lord," and "ye." That is the account of the partnership.

The declaration is that we are in partnership with Christ. That word partnership is used in two ways in our common speech today. It is a business term. Two men go into partnership with each other in business. We use it in the realm also of friendship. When I was a boy it was the fashion of a man to speak of his wife as a partner. We do not hear it used much today. Too often husbands and wives are running separate establishments. That is the highest realm of friendship possible on earth. Business enterprise and friendship as communion—those are the two uses we make of the word. That is exactly what we have here. We are called into business partnership with His Son Jesus Christ our Lord. We are called into friendship with His Son Jesus Christ our Lord.

What does a thing like that mean, whether in the realm of business or friendship? It means at least three things: mutual interests, mutual devotion, mutual activity.

Mutual interests. He is interested in me, my being, spirit, mind, body; He is interested in my development. I am interested in Him, in the mystery and the majesty of His Person, in the wonder and the glory of His purpose. Mutual interests. That is fellowship, whether in business or friendship.

But it is far more, it is mutual devotion. His resources are mine. Just three words I have uttered, and I am almost frightened as I utter them, the wonder is so great. "In Him dwelleth all the fullness of the Godhead bodily"—in *Him*. All His resources are at my disposal, His wisdom, His power, His infinite and far-flung possessions throughout the whole creation. All His resources are at my disposal—fellowship. Then take the other side of it. I will speak of it ideally, even though it may need qualification; all my resources are at His disposal, my personality, whatever it is, my powers whatever they may be, my possessions, whatever they are, all are His. That may need qualification. I am afraid I have to say, all my resources ought to be, and yet, ideally, that is the truth about fellowship. All we have belongs to Him, and all He has belongs to us. We are in fellowship with Him.

And once more, it means mutual activity. What a marvelous thing that is, He accommodating Himself to our weakness. Oh, no, not becoming weak! He accommodates Himself in His government of us, in His goings, to which He calls us in fellowship; accommodating Himself to our weakness, that is His gentleness. And, on the other side, we are rising to co-operation with His power. That is the secret of greatness in fellowship.

He accommodates Himself to our weakness, but not becoming weak. There is a great text from the Old Testament which may be open to question in the matter of interpretation, " In all their affliction He was afflicted." We get comfort from it; and yet I am quite convinced, personally, after close investigation, that this is a mistranslation by the omission of one word, and that what was really written was this, " In all their affliction He was not afflicted." We may think that takes away comfort. But does it? The old rendering sounded very beautiful, but take the other suggestion. He was there with them in their affliction, but He was not afflicted, He was not bowed down, weakened by the way. "The Lord fainteth not nor is weary," and that is true of our Lord. He accommodates Himself to my weakness. He waits for me, and when my footsteps falter, He pauses by my side. I remember hearing a very dear friend of mine in a Conference say that if the Lord leads us into difficulties, He leads us out; but that if we get into difficulties of our own making, we have to get out ourselves. I thank God that is not true of my life. That is not what I have found out. Yes, it is true if He leads me into difficulty, He will lead me out; but if I wander in my own foolishness, He will still follow me, and lead me out. Fellowship, mutual activity; He accommodating all His power to my weakness and my faltering; and I—oh, yes—rising in co-operation with His power through that fellowship. Not only does He accommodate Himself to my weakness, He gives me power that enables me to do things impossible to me outside the fellowship.

That is the great fundamental affirmation, so far as we are concerned. We were called of God into this fellowship, the fellowship of friendship and the fellowship of business with His Son Jesus Christ our Lord.

So we turn to the first statement. " God is faithful." The statement is brief, almost blunt. Its very brevity and bluntness show that it admits of no question. It is eternally attested. " God is faithful." It is important that we should understand the meaning of the word the apostle employed, the word *pistos*, faithful. It does not mean God is true. That is involved. It does not mean God has faith. What does it mean? It can be translated by one English word, trustworthy. God is trustworthy, we can depend upon Him. He has called us into this fellowship. He is trustworthy. "Therefore, my beloved brethren, be ye stedfast, unmovable, always abounding in the work of the Lord." He is trustworthy. Be you trustworthy. We are in this tremendous enterprise, in fellowship, linked up with the Son of God, Jesus, the Manifester; Christ, the Redeemer; the Lord, the absolute Monarch. We are in business with Him. We are in partnership, friendship and enterprise. We need not tremble. God will not break down. God will not fail. He has called us, He is faithful.

So in this one verse there is at once a revelation of the Church's power and the Church's responsibility. What is the Church's power? Her fellowship with her Lord. That is the secret of all her power. What is the Church's responsibility? "Be ye steadfast, unmovable, always abounding in the work of the Lord." Not by our trying to find something to do for Him, but to get into His business. What is His business in the world? Whatever it is, we are committed to it in fellowship with Him. That is our responsibility.

The enterprise of Christ in Corinth, in every place, is shared by His Church, and, consequently, for its carrying out the Church has His companionship, " I am with you, all the days."

A. CORRECTIVE. THE CARNALITIES	i. 10–xi
I. *Divisions*	i. 10–iv
i. " The Wisdom of Words " and " The Word of the Cross "	i. 10–ii
a. The Contrast	i. 10–25
1. The Wisdom of Words	10–17
2. The Word of the Cross	18
3. The Proof—Power	19–25
b. The Application	i. 26–ii. 5
1. No Glorying in Flesh	26–29
2. Glory in the Lord	30, 31
3. Paul in Illustration	ii. 1–5
c. The Wisdom	ii. 6–16
1. Not of This Age The Cross the Proof	6–9
2. Of the Spirit The Revealer	10, 11
3. The Principle of Discernment The Spiritual	12–16

I CORINTHIANS i. 10–17

AFTER his general introduction, Paul commenced his letter by dealing with a matter concerning which he had received careful information from the household of Chloe. The Authorized Version renders it that this matter had "been declared" to him. The Revised Version renders it that "it hath been signified unto me." The difference is slight. The Greek word quite simply means, made plain. These matters had been made plain to him by those who were of the household of Chloe. *Signified* is better than *declared,* and yet even *signified* may fall short in conveying the full value and meaning to our minds. The Greek word indicates a careful account, as distinct from a mere statement, which, after all, might be a rumour. Paul was not dealing with rumours, but with facts about which there were no doubts. He knew exactly what was happening, and with that knowledge in mind he approached his subject.

The matter to which he turned was one of divisions within the fellowship. "It hath been signified unto me concerning you, my brethren . . . that there are contentions among you." Again, to pause with a word, "contentions." The Greek word might more accurately be rendered "quarrels among you," "wranglings among you." It is not merely differences of opinion, but such differences which had degenerated into wranglings, into quarrels. The word "contentions" is adequate, and that church at Corinth, consisting of those who were called saints, who had been put by God into the *koinonia,* the fellowship of His Son, was spending its time in wrangling, quarrelling. The church was broken up in that way into parties and coteries.

In these verses 10–17 Paul dealt with that fact, though not fully and finally. This section dealing with those disputations ends with the third chapter. The section from chapter one, verse ten, to the conclusion of the fourth chapter, is occupied with the terrible fact of these divisions in this church at Corinth. Here, however, in these seven verses the fact is dealt with very broadly, and the paragraph falls into three parts. In verse 10 he made an appeal to them. In verse 12 he described the fact of the trouble. He told them what was actually going on, about which he had received full and careful information. All that follows (verses 13–17) deals with that subject generally, applying it more fully.

First of all, he made an appeal. There is something urgent and touching in the way he put it, in view of the fact of all he had written, that God is faithful, and had called them into the fellowship of His Son—"Now I beseech you, brethren." The word *beseech* is one that signifies appeal and argument in one. It is a word pregnant with meaning, being derived from the same root as *paraclete.* That is one of the great names which Christ gave to the Holy Spirit. Follow out that suggestiveness. The Spirit is at once the Comforter and Advocate.

The advocate, the One Who argues within us the cause of Christ; the Comforter, the One Who by His fellowship, the fellowship of Christ made real, disannuls our loneliness and orphanage. You are no longer orphans, said Jesus. He brings us to the place of strength, the Comforter and Advocate. The word means simply one called to the side of another. The teaching is that He is called to our side to be with us, to be in us for those two purposes. First, as an Advocate. Christ is our Advocate with God. The Spirit is Christ's Advocate with us. He is the Advocate, arguing for Christ always, and so the Comforter.

I once heard my beloved friend Samuel Chadwick say he objected to the name Comforter for the Holy Ghost. He was arguing, rightly, that He was an Advocate, and he said that he should never call his lawyer his comforter. I spoke at the same meeting after him, and I said I differed from him, that if I had to have a lawyer sometimes, I called him my comforter, because it was a great comfort to know my case could be left with him and he would argue for me. Paul said, "I beseech you," as one called to your side, an advocate, and one who would comfort you. It is all there in the word. There is a tender urgency about it that we must not miss. It is the call of appeal and argument.

He says, "I beseech you, through the name of our Lord Jesus Christ." Take the first nine verses and see how constantly he referred to that One, "Jesus Christ," "Christ Jesus," "the Lord Jesus Christ," "His Son Jesus Christ our Lord." The great title occurs nine times in those nine verses. "Now, I beseech you," through that name of the One into fellowship with Whom they had been put by God, in the name of the One through Whom they had received the grace of God and peace; he besought them, he appealed to them. Mark the urgency of it.

What is the appeal? "That ye all speak the same thing, and that there be no divisions among you, but that ye be perfected together in the same mind and in the same judgment." That may be open to different exegesis. Personally, however, I am convinced that when he wrote of the "same mind" and "same judgment," he meant the mind of Christ and the judgment of Christ, the One to Whom he had already referred. What was "the same thing"? Go back to the fourth and fifth verses. There was given to them in Christ Jesus everything; "Ye were enriched in Him, in all utterance"—in the logos—the things to be spoken. "I beseech you . . . that ye all speak the same thing." The reference there is to the message that they had. "Speak the same thing, that there be no divisions among you; but that ye be perfected together in the same mind and in the same judgment."

Notice that carefully in this way. Paul was a great psychologist, in the true sense of the word, and not in the modern sense. He was dealing with these people, and he understood these things. Take, first, the matter of opinion, "the same mind," that you have not varying views upon which you insist, which are causing these wranglings. Get the true outlook. Be of the same mind and judgment. If I am correct in the interpretation here, that "the same mind" referred to the mind of Christ, we have a remarkable interpretation of what that mind is in Paul's Philippian letter, and to what he was calling these Corinthian Christians. He was tracing back here from effect to cause: "Of one mind," "the same mind," "the same judgment," not broken up, not divided, not wrangling, not quarrelling, but united in your thinking and outlook.

And therefore of the same speech, "that ye all speak the same thing," that the expression of that one view shall be a complete, and united and an unbroken testimony. Remember Corinth, and this company of people put into that great city in fellowship with Jesus Christ, responsible for His business, as well as realizing His friendship. Now he says, I beseech you that you get your thinking right, and therefore that you have a right expression, that your speech is what it ought to be. He uses a beautiful word in that connection, "that ye be perfected together." The idea there is not that they shall all become perfect. Perfected together means joined together. That ye be perfectly joined together, that ye be articulated so that there is perfect alignment of the different parts of the body and the Church. The picture is that of a mosaic. It is the idea of a jig-saw puzzle. There is no piece absolutely perfect. When each piece is put in its place the whole is seen. That was what Paul was thinking about, and what he was praying for these people, that having the true view, the same mind and judgment, uttering the true speech, they might be perfected together, so that there would be no break, no disharmony in the body. That is his great appeal.

What was the matter with these people? What caused these wranglings and quarrels? What caused these differing views? I am not suggesting differing views need be wrong. They are wrong only when they produce wrong results, when they divide up the Body of Christ into divisions and sections and quarrels. The reason for these divisions is not given in so many words until the third chapter is reached, and the opening verse, "And I, brethren, could not speak unto you as spiritual, but as unto carnal, as unto babes in Christ." That was the trouble. "I fed you with milk, not with meat; for ye were not yet able to bear it; nay, not even yet are ye able; for ye are yet carnal; for whereas there is among you jealousy and strife, are ye not carnal, and walk after the manner of men?" There he told them what was the real trouble in the church, carnality. They were not spiritual; they were carnal.

There opens a great field for investigation for the Bible student of the New Testament, in order to understand what Christian discipleship really is. Here was the trouble with this Corinthian church. They were carnal, *sarkikos;* they were of the flesh. They were living in the fleshly realm. They had descended to the lower level, and that was mastering their thinking. They were proud of their divisions, their quarrels, and were finding great relief in them. It was fleshly, and not spiritual. There are the two levels of the flesh and the spirit, and everyone is mastered by one or the other in Christian life and experience. I may be living mastered by the lower side of my nature, the fleshly; or I may be living mastered by the higher, which is spiritual, in fellowship with the Holy Spirit of God. These people had degenerated into the lower levels of life. They were not motivated by spiritual values and outlooks, but by carnal and fleshly desires and passions. That is what lay at the root of the whole trouble, and they were rather pleased with their divisions.

Glance now at verse 12, which is an interpretation of verse 17, "Christ sent me not to baptize, but to preach the Gospel." Mark the contrast, "Not in wisdom of words, lest the Cross of Christ should be made void." Later he will take the phrase, "the Cross of Christ," and speak of "the word of the Cross." Now he has referred to "the wisdom of words." That was characterizing these people, and creating all their divisions. No student of this first letter to Corinth can escape from the conviction that the spirit of the city of Corinth had entered into the church. That is always a great peril to the Church. We are sometimes told that we need as preachers to catch the spirit of the age. I deny that emphatically. Our work is not to catch the spirit of the age. It is to correct the spirit of the age. There is all the difference between catching it and being mastered by it, and correcting it. These people were in Corinth not to be affected by Corinth, but to affect Corinth. "The wisdom of words" is a most characteristic phrase. That is a reference, doubtless, to the schools of philosophy in Corinth. The city was full of them. They were all divided, and glorying in their divisions. They were arguing about phrases and human views, or, to use the word of the Schoolmen, they were engaged in endless logomachies, which means fights about words. Paul knew this, and saw that that spirit had invaded the church, fights about words, emphases upon that which was partial rather than upon the sum totality. Perhaps there was the same difference between the logomachies of the Corinthian schools of philosophies and these Christian people in the church. They had contradictory views about the world and so on.

Inside the church they claimed to be Christians still, and to hold the Christian truth, but they were quarrelling, and were divided up, and were indulging, undoubtedly, in false emphases, putting false emphases upon partial truths, and forgetting the value of the whole truth. That is what they were doing, and it is very suggestive. A little group was saying—Paul quotes them here in the singular number—We believe in Paul. Another group said, No, we belong to Apollos. Another said, Oh, no, we belong to Cephas. Then another group—and Paul put them in with the rest—said, We belong to Christ. That little group saying " I am of Paul " were accepting Paul's Gospel. He had founded the church, and they were standing loyal to the founder. Oh, no, said another party. Since Paul founded the church we have had Apollos here, with Greek culture and outlook, and we belong to him rather than to Paul. Then there was another set saying, We had better get back to Jerusalem, the centre. We belong to Peter, to Cephas. Then another group—I do not know whether it was the smallest, but I am quite sure they were very emphatic—said, We belong to Christ.

Paul said, You are all wrong. You are dividing yourselves around these false emphases. Paul, Apollos, Cephas, certainly; Christ, absolutely; but not Paul to the exclusion of Apollos and Cephas and Christ; and not Apollos to the exclusion of Paul and Cephas and Christ; and not Cephas to the exclusion of Paul and Apollos and Christ; and not Christ to the exclusion of His messengers, Paul, and Apollos, and Cephas. They were all wrong. The trouble was, these people were gathering around some emphasis which in all likelihood was correct, but when the partial is made the whole, and cutting them off in fellowship of judgment of mind and utterance from others, then they were wronging the whole Church of God.

Finally, turn to Paul's immediate corrective, with which he will deal more fully subsequently. He says, " Is Christ divided? " It was a sharp word. He has named Him nine times in the introduction. He has also referred to Him in this paragraph. Now he asks, Is Christ broken up? Is Christ divided? Any one element which separates has some element in it of wrong. Anything which breaks in upon the unity of the Christ and His message has something in it that is wrong. " Is Christ divided? "

Then he made a wonderful personal application. He says, " Was Paul crucified for you? " How that arrests us! The crucifixion of Christ was the ground of their Christianity. Where is it? " Was Paul crucified for you? " He left it as a question.

Then he asked a second, " Or were ye baptized in the name of Paul? " The Cross, the crucifixion, was the ground of Christianity. Baptism into the name is not water baptism, water baptism is the symbol of it, and a sacred one. Baptism into the Name is the baptism of the Spirit. Were ye baptized into the name of Paul? When you were baptized in water you were baptized into the name, not in, but into the Name of Christ, the Father, and the Spirit. If the Cross is the ground of Christianity, the baptism of the Spirit is the way in which all men and these people entered into Christian life. How did they come into contact with this life? Was it because they were baptized into Paul's name?

He then went off into that interesting reference: "I thank God that I baptized none of you save Crispus and Caius," and then he remembered another, the household of Stephanas. Yes, he said, I baptized these. His reference was to water baptism, the rite of admission to the Church, but it was the symbol of something he is denying. They were not baptized by him, or anyone else, into his, Paul's, name. They were baptized into the Name by which they received the gift of life, the gift of the Holy Spirit, and their Christian experience began.

So we see the basic unity. First, the Cross, the foundation of their Christianity. Secondly, the baptism of the Spirit of God. They were all baptized by one Spirit into the fellowship and experience.

Then everything ends with these words, "For Christ sent me not to baptize, but to preach the Gospel; not in wisdom of words, lest the Cross of Christ should be made void." Not in wisdom of words, not in this manner to which you are devoting yourselves, discussing views and partial aspects, these logomachies, that you have caught from the Corinthian city, and that are cursing the Christian message. Paul says, I was sent to preach the Gospel, not in that way, the way which has divided you, "lest the Cross of Christ" should have no effect. As we proceed, he deals with that more fully. But here it stands, the contrast, the divisive discussion around words and by words, and the unifying message of the Cross of Christ.

I CORINTHIANS i. 18–31

THE church of God in Corinth was divided into sections and parties. There was schism in the church. Schism means a rent. A sect means something torn off. The garment was still there, but it was rent, and so there were schisms. It had not developed into sectarianism, in the true sense of the word. The one proof is that they were quarrelling, the sure sign of contentions. The word means wrangling, and they were having a warm time, and enjoying it. That was the pity of it, because it was interfering with their work. They were there in Corinth in fellowship with Christ, in business relationship with Him, and in the companionship of sacred friendship. Now the testimony that they ought to have been bearing to Corinth was being hindered and marred because of their divisions.

We have dealt with the beginning of the section concerning divisions, and we now continue with that subject. Paul felt it was a matter of tremendous importance—occupying as it does nearly four chapters of the letter—to deal with those divisions that had crept in.

The first words of this paragraph begin, "For the word of the Cross." One cannot read that intelligently without linking it with something that had gone before. The apostle had immediately before declared that he had been sent not to baptize but to preach the Gospel. Then he had referred to the method, "Not in wisdom of words, lest the Cross of Christ should be made void." In that sentence we have a sharp and remarkable contrast, intentionally so, undoubtedly, on the part of the apostle: "the wisdom of words," and "the Cross of Christ." Those two phrases stand opposite to one another. He had not employed the one method, "the wisdom of words"; and that which was his burden, the Gospel, centered in, and was surrounded by one great fact and message, "the Cross of Christ." Those two things are put into juxtaposition, and the phrases contain contrasted methods and messages. Here was a preacher who did not employ the first, "the wisdom of words," who was burdened with the second, "the Cross of Christ." There is significance between the plural and the singular here. "The wisdom of words," plural—words suggesting disruption, differences; the singular, "The Cross of Christ," suggesting unity and completeness.

The subject, then, with which the apostle was dealing here was that of wisdom. The Greek word *sophia* stood for wisdom, or philosophy. We often refer to the wisdom books of the Old Testament, and find in them Hebrew philosophy, which is perfectly correct. This thought runs all through this section of the letter. From this seventeenth verse of the first chapter to the end of the third chapter the word *sophia* will be found no less than sixteen times. The apostle here is dealing with that wisdom which comes from philosophic inquiry and disputation, "the wisdom of words." On the other hand, he deals with the wisdom of philosophy, or revelation. Those are the two great ideas that run all through the section. I heard my colleague, Dr. Lloyd-Jones, say about two years ago in Albert Hall that the whole drift towards modernism that had blighted the Church of God and nearly destroyed its living Gospel may be traced to an hour when men began to turn from revelation to philosophy. While not enlarging upon it, that is exactly what we find here. Although my friend was referring to what may be described as certainly a recent movement of fifty or sixty years ago, here it is seen at the beginning. In this respect also there is nothing new under the sun. That is one reason why I do not like to call it modernism. It is an ancient antique that is being dug up! It is all here, and it all comes down to this: the difference between the wisdom that results from what is known as philosophy and the wisdom or philosophy that is built upon Divine revelation.

This word wisdom, *sophia*, is used only in the Bible of God or of good men, except in ironical sense, and there it has a qualifying phrase, such as "the wisdom of this age." Here we have the wisdom of the age and the wisdom which is the wisdom of God. Those two things are put into contrast. Those teachers of old were first called Sophists, which meant wise men. It is very interesting to note that in the course of time they did not care to be called Sophists, and it is one proof that they had a certain amount of modesty, for they called themselves philosophers. The word "philosopher" does not mean a wise man, but one who loves wisdom. Today sophism has degenerated in meaning until it now means a false line of argument.

Take this paragraph, and there are four things to be glanced at. The apostle, first of all, declares what is the effect of the Word of the Cross (verse 18). He then shows the futility of earthly wisdom (verses 19-20). From verses 21 to 24 he shows what God's provision is for a world bankrupt in philosophy; and, finally, in the concluding verse of the paragraph he makes that amazing contrast, at which we have often wondered—seeing it was so self-evidently true—that it needed to be stated.

First, then, the effect of the word of the Cross. The word of the Cross, or to give the phrase its full value, the logos of the Cross, is the whole totality of truth contained in and revealed through the Cross. Logos is truth, and not truth merely, but truth revealed, truth manifested. So the Greeks used the word. So it is used in our Scriptures. "The word of the Cross," the truth embodied, embedded in the Cross, and that truth declared and revealed. Paul tells us the effect. "To them that are perishing" it is "foolishness." That is a true and accurate word. Really, the Greek word has more acid in it. We could translate it by our word "silliness," quite accurately, or by the word "absurdity." "To them that are perishing, silliness, absurdity."

What does that mean? Is it absurd to them? Is it foolishness to them because they are perishing? No, they are perishing because they are treating the Cross as silliness and foolishness, as absurd. The reason for the perishing is in their attitude. These people were refusing to examine something outside of, or contrary to, their own thinking, contrary to their own philosophies. They had their philosophies, and they were not prepared to consider something that was outside the realm of those philosophies. It was foolishness, it was silly and absurd, and therefore they were perishing. The effect of the word of the Cross.

"But unto us which are being saved it is the power of God." Again, that is the secret of the saving. Just as refusal to listen to anything outside the realm of their human thinking results in looking upon the Cross as foolishness, so the Cross becomes a saving dynamic, *dunamis*, that is the word. It is a saving dynamic to those giving attention to it and to its message. One cannot do better than quote again the great words, "God so loved the world that He gave His only begotten Son, that whosoever believeth on Him should not perish, but have eternal life." Men and women who believe that, and give attention to that, consider it, and trust themselves to it, know the working within them of dynamic, power. It is the power of God. Notice the difference. Foolishness, the thing of the mind altogether, the thing of opinion. Power, something that throbs and acts, and produces results. The effect of the word of the Cross is thus put into contrast with the wisdom of words.

The apostle then went on to show the futility of earthly wisdom in verses 19 and 20. It is very interesting that he cited Isaiah. We are driven back to see where Isaiah said this. In chapter 29, having uttered messages concerning surrounding nations, he came to deal with the chosen people of God. He was addressing the nation from the standpoint of the capital, " Ho, Ariel, Ariel, the city where David encamped," and at verse 13 we read this:

"And the Lord said, Forasmuch as this people draw nigh unto Me, and with their mouth and with their lips do honour Me, but have removed their heart far from Me, and their fear of Me is a commandment of men which has been taught them" [literally, "learned by rote"] "therefore, behold, I will proceed to do a marvelous work among this people, even a marvelous work and a wonder; and the wisdom of their wise men shall perish, and the understanding of their prudent men shall be hid."

What was the matter with these people to whom Isaiah was writing? They had departed from God, and they were taking His name, professing that they were true, and yet they had departed, and were gathering around their own views and conceptions and their own accommodations; and God said He would destroy the wisdom of the wise. Paul quoted it of these people in Corinth, of whom it was true. They were turning their attention to the thinkings of men, to the philosophies of the hour, and creating within the Christian Church schism in the matter of opinion, gathering around Paul or Apollos or Cephas, or even insisting upon the fact that they alone were true, because they named the Name of Christ.

Then the apostle in satire asked his questions, "Where is the wise?" In other words, what does it all amount to, the wise, generally speaking? "Where is the wise?" What has he done? Where has he arrived? "Where is the scribe?" That is the peculiar word for the Jewish attitude. "Where is the disputer of this world?" That is the Greek attitude. What does it all amount to? The overruling God has made foolish the whole business, has made all this wisdom silly, absurd. These people looked upon the word of the Cross as silliness. God proves by what He has done, and by that very word of the Cross, the silliness and absurdity of all their thinking. In writing to the Romans, Paul said, "Professing themselves to be wise, they became fools."

Paul was now showing these people what God's antidote is for this bankrupt wisdom of the world. In verse 21 he draws attention to this. God is still governing, and overruling. "In the wisdom of God the world through its wisdom knew not God." All its philosophy had failed to discover God, or come to a knowledge of God. That was his charge, the bankrupt wisdom of the world.

Is there an antidote? Yes, God has chosen by the foolishness of the preaching—literally of the thing preached, the message is referred to—to save them that believe. Compare again the futility of all philosophies, discussions of the sages, and the so-called Sophists or philosophers. They had failed to find God. They could not find Him. They did not find Him. They found Him never. Then into the midst of that bankrupt world and its philosophies God sent His Son, and by the Cross He sent out a message, the preaching, the announcement, the declaration, "the foolishness of the preaching"; and by that God is acting in wisdom. How do we know? Because it saves, it acts, it works, it transforms them that believe.

He then referred to the contrasted quest. Jews are looking for signs. Greeks are looking for wisdom. How often in the days of our Lord's public ministry they were seeking a sign, and to them the Cross became not a sign, but a stumbling-block, a *skandalon,* a scandal. A stumbling-block is something men fall over. These Jews looking for a sign, always in the realm of the material, having lost their understanding of the spiritual, always looking for the spectacular manifestation—what they wanted demonstrated who can tell? When they heard of the Cross as the way of human salvation, they stumbled over it. It was an offence to them.

And to the Greeks it was foolishness. But to the Jews and Greeks, that is, to massed humanity that lay behind these divisions, that very Cross which was foolishness and silliness to the Greek, discussing matters, became the power of God and the wisdom of God.

So the apostle gathered everything together in that last remarkable contrast. "The foolishness of God is wiser than men; and the weakness of God is stronger than men." We cannot ponder that without feeling the apostle was still looking at those two ways of men, the Jew and the Greek. A stumbling-block, something in the way, a weakness to the Jew, yes. Foolishness to the Greek, yes. But why? The idea of incarnation as revelation to the Greek was silly. Keep to the use of that word, because that is what it was. It was absurd, outside the realm of all things they knew and discussed. The incarnation of a Man, and such a Man, so evidently of human nature according to the stories they heard from Paul and all the rest; and a Man Who went His way not discussing philosophies at all. And to say that He was God manifest was foolishness, absurd. To tell them that that Cross whereon that Man died was the way of moral renewal and strength in human life, the whole thing was absurd.

There is no need to go back to these people. That was the condition then. That is the attitude of many people towards the Cross today. Talk to them of the incarnation of God as being a revelation, and the Cross as being the secret of moral strength and renewal by dealing with sin, and they say it is absurd, foolish. Yes, but Paul says that that foolishness, according to Greek thought and ideal, that foolishness of God, is mightier than all the wisdom of men. He is wiser. It is the supreme and ultimate wisdom by revelation.

Or, again, the Jew saw the Cross as the proof of weakness absolutely. He knew about Jesus. He heard the story, and he said, Yes, but He was beaten, He was defeated. The Cross is the symbol of defeat. You say that the Cross is the way of victory and of life. We do not understand that. We stumble over it. We cannot follow that. Yes, says the apostle, but the weakness of God in that Cross is mightier than all the strength of men.

What a wonderful contrast it is! Look at men, look at the wisdom of words, and what do we see? A mental strength inquiring, suggesting, debating, arguing, surmising, what? Nothing. That is a very human way to put it. God is laughing at that foolishness, the silliness of men; and He is giving men this great Cross as a revelation and a message and a power. So He is answering it.

If there is anything brought out clearly here it is the futility and the paralysis of all worldly philosophy. So it has ever been, and so it still is. The finality of philosophy is based on revelation, and that is revealed in the Cross. As men come to that Cross, and trust it, they are being saved, for they find it is the power of God.

Continuing his teaching concerning the divisions, and the peril arising from them, to the true fulfilment of the function of the church in Corinth, the apostle now reminded those to whom he wrote that the things of supposed human wisdom are futile and powerless. That summarizes this paragraph (verses 26-31).

The arguments of this section are revealed most clearly, and are crystallized at the end, in the 29th and 31st verses in two statements: "No flesh should glory before God," "He that glorieth, let him glory in the Lord." There is much significance in the word "glory" which the apostle used here. Sometimes another word carries the real meaning more fully. We might substitute the word "boast" there. "No flesh should boast before God," "He that boasteth, let him boast in the Lord." In that word is a revelation of the fact of a good deal of self-satisfaction among those who were boasting in names—Paul, Apollos, Cephas, or Christ.

Paul began by reminding them of the fact of those who were called. "Behold your calling, brethren." That takes us inevitably back to the beginning of the letter, "Unto the church of God which is at Corinth, even them that are sanctified in Christ Jesus, called saints." That was their calling, that was their name, that is what they were. The definition of saintship has run all through. Now he said, "Behold your calling." Look over the ground, look at the Church, look at those who compose that which is called, "Behold your calling," your election. What did he want them to see? "How that not many wise after the flesh, not many mighty, not many noble, are called." Look over your calling. Look at those who constitute your fellowship, and not many wise, not many mighty, not many noble, will be found, after the flesh. Not many wise, mighty, noble.

It is a remarkable thing that Paul asked them to observe. It is something we should do well to remember, and we should not be discouraged by the fact. We can imagine that some of these people in Corinth were, perhaps, sometimes inclined to be a little discouraged. It looked as though Paul knew that, and asked them to face the fact. We have all known churches which felt they would be much stronger if they had some intellectual people in their fellowship. The apostle said "not many," he did not say "none." There are churches which think they would be better off if they had some "wise," highly intellectual people, and "mighty" people characterized by ability and force; and some "noble" (to translate literally, some well-born) people. It is remarkable how things run down the centuries, and human nature is the same. Paul asked them to look round and see "not many." The history of the Christian Church has always begun at the bottom and worked upwards, has never begun upwards and worked down. It always begins with "not many wise," the simple folk. "I thank Thee, O Father, Lord of heaven and earth, that Thou didst hide these things from the wise and understanding, and didst reveal them unto babes."

Those are the words of our Lord, and it has always been true, and that is what the apostle reminded them of now. He asked them first to look around. He did not say there were no wise, after the standard of intellectual ability, and no mighty, after the standard of worldly affairs; and no noble born; but he does say, "not many." Three times over he repeats his phrase.

That has always been the story of the Christian Church. It never begins—I use a phrase I do not like—with "the upper ten." That is a horrible expression. They do not use that in America, they say "the four hundred." I remember when I was a boy some people judged the influential power of the church by the number of carriages at the door after service. I have heard again and again, There were ten, twelve, twenty carriages drawn up outside. Oh, my masters, what an appalling revelation of the fall of people who talk that way, from the glorious supernal heights of the truth concerning Christianity to the low levels of materialism! Oh, no, it always begins and works up, and never begins up and works down.

The apostle then drew a remarkable contrast between the conceptions of the flesh-governed thinking and those of the Divine provision. This is a very arresting paragraph, and very full. "God chose the foolish things of the world, that He might put to shame those that are wise." That is, for the things that in the thinking of the world are wise God chose foolish things to put them to shame. "And God chose the weak things of the world, that He might put to shame the things that are strong." Shame (disgrace is the word), that He might disgrace the strong things, that is, the things which the world accounts strong. "And the base things of the world, and the things that are despised, did God choose, yea, and the things that are not, that He might bring to nought the things that are; that no flesh should glory before God."

Notice the contrast suggested through those verses. First of all, the wise things, strong things, and high things of the world's estimation, the things that are held high, and not despised, and the things that are actual. Look at the foolish things in the thinking of the world, as opposed to the wise things, the strong things, in the estimation of the world, as opposed to the weak things, the things the world looks upon as weak; the high things in human estimation, in the thinking of the world, as opposed to the things the world despises. The things that are, that are real and definite in the thinking of the world, opposed to the things the world does not count at all, that are not.

Take the things he is looking at, the world and its thinking, all that was coming from the philosophers of the time, those discussing philosophy. It is well to remember that at the time Paul wrote these letters philosophy was dead, as decadent and dead as was religion. There had been living, vital voices in philosophy, but at this time they were rather discussing the views of dead men, and if there is nothing to discuss other than the views of dead men, the result will be as dead as the men talked about. So it was with these men. There had been a living period in philosophy beginning with Anaxagoras, and on down, and then two thousand years in which there had been no living voice; and then it had moved on with Bacon and Descartes, on to the present times. Here they were discussing, with brilliance and with a good deal of joy; and they were creating a warfare of words. The Church had become infected.

Paul now asked them to look at and to think over the things held wise by all these thinkers and these disputants, things they looked upon as being strong, things these men held in high estimation, and held as real things, tangible things. Paul says God refuses all those things, and in the wisdom of God they are seen to be utterly futile and worthless.

Mark the contrast. "God chose the foolish things of the world," that is, the things the world looked upon as foolish to that age. We confine ourselves to that for a moment, though it has equal application to our own. That age looked upon certain things as utterly foolish, and the most foolish thing to the wisdom of the world was the Christian, with the central idea of the Cross as the way of human salvation. That was utterly foolish. It was foolishness to the Greek, as we have seen. God has chosen it to disgrace the futilities of human disputation and discussion, and attempts to find out the secrets of life and truth.

The weak things of the world God has chosen. What were they? The weak things of that age were its moral standards. The moral standards were lowered. If Corinth was characterized by its learning—and it was at that time—and its eloquence—and it stood out radiantly in that realm—at the same time its corruption was appalling, the moral standards were gone. They were looked upon as weak, foolish things. God chose them, the foolish things, righteousness and truth and justice and the moral standards, the disgrace of the immorality of the times.

Then, again, the base things and the despised things, and the things that were debased in the thinking of those men and those teachers and those disputants, the base and despised things were the things of purity and sanctity and beauty and truth, and God chose them.

Then that striking contrast to end: "Yea," he says, "and the things that are not," that is, in the thinking of the world. What are the things that are not? The whole realm of the future, the life beyond. It was not certain. No, no, said the philosophers. Let us deal with actualities. Let us deal with facts, with things tangible, things apparent.

We are here right in the midst of these things which are spectacular. Take the life beyond, they are not, they do not exist, they do not enter into our calculations; and God chose those things, all the things that the world held of no value by human wisdom, a wisdom bound by the cosmos, the world, the earthly, the material, all the things that were held high in the estimation—all these things God counted foolish and weak and ignoble and unreal.

All that led to that tremendous passage, " That no flesh should glory before God." Here follows the contrast, " But of Him are ye in Christ Jesus, Who was made unto us wisdom from God, and righteousness, and sanctification, and redemption; that, according as it is written, He that glorieth, let him glory in the Lord."

Summarizing the whole outlook from the Divine standpoint, all this wisdom of words is uttermost futility in the results it produces. There is wisdom, but it is vested in God. It is at your disposal. It belongs to you if you are in Christ Jesus, Who is made unto you wisdom from God. Here is a point where there may not be perfect agreement by equally scholarly and devout teachers. Here I believe everything is summarized in the word " wisdom." It is said sometimes that Paul here describes Christ as being four things to us, " wisdom from God, and righteousness and sanctification, and redemption." That is quite true; but the whole statement as I read it and understand it is this, that everything is included in the word wisdom. And then what is included in the word wisdom is revealed in the words that follow, righteousness, sanctification, redemption. In the Greek New Testament there is a slight difference. Two words are used. We translate " and righteousness, and sanctification and redemption "; but that first " and," the Greek word *te,* may mean " both." The other two occasions it is the Greek word *kai.* " Both righteousness and sanctification and redemption." There are four things here, however they are arranged. What Paul is saying here is that over against all this false wisdom of words there stands the wisdom of God, and that wisdom of God is ours in Christ Jesus. All wisdom is in Him and in His words. What is wisdom? He analyzes it in those three tremendous words, " righteousness, sanctification, and redemption."

What is righteousness? A word becomes more powerful sometimes when it is shortened. Rightness is the same thing. Shorten it again and the word is a little more dynamic—right. What is right? Right is perfect conformity to a standard. What is the standard? There is only one, and that is what the world has yet to learn. What is it? God Himself. Righteousness, or rightness, or right, in human life is conformity to the standard which is found in God and revealed in Christ Jesus. The marvellous thing here is that Paul says Christ is made that to us—righteousness, and that is the root, the very foundation of wisdom.

But he goes on, "and sanctification." What is sanctification? It is purification in separation, a process. I am not going to enter into any theological or doctrinal argument on sanctification. How the Church of God has been divided on that very subject! We have had two schools of sanctification. We have heard the phrase often, the second blessing. It is a most disagreeable phrase. People who have experienced it go around and say they have received it, and they put up their chins so high, and strut around! I do not want to quarrel with anyone's convictions. We may enter into the experience of sanctification by sudden illumination. As a matter of fact, we enter into the experience of sanctification the moment we are born again. Christ is not made first righteousness to us, and we are not made to wait a little while for sanctification. All these things are ours in Christ in the moment we believe in Him and become members of His mystical Body which is the Church.

Yet there is progress. Righteousness, yes, immediately. Sanctification, yes, progressively. And, finally, redemption. Here is a remarkable thing. We might be inclined to put that first, as something inclusive, but Paul concluded with it. As a matter of fact, it is something different. Redemption here means final escape from all bondage. This particular Greek word occurs in the New Testament ten times, and every time it refers to the future, and not to the past or the present. "Now is salvation nearer to us than when we first believed." It is in that sense Christ is made redemption, the assurance of ultimate escape from all bondage and limitation, the complete and final entrance into the meaning of our salvation; and that will never be until He shall fashion anew the body of our humiliation, that it may be conformed to the body of His glory. But it is all there, all provided for us.

Oh, these little puerile, futile discussions among supposedly clever people! They leave the whole fact of human life in its direct need and profoundest necessity helpless. But God has made us who are in Christ Jesus, wisdom, righteousness, sanctification, redemption. Some words were heard in old days more often. Our fathers used to talk about the imputation of righteousness, that it is imputed to us in Christ Jesus. So it is, and that is exactly what takes place when we believe on Him and are born again. He Himself is righteous, the Righteousness of God, and in Him God is imputed to us. We may not be wholly righteous. We may not be wholly clean, or true. Faith is the appropriation of His righteousness. It is imputed to us. This imputation has to do with the spirit, the essential nature of man. Sanctification is progressive. In sanctification Christ is not imputed, but imparted, and that is progressive, that has to do with the mind, the mind being transformed into His image and His likeness. The last, redemption, looks on to the ultimate. What is that? Christ implanted. Everything is done then. That is the final fact, and that has to do, ultimately, sacramentally with our body, when He shall fashion anew the body of our humiliation that it may be conformed to the body of His glory.

That is God's wisdom as opposed to man's wisdom, that wisdom which is ours in Christ Jesus. Christ imputed, righteousness; imparted, sanctification; implanted, redemption. All through here the apostle draws the distinction between futility and power. Human philosophy has no spiritual or moral dynamic. In saying that I am saying something to which the philosophers will all agree. Philosophy does not profess to have spiritual or moral dynamic. It ignores the things of God's wisdom, oftentimes, I am afraid, despises them. But the Word of the Cross, which is the ultimate word of Divine wisdom coming from God for man, has wholly to do with these very things. It is the application of the wisdom of God to the human being, in spirit, in mind, and in body. Immediately it comes back to us the wrong and the shame and the folly of Christian people, who ought to be bearing witness by lip and by life to these great facts but are spending their time separating around these views, while the witness is not being borne.

I CORINTHIANS ii. 1–16

This is a brief paragraph (ii. 1–5) but it is of exceptional value and significance. While still dealing with divisions, Paul turned from the general to the personal for purposes of illustration. In these verses he used the personal pronoun "I" four times and the possessive pronoun "my" twice. In his mind there were two matters of importance, the Church's message, and the method in which that message should be made known. These are the two things illustrated here in a most interesting and arresting way.

A contrast is sharply drawn between the false and the true; the false represented by the wisdom of the world and its disputes; the true by the great Word of the Cross which he and all the Church were called upon to make known. The false is recognized here by reference merely. The true, as to message and method, is stated and described. We are necessarily supremely interested in the true, and only glance at the false as giving the background. The false messages which the apostle had in mind were the words of wisdom, or philosophy of the cosmos, that is, all that teaching which had resulted from an examination of the material order and which consisted of views concerning that material order. The false manner was that of disputation and discussion, in other words, all the philosophies resulting from human thinking coming into contact with each other, and creating all the different schools in Corinth, debating their philosophies and attempting to teach men wisdom on the basis of this kind of investigation. All through this section Paul was showing how false and puerile that method of dealing with life is. The false wisdom is the wisdom of the cosmos and the false manner the disputations and discussions resulting—all the philosophies resulting from human thinking.

But the interesting matter is the apostle's revelation of what the true message is, the message committed to him and to the Church. He is concerned also with the manner of making known that message.

First, then, the Christian message. The first two verses show what Paul felt to be the Christian message committed to him and, consequently, committed to the Church. The message of the apostles was given to them that the Church might deliver that message. In the Ephesian letter Paul said, concerning gifts bestowed upon the Church, "He gave some apostles, and some prophets, and some evangelists, and some pastors and teachers; for the perfecting of the saints," not "for the work of the ministry," as though the gifts were bestowed in order that those possessing them should do the work of the ministry. It is rather "for the perfecting of the saints, unto the work of ministering." The whole Church is in the ministry. The whole Church is committed to the revelation of this tremendous message. So here.

Two phrases in these verses arrest us. The first is "the mystery of God," and the second, "Jesus Christ and Him crucified." The Authorized Version renders the first phrase, "the testimony of God." The revisers have changed it to "the mystery of God." There is no final and dogmatic statement possible on the basis of the MS, whether Paul wrote "testimony" or "mystery," whether *marturion*, or *musterion*. Finally, however, it is not important, for they mean the same thing. I am inclined to believe Paul wrote "mystery." It is possible that some copyist thought the word was *marturion*, testimony; or else *musterion*, mystery. If we take the word "testimony," then it must be interpreted by its occurrence in the first chapter and the sixth verse, "the testimony of Christ . . . confirmed in you." We then saw that the meaning was as to the full Gospel, all the message concerning Christ to which the Church was called upon to bear witness.

If Paul wrote the word *musterion*, mystery, then we must interpret that by his use of the word in other places in his writings, and notably in one. When writing to Timothy he said, "Great is the mystery of godliness; He Who was manifested in the flesh, justified in the spirit, seen of messengers, heralded among the nations, believed on in the world, received up in glory." That is the mystery of godliness. But whether "testimony" or "mystery," the idea is that of the content of truth, of which the Church is at once the depository and the institution for publication in the world. Go back to the passage in Timothy:

> "Great is the mystery of godliness." Look at the context. "These things write I unto thee, hoping to come unto thee shortly; but if I tarry long that thou mayest know how men ought to behave themselves in the house of God, which is the pillar and ground of the truth. And without controversy great is the mystery of godliness."

The Church is the pillar and ground of the truth, the institute in the world with which that truth is deposited, and which she is responsible for making known.

All that certainly was in Paul's mind, whether he used the word "testimony" as covering the whole ground, or "mystery." The reference is to the same thing, and that is the Christian message. "I, brethren, when I came unto you, came not with excellency of speech or of wisdom, proclaiming to you the mystery of God." He had come to Corinth from Athens to proclaim the mystery of God. That is the Christian message.

Consequently, notice here that Paul said, "For I determined not to know anything among you, save Jesus Christ, and Him crucified." I do not know a statement of the apostle that in my view has more constantly been misunderstood and misapplied than that. Personally, I am convinced that the emphasis in that declaration is upon the word "you." "I determined not to know anything among *you*, save Jesus Christ, and Him crucified," that is, those people of Corinth. It was the message for Corinth, because of the carnality of the city which had infested the church. To a city so characterized, either then or today, the one first great word of the Christian message is that of the Cross of Christ. That was the message for Corinth, it was the fundamental note of this great message, but it was not the final one. It is not the final note in the mystery of godliness. Let Paul be quoted again, and this time he was writing to the Romans. "It is Christ Jesus that died, yea rather, that was raised from the dead." The ultimate note in the Christian message is that of the resurrection, in its bearing on the Cross. But it may be that men are not ready for that note, that positive and glorious note. Possibly, Apollos had come and given that note. We do not know. But when Paul came, he said, I could not give you the whole Christian message, "I determined not to know anything among you, save Jesus Christ, and Him crucified." "The mystery" of God is the Christian message in its entirety, but there are conditions in which it is only possible, or right and proper, to give the fundamental note, " Jesus Christ, and Him crucified."

The view I have referred to, which is prevalent in exposition, is that Paul came to Corinth from Athens, where he had failed; and therefore he determined that he would not try in Corinth the same method he had tried in Athens. But was Paul's visit to Athens a failure? Why do people say it was? First of all, read Paul's great address in Athens, one of the most massive and marvellous pieces of eloquence to be found anywhere, and not eloquence only, but reason and philosophy, religion and theology. Did he fail? I go back to the story in the Acts, trying to disabuse the mind of the popular passion for big statistics. It is terrible how the Church of God has passed under the blight of a passion for statistics. " Certain men clave to Paul and believed; among whom was Dionysius the Areopagite, and a woman named Damaris, and others with them." That is all we are told, certain men and one man named, and a woman and a few others; a most insignificant little group. Suppose we take up Church history, what do we find? During the next century, the church at Athens produced Publius, Quadratus, Aristides, and Athanagoras, names that stand out to this hour as men of powerful spiritual ability. Come down to the third century of Church history, and there was a church in Athens characterized by peace and purity; and, again, to come to the fourth century, it was the church at Athens that gave us Basil and Gregory. What about the Corinthian church, where Paul determined to know nothing among them save Christ crucified? It was gone; it had perished, had lost its witness, and there is no single outstanding name among those connected with the Corinthian church. The whole message of the mystery, the testimony of God, could not be preached in Corinth, in that city saturated with voluptuousness, with its carnality; all the people affected by it. He came there, and said—reverently I put it—No, I cannot preach all the facts of the Christian message yet. " I determined not to know anything among *you*, save Jesus Christ, and Him crucified." Consequently, that is the fundamental note with which to face the pagan world. The carnality of the human heart must be faced with the message of the Cross.

There are those who render, and I think quite permissibly there, " Christ Jesus, and even Him crucified." What a message it was, contrary to the wisdom of these disputing philosophers, contrary to the ideals of Messianic power borne by the Jews. Paul had to begin with them there, with the Cross; and the Christian messenger must bring carnality face to face with the Cross. He determined there to know nothing else.

If that is the message, now notice those personal references to the manner of making it known. The apostle denied two methods. Notice the word "not" twice over. "I, brethren, when I came unto you, came *not* with excellency of speech or of wisdom." Again, in the fourth verse, "My speech and my preaching were *not* in persuasive words of wisdom." When he came to that great city, he delivered his message with no excellency of speech or wisdom. That must be interpreted by the times. Corinth was noted then for its eloquence, and the beauty, from the standpoint of literature, of the writings of its pseudo-philosophers. It was so true that when they talked of philosophy in the other parts of the Roman empire, they dismissed it by saying, "They are living as they do at Corinth." There was also another phrase that had passed into the currency of speech. If a man was eloquent in diction and style, they described him as using "Corinthian words." That is the exact synonym for excellency of speech. The apostle said, I abjure it. I did not come to you with a cult of style in phrasing or eloquence or method, so far as style is concerned.

That is most important. Years ago, a great man, a good man, scholarly and a saint, said to me, speaking of another preacher, "Yes, he is a wonderful preacher, but you know he has sacrificed the prophet to the artist." Preachers should think of that. It is possible to sacrifice the prophet to the artist, to be so concerned with eloquence and language and phrasing and beauty of style that the impact of truth is lost. That is what Paul meant. He abjured it. He had not come to them with excellency of speech, and wisdom based upon that kind of thing.

What else? "Not in persuasive words of wisdom." Even in the great subject of his message he had not employed, and refused to employ, the methods of the disputants who were building up their contradictory philosophies. He abjured them. He put them on one side, and declined to use them. But do not imagine that Paul was unequal to persuasion and debate. That is not the point at all. We read in Acts xvii. 17 that he went into the synagogue and "reasoned." That is argument. Again, in Ephesians we read that he "reasoned" and "persuaded." Paul was quite equal to reasoning. He was a great dialectician. One cannot read his writings without seeing it; but in his delivery he did not trust to his dialectics, to his style. He abjured it—"persuasive words of wisdom."

What did he do? Two words reveal his method. In verse 2, "proclaiming to you the mystery of God." Verse 4, "My speech and my preaching were not in persuasive words." Proclaiming and preaching, or rather, proclaiming by preaching. Proclaiming, that is, declaring—*kataggelo*, declaring fully. There was no slurring facts over. He was careful to make them clear in his statement, declaring this mystery of God, this Divine word. And then preaching, *kerusso*, not the word *euaggeliso*, to preach the Gospel, but to proclaim as a herald. It is the language and method of a man who is representing a king. He went to Corinth proclaiming, and he did it by preaching; undebatable authority in the thing he was declaring to them. The note for Corinth was Jesus Christ and Him crucified, proclaimed, declared, and that with authority. That was Paul's method.

Then how remarkable and forceful the double consciousness. Notice first his personal consciousness. In some senses it is almost amazing to read it from the pen of Paul. Yet here it is: " I was with you in weakness, and in fear, and in much trembling." That was not about his message, but about himself. Weakness, that is, strengthlessness of mind or body. That was his consciousness. Fear, alarm, fear lest—may I borrow a Biblical phrase—the trumpet should give an uncertain sound. Trembling! So great was his sense of weakness and fear, and so profound his lack of trust in himself that he quaked, he trembled. Those are the secrets of strength in all preaching.

But there was a relative consciousness, something of which he was quite sure. However weak he felt, however much he feared, however much he quaked, one thing he knew. What he did was in " the demonstration of the Spirit and power." Demonstrating is making plain. He came to proclaim, and the work of the Spirit was to co-operate with him, while he co-operated with the Spirit in weakness, and fear and trembling, and proclaimed, preached. The Spirit co-operating demonstrated the truth of his message in power to those who heard him. It is a great thing for every preacher to realize that. If I thought my making known the truth of this great Gospel depended upon myself and my argument, I should give it up, for I could not do it. That is what the apostle meant. But when I know that when I, submitted to the Spirit, declare the great evangel, the Spirit is going with the message, demonstrating it; it is not my business finally to demonstrate, it is His. It is my business to proclaim, to preach.

Everything is then gathered up to show the reason of his message and method, that their faith might be established in God, and not in human wisdom. That is the mistake they were making. They were trying to pin their faith on him, or Apollos, or Cephas. No, let us get beyond all the words that may have sounded to us as words of wisdom, and get our faith rooted in God.

This is a brief paragraph, but a great one, especially for all preachers and teachers to whom is committed this ministry of the mystery of God.

The first word of this paragraph (verses 6–16) is arresting, " Howbeit." The word might be rendered, " But," though that would not be so good as " Howbeit." However, it does indicate the fact that Paul was now going to make a new beginning, and to say something not in any sense a contradiction of what he had already been saying. He is not even instituting a contrast between something he has already said and what he is now going to say. It is a continuation; there is something else to be said—" Howbeit." It is as though the apostle said, I have written something, but do not hurry, that is not all the truth, "Howbeit." He pulls them up, causes them to pause. It is true that the message does not come with excellency of speech or persuasive words of wisdom. That he had said in our previous paragraph (1–5) by that personal illustration in which he had revealed the nature of the Christian message and the true method of delivery. He had not come to them with excellency of speech nor with persuasive words of wisdom. He had not come with the method of the dialectician or with arguments. All that was true, " Howbeit . . ."

He is therefore going to say something that is vital and important. All that he has said is true, howbeit the Christian message is not devoid of wisdom. They were living in a city where men were discussing their varied schools of philosophy and forming groups around their teachers, and they were imitating them in the Christian Church, were forming little groups around their teachers, some around Paul, or around Apollos, or Peter, or even around Christ Himself. He protested against the whole thing, and yet he did not want them to argue from that that the Christian message was devoid of wisdom. It is not devoid of wisdom. "Howbeit we speak wisdom among the perfect, yet a wisdom not of this world, nor of the rulers of this world, which are coming to nought; but we speak God's wisdom in a mystery." Do not imagine that Christianity is devoid of philosophy, of wisdom, that it is something outside the realm of the intellect. It is not. It has its own wisdom, its own philosophy. Indeed, what Paul is showing here is that the Christian philosophy is the ultimate philosophy. It is not to be tested by other philosophies. They are to be tried by it. "We speak wisdom." He states that with finality—wisdom. All this discussion in the realm of wisdom and philosophy, and all these different emphases, get us nowhere; but we are not lacking in wisdom, " we speak wisdom." Here is the whole truth. They were not to test their Christianity, Paul said to the Corinthian Christians, and to the Church for all time, by all human philosophies, but they are to try the philosophies by the central philosophy, which is the philosophy of God.

This whole paragraph (6–16) is in definition of that wisdom or philosophy, and it divides quite naturally. First, Paul shows that the Christian philosophy is not of this age (6–9). Then he shows that the Christian philosophy is entirely of the Holy Spirit (10, 11). Then he shows what is the principle of discernment in all these matters (12–16).

The Christian wisdom, resident in the Church, of which she is the depository, and which she is responsible for proclaiming to the world, is not of this age. That is the first thing Paul said. Whence, then, is it? What is the fountain head of this wisdom? The Holy Spirit. How are these things to be distinguished? What is the true principle upon which we may know?

Notice, first, that in verses 6, 7 and 8 we have the word "world"—"a wisdom not of this *world*," "nor of the rulers of this *world*," "God foreordained before the *worlds*," "which none of the rulers of this *world* knoweth." Then in verse 12 we read, "We received not the spirit of the *world*, but the spirit which is of God." There is a distinction between these. The first word, in verses 6, 7 and 8 is *aion*, or age; but in verse 12 it is the word *cosmos*, or world. The two Greek words have an entirely different significance. The first word, *aion*, refers to a time period. The second word, *cosmos*, refers to the material order of things. With that distinction in mind, we understand what Paul is saying. He says this wisdom is not of this age. The wisdom of the age is the result of the limitation of thinking within that time period. The thinking that is bounded by the age, limited to the age, is the wisdom of the age. Paul says that is not our wisdom.

Of course, that is an essential characteristic of the Christian religion and of all revealed religion, that it is not bounded by an age, that it overleaps the boundaries of all time periods. It is of all time and of all ages. Whenever we think of these Corinthian days, the state of philosophy was comparatively decadent. It had had its living period. We may look upon the birth of philosophy, of human thinking in its profound attempt to discover the truth concerning the universe, as beginning with Anaxagoras, and on down for about three hundred years, during which period it was virile. Then came a period lasting two thousand years, when there was nothing but the discussion of that living period, until it had a rebirth with Bacon and Descartes, and has been running on since for three hundred years, when it has been a living force. I may add that it is becoming once more decadent. There is nothing new today in the realm of philosophy. But in the whole period stretching over at least 2600 years man has been studying philosophy, and every philosophical school has been attempting to find an answer to one question. What is that? Interestingly and arrestingly enough, it is the question that Pilate asked Jesus, "What is truth?" I know when Bacon wrote his essay on Truth, he began it thus, "'What is truth?' said the jesting Pilate, and did not wait for an answer." I do not believe Pilate was jesting that day. I believe Pilate found himself confronting a Personality and an outlook that amazed him, and when he heard Him say He had come into the world to bear witness to the truth, he blurted out the profound and initial question of philosophy for all time, " What is truth?"

But take the whole history of philosophy, and every new system as it has arisen out of the previous one—it is always beginning again, the period of an age, bounded by an age. That has been the characteristic of all human philosophy. Now, Paul says, Our philosophy is not bounded by an age, is not of this age. He did not merely mean that present age in which he was living, but to all thinking of men circumscribed by a period and an age. Our philosophy is not that. " Howbeit we speak wisdom . . . a wisdom not of this age."

If it is not of this age, and not of the rulers of this age, those great thinkers mastering the thought of an age, which he dismisses with a satirical sentence, " which are coming to nought," which, he says, all perish, what is this wisdom? " But we speak God's wisdom in a mystery." That is the Christian philosophy, the wisdom of God. How can we know that? As Xophar said to Job, " Canst thou by searching find out God?" That is why human philosophy has forever broken down. It has been attempting to discover, to find out. But, said the apostle, it is " God's wisdom in a mystery."

That brings us face to face with a word. What is a " mystery " ? Anyone could intelligently answer that question. We can pick up the newspaper and read about some happening to which there is no explanation, and we say, It is a great mystery. We do not understand it. The word " mystery " never means that when found in the New Testament. Take the Greek word, *musterion*. It occurs twenty-seven times in the New Testament. Three times in Matthew, Mark, and Luke, it is on the lips of our Lord. Really, it is only once, for these three writers give the same account when He used the word " mystery " in connection with His parables. When He uttered parables, He said to His disciples, " Unto you it is given to know the mysteries of the Kingdom of heaven . . . therefore I speak unto them in parables." It is never found in the Gospels again. Paul is the only one who uses this word in the epistles, and in his writings the word will be found no less than twenty times. In the Apocalypse John does use the word, but only four times. Therefore, it is peculiarly Paul's word. It is a word that came out of the Greek schools of philosophy, of the occult, and of science—mystery. Paul fastened on it, and he says, " We speak God's wisdom in a mystery," but he gives it an entirely new meaning. Mystery comes from a word meaning mouth, and it means to shut the mouth. Paul never so used it. That which had been silent has become vocal. That which had not been known and could not be known, as the result of human investigation, has been made known. A mystery in the New Testament always means something undiscoverable by the activity of the human intellect, but revealed, so that human intellect can understand. A mystery is something which has been revealed, so that it may be apprehended by the mind of man, and by the human intellect.

We have a wisdom. We have a philosophy. It is not of this age, bounded and limited by a period, and vanishing when the period ends. It is of all ages, because it is of God. But it is a mystery. It is something which has been manifested. He says the rulers of this world did not know it. Had they known it, they would not have crucified the Lord of glory. And yet this mystery has its greatest marvel in the fact that that very crucifixion, which showed the darkness of the rulers of the world, became the center of light for humanity in the Cross, God's wisdom unveiled and unfolded.

It is very wonderful to see what Paul says of the purpose of this great mystery. "None of the rulers of this age knoweth; for had they known it, they would not have crucified the Lord of glory." Notice then his quotation: "Things which eye saw not, and ear heard not, and which entered not into the heart of man, whatsoever things God prepared for them that love Him." He was quoting from the prophecy of Isaiah. If we turn to Isaiah we find he was referring to the fact that God is the God Who worketh for him that waits for Him. Isaiah says there that things which eye saw not, and ear heard not, and which entered not into the heart of man, were the very things God was preparing for those who wait for Him. Paul took hold of that. Things which eye could not see in watching, in observation, are revealed; words that ear could not hear while listening to all the voices that were sounding could bring that truth. They did not enter into the heart of man; the feeling and emotional nature never fastened upon this deep truth. That is the wisdom of God; but now that wisdom has been manifested.

Next, notice another word particularly. Verse 10 commences, "But . . ." In countless instances I have heard this passage quoted by good Christian people in reference to Heaven. We have no right to do so. They say of the glory of Heaven, "Things which eye saw not, and ear heard not, and which entered not into the heart of man"— and they slip in two little words, "to conceive the things God has prepared for them that love Him." They say, Of course we cannot know these things; they are wonderful, beautiful things. Paul says, "But unto us God revealed them through the Spirit." You *can* know them. The rulers of the wisdom of the world could not know, their eye could not see, their ear could not hear, their heart could not visualize or imagine anything like that; but unto us God hath revealed them.

So we turn to that which is not of the age but of the Spirit. The undiscovered Revealer is the Spirit. What a wonderful passage this is! "The Spirit searcheth all things; yea, the deep things of God. For who among men knoweth the things of a man, save the spirit of the man, which is in him?" Who can know these deep, profound mysteries, the wonder of the Divine Being and purpose? "Even so the things of God none knoweth, save the Spirit of God." But the Spirit has revealed them. The wisdom is unveiled, it is revealed to us. All these things that eye has not seen, or ear heard, and never entered into the heart of man, these things are revealed to us, and are revealed by the Spirit.

Paul then showed the principles of judgment. But we received, not the spirit of the cosmos, not the spirit bounded by the material, which could depend only upon investigation of matter. We know full well that science, of which we speak with profound respect, cannot go beyond that. Whatever it has to say to us is based upon the material cosmos. But this wisdom goes far beyond that. We have not received the spirit which is bounded in the cosmos, but the Spirit of God, that we might know the things which are given to us by God.

"Which things also we speak," our resulting testimony. We have received that Spirit if we are indeed Christian people. If we are called saints, the Spirit is ours, and the resulting testimony; and we are called upon to bear witness, "which things we speak."

Then next, "comparing spiritual things with spiritual," a most important principle in all the investigation of this wisdom of God, that the spiritual should be compared with the spiritual. If that is not done, we shall hear some saying they are of Paul, or Apollos, or Cephas. But if we are comparing, we see what is insured by that, comparing the spiritual with the spiritual, the assurance of the balance of truth. That is a most important principle today. There are people whose Christianity or sincerity is not questioned, but they have become so obsessed by some one view of truth that they see nothing else, and consequently that very view of truth becomes a hindrance instead of a help. We are to compare spiritual things with spiritual, for Paul says, "The natural man receiveth not the things of the Spirit of God." What is meant by "natural"? The Greek word there is *psuchikos*, and we might read the psychic man, mentality, the mental man. That is quite true. The man who is only psychic has no relation with the Spirit, he is hemmed in by the material universe, and then by human thinking. "The psychic man receiveth not the things of the Spirit of God; for they are foolishness unto him." He cannot see them. That is what the Greeks said, as we have already seen.

"But he that is spiritual discerneth all things, and he himself is discerned, judged of no man." If we can discern the things of the Spirit, the natural man will not discern us, he will think we are foolish, and he cannot understand. How often that is borne out! "For who hath known the mind of the Lord, that He should instruct him?"

Everything closes with this tremendous statement, yet so simple to read. "But we have the mind of Christ." There the whole thing is stated. The wisdom, and the wisdom made known by the Spirit, what is it? "We have the mind of Christ." The Greek word is *nous*, which simply means intellect or consciousness. We have the consciousness of Christ, the mind of Christ, the outlook of Christ. That statement should not be confused with another, when Paul says, writing to the Philippians, "Have this mind in you, which was also in Christ Jesus." That is not the same word. The word there means an exercise of mind. It has to do with emotion, inspiring, self-emptying. Here it is intelligent understanding, wisdom.

He summarizes everything. Howbeit, do not make any mistake and imagine we have no philosophy. We have a wisdom, the wisdom of God in a mystery. "Great is the mystery of godliness, He Who was manifested in flesh, attested by the Spirit, seen of messengers, proclaimed among the nations, believed on in the world, received up in glory"—that to quote Paul again. That is the whole mould of the mystery; and whatever else there is, there we have the mind of Christ.

To return again to the introduction. The Christian message is the ultimate philosophy. There is a simple Gospel, thank God. We hear people talk about the simple Gospel, and they are quite right. There is a simple Gospel. But do not forget that the simple Gospel is sublime and profound in its ultimate content. It is rooted in the deep things of God, and its simplicity is created by the fact that it has come into manifestation through Jesus Christ, so that our little children can hear it and understand it, love it and grow up into it, until the years having run their course, they will say at the last what Sir Isaac Newton said in the presence of the universe of which he was a devout and earnest student, "I am like a little child, standing by the seashore picking up a pebble here and a pebble there, and admiring them, while the great sea rolls in front of me."

ii. Causative Carnality Corrected   iii, iv
    a. The Cause of the Schisms   iii. 1–4
        1. Carnal. Not Spiritual
                  Not Discerning
        2. Babes. Arrested Development
        3. Jealousy and Strife
    b. The Correction   iii. 5–23
        1. The Ministry and God   5–9
        2. The Ministry and the Church   10–15
        3. The Church and God and the Ministry   16–23

I CORINTHIANS iii

PAUL has been aptly called a great doctor of the soul. I use that figure of speech in coming to this paragraph. As a layman, I should say there are two things of supreme importance in the work of a doctor or physician: one, understanding the malady, and the other, providing the remedy. If that be true, surely Paul was a great doctor of the soul. How he understood the malady of human life and history, and, thank God, how he understood the great remedy that has been provided!

The justification of this description is often seen in his writings. Perhaps we are sometimes permitted to indulge in speculation which may have no warrant. I have wondered if Paul did not owe something to Luke after all. Luke owed something to Paul. He so often travelled with him. Constantly in Paul's writings the justification of the description of the doctor is found, and notably so in this passage. We shall look at it from that standpoint.

Paul was still dealing with the divisions in the Corinthian church, and wherever such divisions may show themselves, for this letter was not written for the Corinthian church alone. It was written to you, to me. Paul said so at the commencement of the letter. It has a universal application so far as the Church is concerned. In this paragraph he reveals the underlying cause of the divisions, names the proofs of his contention as to the underlying cause, and shows how the wrong may be corrected. That is the method of the doctors. I adopt their very terms. First of all, there is diagnosis (verses 1–4), and in the same verses we see the revealing symptoms that prove the correctness of the diagnosis. Then in verses 5–8 he shows how the malady is to be corrected. Paul the doctor is dealing with a malady which is destroying the influence of the Christian Church in Corinth and in other places; and he first gives the diagnosis, shows what is the underlying cause and nature of all the trouble; and then he gives us certain symptoms which prove the accuracy of the diagnosis; and then he gives an account of how that matter is to be corrected.

I have used that word "diagnosis." It is a wonderful word, which has become the word of the medical profession almost exclusively. I do not know that we hear it in any other particular realm. What does it mean? Knowing through, knowing completely, *dia gnosis,* thoroughly understanding. It is an interesting fact that the Greek word diagnosis occurs only once in the New Testament, and there it is not used of a doctor at all. When Festus brought Paul before Agrippa, Festus told Agrippa he was greatly puzzled by this case, and he did not know what he should do with him. He said Paul had appealed to "the decision of the emperor." So the Revised Version. The Authorized reads he had appealed to the "hearing of Augustus." The revisers have rendered *diagnosis* "decision" in this one case, and the Authorized, "Hearing." I think they are both wrong. The word means simply the investigation by the emperor of his case, as every Roman citizen could appeal directly to the emperor, for the emperor to make the diagnosis. It means the same thing, knowing through.

What does Paul say about the divisions with which he has already been dealing in the Corinthian church? First, he addresses them as "brethren." "And I, brethren, could not speak unto you as unto spiritual, but as unto babes in Christ." Whatever he is going to write, he is writing to them as brethren, those who are his fellow believers, who are babes. That shows the presence of life. He is not writing to those dead, to those people who have no apprehension of the things he is saying. You, brethren, you are babes. You have life, you are born. He began there.

What was the matter with these people? "I . . . could not speak unto you as unto spiritual, but as unto carnal." There is the underlying truth. He is not writing to men of the world, outside the Christian fact. He is writing to those within the Christian fact, to those born again, who have life. Yes, he says, they are babes, but they are brethren. The trouble with them is that they are not spiritual, but are carnal.

The statement demands attention. What is the difference between the spiritual and the carnal? I turn to one of the most wonderful things in the New Testament, the analysis of personality that came from Paul's pen when he was writing to the Thessalonians. He certainly understood men and human nature. He prayed that their "spirit and soul and body be preserved entire, without blame at the coming of our Lord Jesus Christ." Not three entities, perhaps in some senses only two, the spirit and the body. What is the soul? The consciousness, the mind. There are the three Greek words—*pneuma* for spirit, *psyche* for soul or mind, and *soma* for body. There is the whole of human personality. There are the three phases, or sides, or aspects, or entities. The essential thing in human personality is not the body, and it is not the mind. It is the spirit. God is a Spirit, and man is made in the Divine likeness, and man must worship in spirit. Of every person, every human being, whether in the Church or outside, the supreme fact is the spiritual fact. What is the matter with the world? It has forgotten that.

Then there is the body, an equally definite fact; but the body is there as the instrument of the spirit. Through the body the spirit receives and makes contact with others. Through the body it expresses itself to others. The body, an ideal personality in the Divine economy, is secondary.

What is the soul? The consciousness, the mind, the intelligence, although, finally, intelligence is vested not in the body but in the spirit. That great surgeon, Dr. Howard Kelly of Baltimore, who read his Hebrew Bible every morning with his ten-year-old daughter, said to me once, "They tell me the seat of memory and consciousness is in the brain. Nothing of the kind, it is in the spirit. The brain may act in that way as a medium, but it is not my brain that knows, it is I that know, and the *I* is the spirit." He gave me a somewhat gruesome illustration. He told me of a man terribly smashed up in an accident. Dr. Kelly cut off a large part of his brain, and the man recovered, and never forgot anything! The doctors can discuss that. At any rate, I believe it is true, and that the final seat of consciousness is the spirit.

But mark you this. What is the Bible account of man? It is that God formed him of the dust of the ground. That is the body, but that is not man; and He breathed into his nostrils the breath, the *ruach*, the breath of life, that is the spirit, and so he became a living conscious soul. Here we have three planes, the spirit, the mind, the body; and every man and woman is living, either mastered by the body, which is the lower, or by the spirit, which is the higher. The mind is affected by that part of personality to which the mastery of the person gives himself over. If I descend to the level of the material, if I consent to that, then all my thinking is fleshly, carnal. That is the word. On the other hand, if I lift my whole personality to the spiritual, then my thinking is spiritual, mastered by the spirit. I am not referring to the Spirit of God for the moment. Of course, He enters in the Christian experience. The Spirit of God comes when I am dead in trespasses and sins, and gives me new life, and it is when the life of the indwelling Spirit takes possession of my spirit that all comes under the domination of that Spirit.

We see, therefore, the reaction of these: the spirit or the body dominant, and the mind or soul governed thereby, either to carnal things, the lower; or to spiritual things, the higher. Writing to these

Corinthians, Paul says, I will tell you what is the matter with you Corinthian people. I cannot write unto you as unto spiritual—you are not living in that realm—but as to carnal. You are living under the mastery of the flesh. Oh, you are children, you are babes. You are born again. You have life, but you are yielding yourself to the carnal side of your nature, instead of the spiritual. To refer to another of Paul's letters, he wrote to the Romans, " For they that are after the flesh do mind the things of the flesh; but they that are after the spirit the things of the spirit. For the mind of the flesh is death; but the mind of the spirit is life and peace."

The whole trouble was just there. These people had received the gift of life. They were babes in Christ, but mastered by the lower side of life; and their thinking was under the mastery of that which was fleshly and material and carnal. It is a severe diagnosis, and not at all popular. I do not know that it was there in Corinth. I know it would not be today, but who will doubt the accuracy?

Well, Paul, how do you prove this? He gives proof. First, they were " babes," undeveloped, immature. They were not full grown. Paul had already said, " We speak wisdom among the full grown," for the developed. These people were not there. The trouble was this, that they were in a condition of arrested development, and that always means failure to function according to intention. That may be illustrated in life. Take a child, a baby, how beautiful, but if that child is seen in sixteen years' time, and it is still a baby, we should say it is undeveloped, immature, not grown up, and it cannot function. That was the trouble with these people in Corinth. Paul was not speaking only of them, and their peace and joy and blessedness. He was thinking of Corinth, that great city in which God said He had many people who were uninfluenced by the Church because those within the Church were quarreling. What was their function? God had called them into the fellowship of His Son Jesus Christ. That was their function in Corinth. They were not fulfilling it. Why not? Arrested development. Why?

Then there were other signs—" jealousy and strife." The word " jealousy " may be rendered envying, and that marks personal pride and pique if one did not agree with them. " Strife " is a strong word, positive quarreling and wrangling. That was the positive outcome of the jealousy. These people who ought to have been functioning in the fellowship of Jesus Christ were quarreling among themselves, forming themselves into little groups, with a very pious sound, Paul, and Apollos, and Cephas.

He says they are walking " after the manner of men," acting as men of the world are acting, influenced by partiality for human teachers such as Paul and Apollos; and all that proves that they were living on the lower level of life, in the realm of the carnal. It is well we should ponder that for ourselves. People say, We understand what carnality is. It is vulgar, fleshly indulgence. What is fleshly indulgence? We can name all manner of things, and start all kinds of societies not to do this, that, and the other, and we are cutting off, and not touching the deepest meaning of the fleshly and material. Arguments that deflect the mind from the centrality of Christ and His Cross are fleshly and carnal. They hinder development. They prevent the Church fulfilling its function, and all these things result from the yielding to the flesh, the lower side of the nature. That is the diagnosis and the symptoms that prove it, as Paul saw them in Corinth.

What are the facts about the case? What about these men around whom they were forming their little coteries, Paul and Apollos? He said, "What then is Apollos? and what is Paul?" He tells us who they are. They are ministers serving the Lord, deacons, not in our modern sense, but in the simple sense, errand boys, *diaconoi*, the men who run errands for someone else, under authority, going where they are sent, doing what they are bidden. That is what we are. That is what Paul and Apollos were.

What are these men, and what do they do? He said, in the case of Corinth, "I planted." Now, planting is a very important work, but the life principle is not in the man who plants. It is in the seed he plants. It is tremendously important work to put that seed into the soil, but the man cannot communicate life to it, and never does. All he does is to put it in the soil. I am not minimizing that. It is one of the most tremendous conceptions in the world that I may be allowed to plant, to put the seed into the soil. But that is all I can do. And Apollos may come along, and Paul says, "Apollos watered." What is that? Watering is splendid, that which is necessary to growth and development, but the secret of growth is in the seed itself. It needs to be put into the soil. It needs watering, but the life principle that presently is to express itself in harvest is not in the man who plants or the man who waters. I go so far as to say, it is not in the soil, it is not in the watering, it is in the seed.

In the presence of this figure of speech stand back, as in the presence of all Nature. We see not the plower ploughing, and the sower sowing the seed, and the harvester putting in the sickle, but God. It is true in all Nature. It is true in grace. It is true everywhere. Their service is co-operative service, and the reward of each will be individual, according to the work each is called upon to do. They are ministers, carrying out the Divine commissions; but as for God, He " giveth the increase." Go back in the New Testament and take the phrase, "the seed is the word." I planted it, said Paul. Apollos came along and watered it, but God gave the increase. It was by the act of God that there was first the blade, and then the ear, and then the full corn in the ear. Man's work is wonderful, glorious, important, but he is out of it finally. Then imagine forming sects around the planters and waterers! That is what they were doing.

So Paul summarizes at the close of those wonderful words, "We are God's fellow workers," a tremendous declaration. More interesting is what follows: "Ye," you Christian men and women, you babes, whose development has been arrested, and who cannot be fed with strong meat, "Ye are God's husbandry, God's building." God's. All the emphasis is there. You are God's husbandry. Our minds go to words of our Lord. "I am the true vine; My Father is the husbandman." "Ye are the branches" in that vine, you are God's husbandry. He is watching over you. He is cultivating, He is preparing the life force that it may produce the fruit that shall glorify Him. And you are God's building. He takes that figure of the building up and elaborates it, as we shall see in our next paragraph. But the trouble for the moment, wherever there are divergences of opinion—and there will be divergences of opinion so long as man remains—but where there are divergences of opinion that make cliques around human personalities that result in strife, envy and wrangling; know this that the inspiration of that kind of thing is never spiritual, it is of the flesh, it is carnal, and that is the trouble.

Paul was still dealing with the subject of divisions existing in the Corinthian church in verses 10–15. He was profoundly moved by the significations of such divisions. The first nine verses of this chapter showed the root of the trouble, and declared that it was carnality. Those forming these separate parties were gathering themselves around men and their views. Certainly every man was of value, and did work of importance, and their views were accurate. But alone, any one of these men and the message he bore were incomplete. A devotion to the partial around personalities and views obscured the vision of the whole fact. It is that whole fact of the Church of God and her calling, whether it is thought of universally, or in any locality, whether to employ the opening words of the letter, of the church in Corinth, or those in every place who call upon the name of the Lord Jesus. He saw the whole meaning of the Church. The whole value of the Church was being not only hindered but injured, harmed, spoiled by reason of these divisions.

Our previous paragraph ended with the words, "We are God's fellow workers; ye are God's husbandry, God's building." In this section (verses 10–15) Paul takes that second figure, that of building, and develops it, and shows the relation between those who he declared are fellow workers with God, the ministers as he called them, and this building of God. There are two figures of speech, "God's husbandry," "God's building." He now takes the second figure in applying and showing the relation between those who were ministers and the whole Church.

The whole Church is in view when he says, "Ye are God's building." That word may have two significations. It may mean God's structure in the sense of His erecting it. It may mean God's possession, that the thing created, built up, belongs to Him. The two meanings are undoubtedly true. He is the Builder, and He owns that which He has built. That is the double signification of the word, and properly so. The Church is His work and His possession.

But while it is His work, He is acting through others, those whom Paul designates as His ministers, His servants, the *diaconoi*, quite literally, errand boys, that is, those who do what they are told and do not ask the reason why. That does not apply to the minister of the Church today, for he is one of them. No, it applies to the Lord, the One Who is the supreme Worker. God is working through these whom Paul here described as His "ministers." There are three things quite clearly in this paragraph. First of all, he shows the co-operation of these ministers with each other. Then he shows the possibilities that there are in carrying out the building, the possibilities to those who are the coworkers. God Himself is the Worker employing others to do the work. In a significant passage Paul shows an alternative of possibility. A man may be a minister, a worker, and may build unworthily. On the other hand, he may build truly. He shows how this marvellous building is set in the light of the great ultimate, the testing time for all such work, that is yet to come.

Mark carefully the opening of this paragraph. "According to the grace of God." He is recognizing his debt to grace. What had Paul done? "According to the grace of God which was given unto me, as a wise master-builder I laid a foundation; and another buildeth thereon." That is the view of co-operation. Paul says as a wise master-builder he laid a foundation. Master-builder means an architect, and one who carries out his work. He is careful to show what the foundation is— "Jesus Christ." He said in the previous chapter that he determined to know nothing among them "save Jesus Christ, and Him crucified." The necessity of the occasion limited the message at the beginning. They were carnal, sold under sin, and he could do no more than teach that. That is how the work began. He says, Here is the foundation, and "other foundation can no man lay than that which is laid, which is Jesus Christ." How much opens up there! How much of other

Scriptures seems to shine upon that great declaration in the light of the consideration that God is the Architect, God is building! He is the supreme Worker. He is responsible for the whole building, the whole institution. God is the Builder, and the foundation of that building is Jesus Christ.

When Paul went to Corinth from Athens, we see exactly what he did. In his preaching and teaching, he, first of all, "reasoned and persuaded." But when two men came down to see him, he was caught up by the Spirit and the Word, and he proclaimed them. There are the two aspects of preaching. There was the day when it was hard and difficult, and he reasoned and persuaded. There was a day when the Divine afflatus came upon him. But it was the same Word in every case. He was preaching Jesus Christ. We are told that Crispus, the ruler of the synagogue, believed. We are told that many of the Corinthians believed. Paul here said, "I laid the foundation." That is where the whole thing began, and the foundation was Jesus Christ. Take the twelve letters from his pen, and study them all, and find exactly what he meant by that. The whole fact of our faith, and of our holy religion, is built upon Jesus Christ. Paul said here that he started the work. He laid the foundation, and others built thereon. There is no conflict at all. He does not name another now, Apollos or Cephas or any other that should come along. They all built upon the same foundation. The verb here means to compose in co-operation. There is the position occupied by those men, Paul and Apollos and Cephas; but all they did was in the light of God's building, and they were all working together towards the realization of a Divine plan and a Divine purpose. That was never lost sight of.

We see at once therefore the trouble in the Corinthian church was that that whole vision of the Divine purpose in building had been lost sight of by men who gathered round individuals. They had lost the vision of the whole, and were obsessed by that which was partial, and, therefore, being partial, was a hindrance rather than a help. Think of the idea of building again. There are all kinds of workers in a building. There are carpenters and stone masons, plumbers and decorators. Suppose, in the course of the building, some people gathered round and said, We belong to the carpenters. We have no connection whatever with the stone masons. I need not go on with the supposition. We see the absurdity of the sect of the carpenters, or stone masons, plumbers, or decorators. In the work of building they work together, and all work with the ultimate building in mind. Not every stone mason can see all the building, but he is working under the direction of those who can, and it is a great sense if he has the conception of the building as he carries on his work. Many years ago there was a big contract being carried out, a large building erected, and hundreds of men were employed. There came a boy who wanted a job, and someone gave him something to do. He was bright-eyed, had no shoes, and his trousers were ragged, and he was going about his job. One of the head contractors met him, and said, " Come here, what are you doing here? " To which the boy replied, " Didn't you know I was on the job? " I love that story. He was *on the job*. That boy had a sense of the bigness of the thing, and therefore the importance of the little thing he was doing.

That is what they had lost in Corinth. They had lost the vision of the big in their devotion to the partial. Paul is here showing that the builder (himself) and another, whether Apollos or Cephas, or any other, were building under direction, with the ultimate in view. " Ye are God's building, we are God's fellow workers."

The next paragraph is really a very searching one. It should be looked at when we are alone, especially if there is committed to us something of this sacred ministry. " Let each man take heed how he buildeth thereon." If we are going to build on this foundation, we must take heed, remembering the foundation. That means that we can go on building unworthily. Paul shows us the two ways. There can be the permanent—gold, silver, costly stones. There can be building that is perishable—hay, wood, stubble. Take heed how ye build. Remember that no other foundation can ever be laid than Jesus Christ.

I ask myself, How am I to build that which is permanent? How am I to build that which is gold, silver, or precious stones upon that foundation? Worthy building, permanent building is that which develops and applies all that is involved in Jesus Christ. That is no small matter. That is a life work for any man whom God calls into the ministry. No man will ever finish it, but that is worthy building; and that becomes the more apparent if we ask in the same way what is unworthy building? Anything that qualifies or contradicts the eternal verities concerning Jesus Christ. Any supposed instruction given to Christian people that calls in question all the authoritative Gospel of the Person of our Lord, and the purpose of our Lord, and the passion of our Lord, anything that calls it in question, anything that lowers Him in thinking, perhaps almost unintentionally, is unworthy building. It is building hay and wood and stubble.

I suggest that this be pondered when we are alone, all that is suggested by that name and title, " Jesus Christ." Jesus, that name which is our brief English form of a Greek word, with the tremendous thought, Jehovah saves. Where did the name come from? Jesus is Joshua. Go back in history, and we find Moses gave that name to Hoshea, the man who was to succeed him in leading the people, and to carry on the work he left, that he could not do, and someone else must do. The name was Je-hoshua. It was a combination of the Hebrew name Hoshea, and part of the Hebrew name for God. Je-hoshua, salvation. That boy's parents were in Egypt, in slavery, and he was born there, and they called him Hoshea, which meant Salvation. I always think it is a wonderful thing to remember. In the heart of that Hebrew man and woman in slavery, in Egypt, there were hope and expectation, and when the son was born they gave the name that spoke of their spiritual hope. Moses said, He is salvation, but we will link it with the other name for God—Je-hoshua, Joshua, Jesus. All that is implicated in that name.

Then in the title too, for *Christus* is a title, the Greek form of the great Hebrew word "Messiah." This Jesus is the Messiah, the Messenger of God, the Man, the One Who has come to establish the Divine rule and reign and authority and Kingdom in the world. It is He, Jesus, and "Thou shalt call His name JESUS; for it is He that shall save His people from their sins." That is the foundation on which the building is built, and the Church is being built. Paul says, No other man can lay a foundation. There is no other foundation upon which there can be erected such a building as the Christian Church. But we can build on it unworthily. If we take that great name and title, and in any wise qualify all the suggestiveness of it, or contradict the truth for which it stands, we may think we are building, but it is hay and wood and stubble. We can give our whole life up to the holy and sacred and blessed business of developing the truths that lie implicitly in that great name and title and Person, and we are building gold and silver and precious stones, the things that cannot perish in fire, instead of the things that perish immediately therein.

So he glanced on to that very fact, the testing day. "The day shall declare it." It is the onward look. It is the consummation. He sees beyond all the processes of God's building through His workers, some of them building unworthily, many of them building worthily, and he sees through it all a day of testing when everything is to be revealed, and it is to be a day of fire. One can hardly read that without being reminded of a description of our Lord found in the New Testament, that description of what John saw as he was in the isle called Patmos. Take from all the glorious beauty of that description one phrase, "His eyes were as a flame of fire." Keeping that in mind, come back to Paul in the second letter (verse 10), "We must all be made manifest before the judgment seat of Christ, that each one may receive the things done in the body, according to what he hath done, whether it be good or bad." That passage is often quoted as applicable to men everywhere, but it does not so apply. There is a great white throne, which is the ultimate seat of judgment, the great assize, but that is not what is referred to here. The judgment seat is the *bema,* and the "all" here refers to all believers and workers, and all believers ought to be workers. In that sense "we must all appear at His judgment seat that we may receive the things done in the body," whether they "be good or bad," whether gold, silver and precious stones, or hay, wood, stubble. The testing for us is the *bema,* the judgment seat of Christ, and that which tests is fire.

Putting those together, we see an almost appalling picture, and yet one full of comfort to the soul, that at last we are to appear before Him, and His eyes are to search the things that we have done. Paul tells us that as He looks, and as He searches, as He tests by fire, all that is unworthy will be shrivelled up and destroyed, the hay, wood and stubble. And everything that is worthy, gold or silver or precious stones, what effect will fire have upon them? Only to purify them. That is the testing day.

The vision of the whole building, and the certainty of that testing day are to have their effect upon all the service that His ministers render. In that day, we are told, the true builder will be rewarded, but the false builder, he will be saved, but "so as by fire." His work will be destroyed. That whole conception gives some warrant to a hymn that we used to sing: "Must I go, and empty-handed?" There is a possibility. But the comfort is that he himself shall be saved, even though it be by fire.

This paragraph teaches us that the supreme thing in all service, whether of Paul, or Apollos, or Cephas, or us—the principal thing is the building, the whole building, God's building, God's Church. How wonderful is this conception of the Christian ministry! We are His fellow workers. Let every preacher, every teacher remember that, and then let every man take heed how he build, and recognize the folly of taking some one man, or some one idea, and gathering round it as though it were the whole, when the vast glory of the building is lost.

Verses 16 and 17 are separately printed, constituting an exclamatory passage full of tremendous significance. The opening words, "Know ye not," show that in the mind of the apostle was the failure of the Church to fulfil its true function, or to recognize the truth concerning itself. One can almost catch the accent of the writer as he dictated this, or as he wrote it. Do you not know? Are you ignorant of this tremendous fact? On the other hand, if indeed you know it, do you not know it practically? Have you allowed it to drop behind until you have lost the power of it? Do you not know? "Know ye not?"

The previous paragraph (10–15) had dealt with the relation of the work of the ministers to the purpose of God. Paul had made two statements concerning the Church, "Ye are God's husbandry, God's building." Then he had elaborated the second figure, that of building, and had shown how in this work, which is God's work, ministers are His fellow workers. He is speaking for himself, and Apollos, and Cephas, and any others, serving ministers in the Church, of whom he makes that glorious announcement, We are "His fellow workers."

In any building there is a purpose, a meaning in it; or there ought to be. I suppose there are buildings that have no purpose. But the general idea is if a building is put up, it is for some purpose. That is what was in the apostle's mind. The Corinthians had not only been misunderstanding the function of Christian ministry, they had not only misunderstood the function of Christian ministers, they had also been forgetting the real meaning of the Church, and her true function. So he broke out, "Know ye not?" He arrested their attention by that very phrase. In this paragraph (16–23) therefore we have first the two verses standing alone (16, 17) in which the fact is stated concerning this building of God, in the activity of building which His ministers are fellow workers with God. Then he passes to an admonition based upon that fact of building (18–21a). He concludes with that marvellous and glorious statement (21b–23).

"Know ye not?" Ye are this building that God is building in co-operation with those who are His ministers—"ye are a temple of God." We must keep this in connection with all that has been written, and we must go back to the opening chapter, to the fundamental proposition which we saw was so important. "God is faithful, through Whom ye were called into the fellowship of His Son Jesus Christ our Lord." That is fundamental. In that statement we found what the true function of the Christian church is in Corinth, or anywhere in the whole catholic Church. What does it exist for? These people were formed into one, for what purpose? God has put us into business partnership and fellowship and companionship with Jesus Christ. That is what fellowship means. There is a privilege of companionship. There is the responsibility of service, and the Church is put into that business.

We go behind that, and ask, What is His business in the world? What is He doing here? What is He seeking therefrom Himself? Go back and listen to things Jesus said about His work. Watch Him at His work during the days of His flesh. We hear Him say that during that period He was straitened. We see Him passing through His passion-baptism and emerging therefrom in victory, carrying on the same things that He had been doing. So that when Luke writes the story, the continuity of the story of Jesus, he says, "The former treatise I made . . . concerning all that Jesus began both to do and to teach." Not what Jesus did and said. We must not misread that. He began.

What is the inference? That He is going on. Go back and read what His work was, including the whole of that mighty work; and perhaps there is no better way of getting a picture of it than to read the fifteenth chapter of Luke. There we find the work of the Lord. The Church is in partnership with Him. In order that she may carry out the responsibility, she is in partnership with Him, in companionship.

Paul then broke out suddenly, and said to them, Do you not know? Do you not understand your position? Do you not know what this Church of God really is? "Know ye not that ye are a temple of God, and that the Spirit of God dwelleth in you?" We are fellow students and believers, but I am inclined to think if that truth broke upon us today in all its power, it would have a remarkable effect on the life of everyone. Dare to examine it. "Ye are a temple of God." There are two words in the New Testament translated "temple": one, *hieron*, which refers to the temple as it then stood, the whole of it, all its precincts. It was a marvellous temple which had been building forty-six years, and was not even then finished, and was not completed for another ten years. But there is another word, *nahos*, which refers, not to the whole temple with all its precincts and its courts, but to the inner shrine, the very Holy of Holies. That is the word Paul used here. That is also the word our Lord used of His own body, when in that first year of public ministry He was challenged as to His authority. He said, "Destroy this temple, and in three days I will raise it up," the inner shrine, the very dwelling place of Deity. Destroy that, and in three days I will build it up. That is an illustration of the word.

Look for a moment at the ancient sanctuary of God. The pattern of it is in the Old Testament, the tabernacle. That was God's place of worship. The temple was an accommodation to human weakness, just as kings were also, and priests. But the ideal was the tabernacle. Go back and look at it in the wilderness, with its outer court and enclosure. Cross the court and enter the Holy place. Beyond that is the Holy of Holies: those two chambers, the Holy place, where was the altar of incense and the table of shewbread and the golden lampstand; and the Holy of Holies, where were the ark of the covenant and the overshadowing cherubim, and the shining of the Shekinah glory. That was the *nahos*, the sanctuary. What was that to these people? It was the place of Divine manifestation, and it was the centre of Divine activity. Paul says, Do you not know that is what you are? That is what the Church really is. It is the centre of Divine manifestation. It is that institute which is in the world through which God is to be manifested.

There again we see the door that is opened. In His holiness, in His righteousness, in His infinite compassion, in His abounding mercy, in His eternal lovingkindness, God is to be manifested in the Church.

That is what Peter meant when he said, "Ye are an elect race, a royal priesthood, a holy nation, a people for God's own possession, that ye may show forth the excellencies of Him Who called you out of darkness into His marvellous light." It is the same thing. Do you not know that the Church is the sanctuary, the place of Divine manifestation, and the centre of the Divine activity? The ark with the overshadowing cherubim was the throne of government, as well as the place where the glory of God was manifested. Do you know you are that? Have you forgotten that? said Paul. Do you not know it? That is the great truth about the Church.

Then to emphasize it, not to change it at all, he added the words, "For the Spirit of God dwelleth in you." Ye are the dwelling-place of the Spirit of God. Later on, he takes that statement and applies it to every member of the Church, when he says, "Know ye not that your body is a temple of the Holy Spirit?" It is the same word. But here he is looking upon the whole company, united to one another because united to Christ, and constituting the institution. Do you not know you are the temple of God? Do you not know that the Spirit of God dwells in you, and hence the peril of destroying it? The word "destroyeth" is not the best word to use there. When Jesus said, "Destroy this temple," He used a different word, meaning to loosen, to break up. But this word here means to injure, spoil, mar, harm. Paul distinctly affirms that if any man spoils, hinders, injures, or harms the temple, him will God spoil. To look at those words, consider them, and think through them is to feel it is an exclamatory paragraph of profound significance. That is what the Church is, for "the temple of God is holy."

Then comes the admonition. "Let no man deceive himself." Notice the two expressions, "wise . . . in this *world*," "the wisdom of this *world*." The two words are not the same, while they move in the same realm. The first is, wise in this age, the clever people according to the standard of the age. If a man thinks he is clever and wise in this age, *aion*. The next, "the wisdom of this world," is the *kosmos*, the wisdom of the material. The two phrases put together reveal the peril. The wisdom of the age, which is wholly of the age, is always the wisdom of the material, which forgets the spiritual. What Paul was warning them against was, if a man thought he was wise, and was puffed up in intellectual apprehension according to the standards of the age, let him become a fool. Let him take the place of ignorance, let him confess he is ignorant; because the wisdom of the world, the wisdom wholly in the material realm, sees nothing beyond it, and it is foolishness with God. That is a great word used twice in different ways. It is foolishness, silliness. That second word is not so forceful, and yet I do not know; it is stupidity, it is foolishness. That is what the word means. My American friends use a word of certain people when they say they are morons. That is a transliteration of the Greek word here. They define a moron as an adult with the mentality of a child of twelve, as someone who has not grown up and developed. All the wisdom of the moron is indeed stupidity with God. That is what some of these people were doing in Corinth. They thought they were clever, listening to the accents of the schoolmen, instead of fastening upon the message of Paul and Apollos and Cephas. They had constituted themselves and formed little parties, and had gone back to childhood. As a matter of fact, Paul had already told them they were babes, were not fully grown, and had not taken the stages toward spiritual maturity. Oh, there are thousands of morons today in the Christian Church in that sense! In view of the fact that we are the sanctuary of God, this sanctuary may be spoiled and injured by people listening to the wisdom of the age and the material world, through unutterable foolishness. Let such become fools, and, finally, let no one glory in men.

In the last brief and yet pregnant and marvellous passage Paul reminds them of what this all meant to them. They had been saying, We are of Paul, we are of Apollos, we are of Cephas. He says, in effect, Why will you be so niggardly with regard to the things you claim are yours? "All things are yours." As a matter of fact, he makes a threefold statement: "All things are yours; ye are Christ's; Christ is God's." The first he illustrated. "All things are yours." It is very beautiful to see how he does it, whether Paul the planter, who first brought the message of the Gospel, he is yours. All his teaching is yours. Apollos came after, and others. He is yours, he belongs to you, and all his teaching. And Cephas, whatever there was of value in him and his work, he is yours. He goes on and says, all the cosmos, the wisdom of the cosmos; and if you are hidebound by the material in your thinking, and you are fools, yet that whole world belongs to you. "Blessed are the meek, for they shall inherit the earth." Do we believe that? I once heard Dr. Parker use this illustration. "I began my ministry in Banbury, and my upper window looked over the vast estate of a wealthy man. It was I who inherited that estate. I did not own a foot of land, but it was all mine." He said, "The owner came down to it once a year for ten days, and shot over it. I walked its miles day after day. The meek shall inherit the earth!" The world is yours. The flowers are yours, the hills and the valleys and the rivers, they are all yours. "All things are yours." They are your Father's. They belong to the One Who is indwelling the sanctuary, and they belong to you. And not only the world, but life, and the simple word is used, *zoe*, in itself, in essence, it is yours. It does not say any particular manner of life, but life. But that will not last, Paul. Very well, death is yours. It belongs to you. Death is not going to master you. You are going to master it. Death is yours. Then he looks all around. " Things present," they are all yours; and the " things to come," you are expecting them, they are all yours, " and ye are Christ's, and Christ is God's."

Do you not know that you are the temple of God, His dwelling-place? Let us listen to those three words, " Know ye not?" Are you ignorant of the fact, or have you forgotten it, or failed to respond to it, so that it has no living power with you? Do you not know? There could have been no divisions in that church at Corinth, or there can be none anywhere if that truth had been, and is known, or remembered. The lost sense of the marvel of the Church as the sanctuary of the Holy Spirit is what has alienated us, and caused our divisions, and paralyzed our powers. It has caused divisions and disputings. " Know ye not?" Oh, for a practical rediscovery of this fact that the Church is the sanctuary of the living God!

c. The Appeal	iv
1. The Attitude of the Church to the Ministry	1
Ministers	
Stewards	
2. The Consequent Attitude of the Ministry	2-5
Independence	
Responsibility	
3. Direct Appeal	6-21
Severity	6-13
Tenderness	14-17
His Visit	18-21

I CORINTHIANS iv

CHAPTER four concludes the apostolic dealing with the subject of divisions. The teachers in Corinth—Paul, Apollos, Cephas and others—were unwittingly the cause of these divisions. All unconsciously, there is no doubt, the divisions had arisen around these teachers. Paul had mentioned four factions in the earlier part of this section. Some said they were of Paul, and some of Apollos, some of Cephas, and others of Christ.

Paul now referred to two of these, himself and Apollos, to those who had been the principal instruments in the history of that church. Paul had planted, and Apollos had watered. Of the church and its founding, from the Acts of the Apostles briefly, and yet completely, we know these were the principal two. There is no report that Peter ever visited Corinth. He may have done so. But there were other teachers who had arisen, and had exercised the function of the teacher in the Church.

All that Paul now says is equally applicable to all teachers. Apollos and himself are illustrations. Verse 6 tells us exactly what he intended to do at this point. "Now these things, brethren, I have in a figure transferred to myself and Apollos for your sakes; that in us ye might learn not to go beyond the things which are written; that no one of you be puffed up for the one against the other." Paul is using himself and Apollos as illustrations of certain principles which it was of the utmost importance that these Corinthian Christians, and all Christians for all time, and all believers should remember. It is important to understand clearly the truth about their teachers, and the truth therefore about themselves in relation to the teachers. A true view of these teachers will deliver from pride, and prevent the creation of any party spirit. Had these Corinthians been mindful "of the things which were written" they could not have been so divided. In effect, Paul said that all their divisions were due to the fact that they had not recognized these principles as revealed in the things written.

To what was he referring? Certainly not to his own letters. He was surely referring to these writings which had been given to the Hebrew people, and although those Corinthians were not Hebrews, it is true that these Hebrew Christians used the Scriptures in all the beginning of their work, as the Lord Himself did. Paul suggests here the very same principles underlying all the writings of the prophets and seers and psalmists that he is now laying down are still obtaining and applicable to the Christian Church.

This paragraph (1–5) is specially for ministers in our sense of the word. But it is also for all the Church, because it deals not only with the ministerial office, making clear what it is, but it also shows the bearing of the ministerial office on those who constitute the Church itself. Here there are three distinct parts. In verses 1 and 2 he declares what are the facts concerning the ministry. In verses 3 and 4 he shows the results of these fundamental facts in the experience of the minister. Then in verse 5 he appeals to the final test of ministry.

The supreme value of these verses is to those who are called, as were Paul and Apollos, or to those whom Christ gives the gift, whether apostle, prophet, evangelist, or pastor and teacher. We cannot get away from the fact that there is a ministry within the Church. There are some people who seem to object to the word. In some senses I do also. Sometimes when I hear someone praying for me, and they say, "God bless our minister," I say to myself, I am not their minister.

THE CORINTHIAN LETTERS OF PAUL 69

This fact of the ministry is created by the fact that the gift has been bestowed upon certain men and women with a capacity for doing certain work. That comes out more clearly in Paul's letter to the Ephesians. "He gave some apostles, and some prophets, and some evangelists, and some pastors and teachers." The trouble is, we have come to such a time when we think every man ought to be a bit of an apostle, a bit of a prophet, a bit of an evangelist, and a bit of the pastor and teacher; and the minister has got to do everything under the sun, and, to quote that old and somewhat flippant saying, he may become Jack of all trades and master of none. I still believe even in this day God does give some apostles, and some evangelists, and prophets, and pastors and teachers. Do not let any man who has the apostolic gift look with contempt upon the evangelist, and so forth. These gifts were bestowed. They had been exercised in Corinth by Paul and Apollos, Apollos not in the same sense as Paul, a pastor and teacher and an apostle. The difficulty of the divisions was that some were impressed with Paul; others said, No, he is all right, but give us Apollos. Is that not modern! It is still among us.

Paul was therefore pointing out at the close of the section the truth about these men. Of course it reflects light upon the true attitude of the Church towards them. Take the first two verses. They are very beautiful and simple. "Let a man so account of us." Let him estimate us. Let him see the truth about us. They had been accounting Paul in one way, and Apollos and Cephas in other ways. Get down to see the truth. "Let a man so account of us as of ministers of Christ, and stewards of the mysteries of God. Here moreover"—whether that means in this world, or in this case also is a question. I think it is an illustration of the steward, of the men on the human level. "Here, therefore, it is required in stewards, that a man be found faithful." That is a tremendous revelation of the true place of the minister. What is he? He is a minister of Christ. He is a steward of the mysteries of God. One thing is required of him, trustworthiness. That is the meaning of the words.

"Ministers of Christ." That is an interesting word used by the apostle here, "ministers." Literally, although that would convey very little meaning to us, under-rowers, that is, servants, under authority, completely under authority, under-rowers. It is interesting to notice how that Greek word is translated in the New Testament. It is most often translated "officers," servants in that sense, ministers. When Jesus stood before Pilate, He used it of those who were round about Him when He said, "If My Kingdom were of this world, then would My under-rowers, servants, subalterns, fight." When Luke wrote his preface to the Gospel he said he was writing as the result of his investigation by "eye-witnesses and ministers of the Word," he used the same word. When in Acts in the thirteenth chapter we have the account of Paul and Barnabas going away, we read "they had Mark as their attendant," their minister. Once again in Acts I find that Paul is telling the story of his own life and of what the Lord had done for him. He says, "The Lord said unto me, I have appointed thee to be a minister and a witness." Again it is the same word.

Quite literally, the meaning of the word *ministers* is one who acts under direction, and asks no questions, one who does the thing he is appointed to do without hesitation, and one who reports only to the One Who is over him. " Let a man so account of us, as of ministers of Christ," not of you Corinthians. In effect, Paul said, Neither Paul nor Apollos is your minister. There is another passage in which he says, "your minister for Christ's sake." But a minister *for Christ's sake*. He is to act under His direction. If I am to act under His direction I must keep in touch with Him. I must seek to know His will. I must not run ahead of Him or lag behind Him. I must live in daily contact with my Master. I am only an under-rower, but I am that; I am a minister of Christ. All I have to do is what He tells me, His work; and when the day's work is over, I never report to a committee, I report to Him:

> "Go labour on, spend, and be spent,
> The Master praises, what are men?"

What a wonderful position! What a wonderful picture! The days are running on. Time is flying. The sun is westering. I want the last lap to be the lap of a man who never forgets he is a servant of Jesus Christ, taking orders from Him, doing His work, and, what is very important, reporting to Him only.

That is so beautiful a story of the days of our Lord in the flesh, when He sent His disciples out. When they had been out, they came back, and they reported to Him. It is a great thing to learn that lesson. I am not sure it would not cut short many May Meetings, but I will not stress that. Think rightly of us, said Paul. We are ministers, under-rowers of the great Captain.

Then next, " Stewards of the mysteries of God." If the first phrase, " ministers of Christ," reveals responsibility, this phrase takes up that thought and reveals what the peculiar and specific work is to which we are committed, and for which we are responsible. " Stewards of the mysteries of God." To translate literally sometimes is rather to rob a word of its strength and beauty, and yet it is helpful to remember that the meaning of the Greek word is housekeepers. The women could interpret that better than I could. Yet I have lived long enough in a home to know what it is. The same thought is in the estate. What does the housekeeper do? He or she is in charge of the stores, and is responsible for their distribution according to necessity. That cannot be improved upon. "Stewards of the mysteries of God." Said Jesus to His disciples when He had uttered the great parabolic discourse on a certain day, Have ye understood these things? And they said, Yea. I never read it without wondering. Oh, they meant it! They thought they had. But had they? Jesus did not say they had not, but He said, "Therefore every scribe who hath been made a disciple to the kingdom of heaven is like unto a man who is a householder, which bringeth forth out of his treasure things new and old." That is the steward. That is the housekeeper. That is the officer in charge of the estate who has to arrange it and distribute it according to necessity. We are stewards of the mysteries of God.

What are the "mysteries of God"? We have seen previously how constantly the apostle uses that great word "mystery," which in the New Testament always means some truth, some fact that human cleverness or human minds cannot and never could discover, but which has been revealed. Again, to quote the central passage in all Paul's writings, "Great is the mystery of godliness; He Who was manifest in the flesh, justified in the spirit, seen of the messengers, preached among the nations, believed on in the world, received up in glory." That is the mystery of godliness. We are stewards of the mystery of God; the essential truths of the Christian Gospel, the things undiscoverable by human intellect, are committed to us, and perhaps we shall never be able to explain them to human intellect apart from the presence and guidance of the Holy Spirit. We are not responsible. They are bestowed in the Gospel, and in proportion as we take these great things and interpret them so that Christian men and women, born again, can growingly see their value and force, and respond to them, in that proportion we are doing our work as it ought to be done.

Paul ends by saying, "It is required in stewards, that a man be found faithful." That refers to his trustworthiness as minister and steward. What a wonderful revelation this is of the Christian ministry! Servants of Christ, to take the unfathomable riches that lie in the great mystery of godliness, and bring them out of our treasure-house, and make them known! We may change the figure, "to feed the flock of God." That is the great work of the ministry. Oh, what a terrible thing if Milton's description ever becomes true of me, of you, of any who are in this ministry, that "the hungry sheep look up and are not fed." We are stewards of the mysteries of God.

In verses three and four Paul shows the result of this conception, and the realization of this fact in the experience of the ministers. Notice the recurrence of an idea indicated in a word, " judged," " judgment," " judgeth," " judge," " justified." That brings us into the atmosphere of what he is thinking, of opinion formed, judging. The scrutiny of a thing and discernment, and the expression of an opinion concerning it. He is writing about that function in the presence of this work of the Christian ministry. Notice his magnificent independence. " It is a very small thing that I should be judged of you," or of any man. They had been forming judgments about him in Corinth. It did not trouble him. His independence of the criticism of human judgment is the very stronghold of the true minister of Jesus Christ. But that is not all. He is not only independent of the judgment of others. He is independent of his own judgment of himself. My own opinion, my own scrutiny of myself, my discernment concerning myself, may not be worth having. Then he wrote that remarkable fact, " I know nothing against myself." How many could write that? I wonder. He did. Yet he said, Because I know nothing against myself, I am not thereby justified. A minister of Jesus Christ is not asking for the judgment of men, and he certainly is not going to accept the judgment of himself on himself, though he have nothing against himself. That is not sufficient ground for this justification. He is quite independent of men's opinion, or his own. The ultimate judgment is postponed, but it is present. " He that judgeth me is the Lord." There is One Who judges. He sees, He knows, He appraises the value of my work and your work. The Lord judges. What does the judgment of man matter? The Lord is judging. He is watching. The great Master is watching His under-rowers. The Owner of the wealth of the great mystery of godliness is observing how His stewards are dealing with it. It is the Lord that judgeth.

So we come to verse 5. There will be a day of final testing. We have already seen that by reference, in another connection. Look at it again. " Judge nothing before the time, until the Lord come." He is coming, and when He comes He will bring to light " the hidden things of darkness." I do not personally think that the apostle there is referring to evil things. I will not dogmatize. Jesus once said to His disciples what they heard in the darkness was to be proclaimed in the light. There is a sense in which all these were servants of God, listening in the darkness, and they were to go out and proclaim it on the housetop. He will bring to light these hidden things, " and make manifest the counsels of the hearts." That is the supreme thing, the reign of Jesus.

Do we sufficiently realize that the great master force in any life is desire, not intellect, not volition, not emotion, but desire. What do we want? What are we after? What is that inner counsel of the heart—which all the time is illuminating or darkening our understanding, or inspiring our action? There is coming a day when the hidden counsels of the heart will be made manifest, and in that day "each man shall have his praise from God." That will be the day of vindication for very many misjudged people. We go around judging, and we do not know anything, and had better shut our mouths. There is a day coming when the inner counsels of the hearts will be brought to light, and Paul says all opinions wait for that great day.

What a wonderful paragraph! What a dignity there is in its conception of the ministry! Every other is trifling. Those in this ministry are above the judgment of men, beyond the opinion of self, and submitted to the appraisal of Christ. Those men in Corinth, who had usurped this sole right of Christ, judged, and expressed their views and judgments, and had thereby created divisions. Wherever there is a recognition on the part of the ministry of the truth concerning its function, "ministers of Christ," "stewards of the mysteries of God," and when that is recognized by those who make up the Church, then they who constitute that ministry hold the Head at all times as supreme. And they, members of the Church, remember to obey those that have the rule over them in these spiritual things, in so far as they are trustworthy stewards of the mysteries of God.

This section (verses 6–21) concludes the apostle's dealing with the divisions that had arisen in the church at Corinth, and the divisions which are always likely to arise, and have arisen in the history of the Christian Church. We commence at the sixth verse, in which Paul told what he was doing, that he was employing Apollos and himself as illustrations of great principles that affect the relationship between ministers, teachers, and the whole Church. In our previous paragraph we saw the definition of the ministers, "ministers of Christ, and stewards of the mysteries of God." He now shows how that view of the ministry, that conception of his work as minister, makes him independent of the opinions of others. Although he was able to write "I know nothing against myself," that does not justify him. He emphasized the responsibility of the minister of his Lord, and that in order that the church might understand what the position of those called to minister really is, and consequently what their true relationship to such as minister abidingly is.

At the seventh verse we come to his direct appeal to these Corinthians. Glancing over the whole movement, we can divide the section into two parts. The first part was characterized by its severity (7–13). The second part is characterized by its extreme tenderness. We have merged in this final appeal to the apostle to these Corinthian Christians and all others the tones of severity and tenderness. The two things are always together in Christian faith and in the Christian messages and teaching and preaching. They are always together in the fact of God. The severity and the infinite tenderness of God come out all the way through the Bible. Think of the whole mass of the teaching of Jesus. It is complete, and final. Nothing more need be added to it, and the apostolic writings in the last analysis are interpretations of things He said. But notice how those two things merge. There is nothing more important than that a preacher should have the wooing note in his preaching; but the Master had another note, a terribly warning note. If by the wooing note He was winning men, by the warning note He was winnowing the crowds that came to Him.

Here Paul was writing to these Christians and to this church that, because of certain reasons, had lost its power. The first subject he has dealt with at greatest length, this fact of divisions that had arisen in the church. Having emphasized that ministers are ministers of Christ, not of the Church, and that they are stewards of the mysteries of God, now he made his final appeal to them. The first note was a severe one. It is impossible for us to read those verses without being conscious of their caustic character. Paul realized the incalculable injury that was being done to the purpose and power of the church by these divisions, and that gave rise to this severe note, merging into the note of infinite tenderness. But the severity is there. Remember the great fact lying behind all this, the great fact of the Church and its function as it was declared in the first chapter: "God is faithful through Whom ye were called into the fellowship of His Son Jesus Christ our Lord." The church in Corinth was called into fellowship, friendship, and business partnership, *koinonia,* fellowship. Paul saw how these divisions were hindering that, cutting the nerve of power, spoiling their witness, making it ineffective in the life of the city. That is why he used this severe and very necessary note.

He began with challenging questions. He says, "For who maketh thee to differ?" It is as though he was addressing himself to one individual. He had said to them he had "in a figure transferred to himself and Apollos for their sakes; that in us ye might learn not to go beyond the things which are written; that no one of you be puffed up for the one against the other." We see the element of division there. They were puffed up, everyone proud of his own view, and prepared to argue for the view. Paul now says, You are not all alike. You have not all the same gifts. That is what he meant when he said, "Who maketh thee to differ? and what hast thou that thou didst not receive? but if thou didst receive it, why dost thou glory, as if thou hadst not received it?" These are challenging questions.

First of all, "Who maketh thee to differ?" What right have you to separate on the ground of differing opinions and differing capacity? Granted that there is a distinction. Paul does grant that, of course. You do differ, but who made you differ? That is the challenging question. What caused the difference between Paul and Apollos and Cephas, and any one of you, or every one of you? The differences in way and characteristics and outlook? Who caused you to differ?

Then his next question practically answers his first. "What hast thou that thou didst not receive?" Whatever you have that marks you as different from others, whatever it be in the way of a gift or a characteristic, you received it. You are not the origin of the peculiarity that you have. It is something that makes you differ from others, but you did not create it. It is not your own work. "What hast thou that thou didst not receive?" Once more we go back to John the Baptist. In the third chapter of John we have the record of what he said, a very general statement, but a tremendous one. He said this about himself, and about Christ, when some people were putting them into contrast. "Man can receive nothing except it be given him from heaven." That is the principle. That is what Paul is reminding the Corinthians of. And, once again, James said, "Every good gift is from above, coming down from the Father of lights." "Who made you to differ?" What has created the differences among you, not in divisions and opinions and quarrels, but the distinct difference between personality and personality? Out of one man's personality comes a line of interpretation, and another from another, and the interpretations finally merge, but you are emphasizing the personality of the one and gathering yourselves around it and arguing, We belong to Paul, we belong to Apollos. Well, you are different. Grant it. Who made you different? Recognize, as though Paul had said it, that you have nothing, no gift that is peculiar that you have not received, for every good and perfect gift cometh down from God. "What hast thou that thou hast not received?" To put this in another way, Paul says, Why go strutting in conceit, as though you had a right to boast? The very things you are putting to an improper use, causing differences, they are gifts, and you have received them from the same God. Later on, Paul enters into that in another connection, in a remarkable and emphatic way.

Then he drops into satire in verse 8. He was laughing at them with holy laughter, and yet with utter contempt for what they had been doing. You are filled, you are rich, you are regnant! Then that one little sentence that flashes its light back upon all of it, "I would that ye did reign, that we also might reign with you." You are rich, you are full, you are satisfied, you are glorying, you are reigning, declaring the sovereignty of your own personality. I wish you understood what it is to reign, said Paul, then you and I could reign together in the true sense of the word. It is a piece of matchless satire.

Then he gives them this marvellous statement of his estimate of the apostolic position in verses 9 to 13. "For I think God hath set forth us the apostles last of all." The "last of all" refers to all the messengers of God who had gone before the Christian era. Paul always had a great historic outlook. He was always looking back, and looking around, and linking the near to that which had preceded it and to that which should follow it. God had had His priests, His kings, His prophets. He had come to man through the ministrations of these varied orders of gifts. Now, he says, it seems to him "God hath set forth us the apostles last of all." Notice his recognition of God. Whatever position he occupied, or Apollos occupied, or other members of the apostolic band, God had set them forth; it was by the Divine authority and the Divine overruling. God had "set us forth," that is, He had exhibited them, and it means also He had accredited them.

Then that amazing word, "We are made a spectacle." The Greek word is our common word today, transliterated, as a theatre, as a place for looking upon things and seeing them presented. We, the apostles, are set forth as a spectacle to the world—as I think it should read—"both to angels and men." What a remarkable statement, "Men doomed to death"! Why? Because "we are made a spectacle to the world, both to angels and men." The things to be manifested through the apostles were the same things which were manifested through the Christ, Whose message they were delivering, Whose Gospel they were preaching, and such things manifested to the world bring death. "In the world ye have tribulation," said Jesus, "but be of good cheer." God has arranged this "doomed to death," to be a theatre for the exhibition of the things for which we stand to the world, both of angels and men.

Then, again, he dropped into satirical speech. "We are fools for Christ's sake, but ye are wise in Christ; we are weak, but ye are strong; ye have glory, but we have dishonour." Mark the satire of it all. It is a passage of great severity.

Paul next gives the facts of the experience of the messengers in those olden days. "Even unto this present hour we both hunger, and thirst, and are naked, and are rebuffed, and have no certain dwelling-place; and we toil, working with our own hands; being reviled, we bless; being persecuted, we endure; being defamed, we entreat; we are made as the filth of the world, the offscouring of all things, even until now." That is a most remarkable passage. These men who were the servants, the ministers of Christ, who were stewards of the mysteries of God in this world; all that tells the story of their experiences. Paul is most evidently setting up a contrast between the conceited folly of those seduced by the wisdom of words, and so creating divisions, and the self-emptying sacrifice of those knowing the Word of the Cross, and being the messengers for its proclamation. The whole passage is characterized by severity. But who can gainsay it? The only way in which we can differ from it is that we do not seem to know this apostolic sense in these days. Certainly this was true about those early teachers. They suffered hunger and thirst, they were naked and buffeted, they had no certain dwelling-place. They toiled, working with their own hands. They were reviled and persecuted. It was true then. I wonder what application that has to us. At any rate, we ought to be able to go on. "Being reviled, we bless." That is the attitude of the messenger of Christ, "being persecuted, we endure," and carry on. "Being defamed, we entreat; we are made as the refuse of the world, the offscouring of all things, even until now." The contrast is always between a conceited, puffed-up attitude of those who have turned from the great evangel and the word of the Cross to discussions and disputes among themselves, so that they go round, every one of them, proud in his own supposed cleverness, and the true minister of Christ, and steward of the mysteries of God, whose pathway is one of self-denial and sacrifice.

In the last verses (14–21) we find a new note. Paul began, "I write not these things to shame you, but to admonish you as my beloved children." Lest his anger against the folly of the schism-makers should be misunderstood as personal, Paul closes the subject on a note of tenderness: "I write not these things to shame you." What did he mean by that? Surely such writing would make them ashamed. Shaming might here mean simply humbling, making them acknowledge and bow down, and take the place of cringing. I do not want you to do that, said the apostle. It is not a personal matter that I have in view. I am not writing to shame you, but I am writing to admonish you as beloved children. No real father ever wants to shame his child. He may have to say some caustic things to that child, but he does not want to make the child ashamed, merely cringing in front of him. No, said Paul, I am writing to admonish you, to put you in mind of these great facts, to warn you.

Then he made a tremendous appeal. "Though ye should have ten thousand tutors in Christ, yet have ye not many fathers; for in Christ Jesus I begat you," as the result of my Gospel which I preached in Corinth. The word does indicate a strong relationship that does exist between any man or woman who is the means of leading others to Christ. If indeed they have passed from death unto life, they cannot forget the one through whom the message came, and the vision came, and light broke upon them.

Paul told them he was sending Timothy to them, and again he adds a startling thing, that Timothy is to put them in remembrance of his ways which be in Christ, that he may remind these Corinthians of his doing and teaching. "I beseech you therefore be imitators of me." That is the point of the appeal. That pulls us up when we read it. Paul could say that his life and teaching were such that he could say, " Be ye imitators of me." All I have to say to my own soul, and to those associated with me in any form, in this high and holy form of ministry, is, Let us see to it that we can say this. It is a great thing. " Be ye imitators of me." He called them to obedience to his teaching and his life, and Timothy was sent to them to help them in this regard.

Then again the local tone. " Now some are puffed up, as though I were not coming to you." You are wrong. I am not coming at your dictation. I am coming when the way is made clear. " I will come to you shortly, if the Lord will."

Paul ends the whole section again by that searching question, though while it searches, yet has in it a touch of beauty and tenderness. How do you want me to come? When I arrive, shall I come with a rod, or in love and a spirit of meekness? As though he said, That depends entirely upon you. If you profit by what I have written, if you turn from all the folly and stupidity of these discussions and this puffing up of the flesh and pride, and thinking you are rich and filled and are reigning, and take the place of true humility through my teaching, I can come in tenderness. But if not, then I am prepared to come with a rod. Which shall it be? said Paul. He has finished now with the subject of divisions. Presently he gets to the great subject of unity that is corrective for all this wrong, in its fact of division and disunion.

II. *Derelictions*	v, vi
i. Discipline	v
a. The Need	1, 2
1. The Particular Sin	1
2. The Church Attitude	2
b. The Method	3–5a
1. Apostolic Authority	3
2. Church Authority	4a
3. The Lord's Authority	4b
4. The Act	5a
c. The Reason	5b–8
1. Salvation of the Man	5b
2. Purification of the Church	6–8
d. The Limits	9–13
1. As to the World	9, 10
2. As to the Church	11–13

I CORINTHIANS v

WORDS of our Lord recorded by Matthew have a bearing on this study. "If thy brother sin against thee, go, shew him his fault between thee and him alone." Some of the oldest MSS. leave out the words "against thee."

> "If thy brother sin, go, shew him his fault between thee and him alone; if he hear thee, thou hast gained thy brother. But if he hear thee not, take with thee one or two more, that at the mouth of two witnesses or three every word may be established. And if he refuse to hear them, tell it to the church; and if he refuse to hear the church also, let him be unto thee as the Gentile and the publican. Verily, I say unto you, What things soever ye shall bind on earth shall be bound in heaven; and what things soever ye shall loose on earth shall be loosed in heaven. Again I say unto you, That if two of you shall agree on earth as touching anything that they shall ask, it shall be done for them of My Father which is in heaven. For where two or three are gathered together in My name, there am I in the midst of them."

We have taken this whole chapter because it is complete in itself. The latter part of the chapter has a bearing on the first part in a remarkable way. To summarize at the beginning, it is the story of the necessity for discipline in the Christian Church. Disorder in the Corinthian church was more than intellectual, it was distinctly moral. Men had become obsessed by the "wisdom of words" to the forgetfulness of "the Word of the Cross." The disorder was distinctly moral dereliction, moral delinquency, not on the part of one only, but on the part of the whole church, because of the one. Possibly there is ever a close connection between intellectual failure and moral delinquency. False thinking issues constantly in wrongdoing. Obsessed with discussions in the realm of the wisdom of words, we are always in danger of becoming careless as to the implication of the Word of the Cross, and what that Word of the Cross ought to mean in moral character and standards.

When Paul comes to this matter, he makes very clear something we must notice. This matter was known generally. The Revised Version reads, "It is actually reported." The Authorized, a little more accurately from the standpoint of translation, reads, "It is commonly reported." To take the words that Paul used and literally to translate them, this is what he said, "It is everywhere noised abroad." The Revised rendering is not strong enough. Paul said, This thing is known everywhere, it is everywhere noised abroad; as we should say, the case he was referring to was of common notoriety.

We break up our chapter, not arbitrarily, but for the sake of study. First of all, Paul names the particular case in his mind (verse 1). Then he turns to the church attitude in the presence of that particular case (verse 2). Then continuing, he shows what the church's duty is in such a case (3-5a); and, finally, he shows the reason why the church should take that attitude, and do what he instructs that they should do (5b-13).

There is no need to tarry at any length with this particular case, save to notice that it was a most flagrant violation of the moral law. It was a case of incest, and evidently it was not only a well-known case, for Paul told them that it was a carnal sin of deeper dye than that of the Gentiles. Even in that Corinthian church, created as it was, Paul says that among the Gentiles, that is, those outside the Christian faith, there was no such case of depravity so definite, flagrant and outstanding. The whole point was that it was a case of moral depravity on the part of a member of that church, and that was the whole reason of dealing with it here. Not that Paul was not concerned about that failure on the part of this particular man, but he was far more concerned about the influence of that sin upon the church which was not dealing with it. This was the apostle's great concern, the effect produced by the presence of that man in that community separated to Jesus Christ, on the basis of the great Word of His Cross, and their fellowship with Christ.

All that was intended by that word fellowship, not only as to privilege, but especially as to responsibility, was placed in danger, dire danger by the fact of the presence in that church up to that time of this particular case. What was their attitude? Paul goes on with almost startling suddenness. "Ye are puffed up," you are haughty, proud, you are conceited about this very thing. That does seem almost impossible. Yet that is exactly what the apostle meant. Were they proud of the sin? One would not like to think that. The word describing them in that connection may mean they were so occupied with their discussions that they ignored the fact of this sin. It was well known, it was commonly reported. Everyone knew about it, about this man and the sin in which he was living, but they were puffed up. In our previous study we found how they were puffed up, why they were quarrelling, and were divided; and it may be they were so occupied with their discussions, though everyone knew about this, it did not seem very important. It may have even a stronger meaning than that, that they were rather proud of the very case, though they were not proud of the sin, that there was a man who dared to commit the sin, and they were proud of their own toleration of it. They could not agree, and they admitted this was a deflection from morality, but they did not do anything, they were tolerant. Compromise! What a word it is!

I was greatly challenged some thirty years ago by something John Morley once said about "compromise." Not that I agree with it in all its applications, but there was a tremendous element of truth in it. He said, "'Compromise' is the most immoral word in the English language." I leave that to the consideration of others in these very perplexing days. But it is here, compromise of that sort, the most evil thing possible. They were puffed up instead of mourning, proud, haughty, going on with their discussions. Whether they were proud of their toleration cannot perhaps be decided, or whether they were conceited over their discussions. One was true, perhaps both entered into it, and thus prevented their feeling the smart of it and the shame and wrong and agony of it. In the church they should have been mourning and grieving over the defection of one of their own members.

Paul ended by saying that they had failed in their duty. "Ye are puffed up, and did not rather mourn, that he that had done this deed might be taken away from among you." That was their duty. That is what ought to have happened, that this man ought to have been taken away, placed outside the communion, placed outside the fellowship, excluded. Or to use the other word, which in some senses we do not love very much for its evil associations, excommunicated. That is exactly what Paul says they should have done. Discipline was lacking. That was the trouble with this church, and that is why Paul devoted a whole section to the subject. The case of the man individually might be dealt with briefly; but this was the Church, its failure to exercise discipline and maintain the standard of purity within it. The Church knew, as everyone else knew, of the flagrant example of immorality that was in her own borders. They had not mourned, they were puffed up. They had not excluded that person from their holy fellowship.

Paul then showed them exactly what their duty was. "For I verily, being absent in the body but present in spirit." I was not there in body, but I was there in spirit. The Church is one and indivisible. Though the apostle may not be there, he is there in spirit. They are of one spirit. But those joined to the Lord are one spirit, and one spirit with the Lord; and all such are joined to Him. Paul was there with them in spirit, and as though he were present he had already "judged him," had already decided what should be done. "In the name of our Lord Jesus, ye being gathered together, and my spirit, with the power of our Lord Jesus, to deliver such a one unto Satan for the destruction of the flesh."

That was their duty. This interprets our Lord's instruction on the whole subject of discipline. If thy brother sin you are not to countenance the sin, condone the sin, to say, It has nothing to do with me. You are a member of the Church. It is not a question to do with you alone. It has to do with the Church. If thy brother sin, go and see him by himself. If he will hear you, you have gained him. Mark that carefully. The object of the visit to the brother in discipline is to gain him. But if he will not hear you, take two or three with you, and if he will hear them, you have gained your brother. That is the object of the going, not excommunication, although that may be necessary. Then if he will not hear them, tell it to the assembly, the ecclesia, the Church. The Church is called in now to act. If he will not hear the Church let him be unto thee as a heathen man and a publican. One can say the same thing in different tones which have a different revelation of personality. Do not utter that with the malediction of Rome and its Bulls. That is not Christ with His infinite compassion. The man must be put outside, and cut off. We cannot permit continuation of membership within this holy circle of membership of Christ's Church. Who was the heathen man and the publican? The man for whom Christ died. All the throbbing heartbeat of Calvary was in it when He said, You must put him out, you cannot tolerate the wrong. You must not allow it to remain within the holy fellowship of My Church; but do not forget when he is outside, he is the man for whom I died, and therefore the man after whom you are to go, that he might be brought in again. I think Paul was familiar with all this, when he wrote this letter, In the name of the Lord Jesus, you being gathered together. When our Lord said that about discipline He went on, "Where two or three are gathered together in My name, there am I in the midst of them." "In the name of our Lord Jesus, ye being gathered together." That is the Church, and the Church is to remember that. Paul was absent in the body, but there in spirit, and with apostolic authority; and they must act when "gathered together in the name of the Lord Jesus."

What were they to do, being so gathered together? "To deliver such a one unto Satan for the destruction of the flesh." Here I join issue with many expositors. It is said repeatedly that Paul was saying there was to come to this man, as the result of his authority and the authority and action of the church, some bodily ailment. It is often quoted, that as Ananias and Sapphira were smitten to death in the fierce fire that burned in the holy company of the church at the first, so this man was to have bodily affliction. I do not so understand it. Paul does not say, for the destruction of the body, but "the destruction of the flesh." The flesh had become a master thing in his life. We have seen the carnal man, and the spiritual man, and the carnal man was one completely yielded to the carnal, the lower, and the fleshly side of his personality. That is what is to be destroyed, the being yielded to that. He is to be put out, surrendered to that to which he has already surrendered himself. Hand him over to the dominion of the one Satan, to whose rule and authority he has bowed the neck in the act of his sin. Yield him, surrender him, cut him off from the fellowship, and so exclude him from the ægis of the Church, from the sense of security that comes to him, and the opinion that is held by the world that the Church can tolerate these things. Hand him over for the destruction of the flesh, not the body, and of course, yield him under the dominion of Satan to that which he has chosen. That always follows. If a man yields himself to the mastery of the evil one on the low level of the flesh, sooner or later that very desire of the flesh withers and perishes and dies, and the man suffers from satiation. Put him outside. He has chosen the dominion of Satan. You cannot tolerate him here in this holy fellowship. Put him out for the destruction of that very thing in him, that very desire in him, that very carnality of his thinking and acting, that is the basis of his wrongdoing. Hand him over to Satan for the destruction of the flesh.

But is that all? No. The reason of it all is now given, "that the spirit may be saved in the day of the Lord Jesus." That is the first reason for discipline, the first reason for the excommunication of a sinning man within the fellowship. Put him outside that he may know the full power of the flesh until it master him, because his spirit is there, in order that his spirit may be saved, and for the purification of the church.

The apostle then used that figure of leaven which is always a figure of evil. There is no passage of Scripture where leaven is anything other than destructive. It is always breaking up. Put out the leaven of malice, pride, impurity. Purge the Church from that which is the secret of deterioration, and brings about a paralysis and lack of power. There must be separation of the Church, and Paul is careful to point out that that does not mean that we are to have no dealings whatever with the world. We are in the world. To take up the position of having no dealings with those guilty of immoral conduct we should have to come out of the world altogether. We are to stay in the world, but we are to have no fellowship within the borders of the Church with such guilty of such sin, no social dealings, not even so much as to eat with them.

This cannot be studied without seeing how Paul felt the tremendous importance of the Church, and the necessity for her purity, therefore the necessity for discipline. Note the connection here in what Paul says, "that the spirit may be saved." The heathen man and the publican is the man for whom Christ died, and when for the sake of discipline a man, an individual member of the Church, must be excluded, he is not to be abandoned and left. He is the man for whom Christ died. As for the world, with that I have nothing to do, says Paul. God judges them; but we have to do with the matter of judgment within the Church. "Judgment" must "begin at the house of God."

We may be inclined to say that such flagrant sin is not existent today within the Church. Or if it is existing and known, certainly it does not cause pride. Yet there are times when I think that in the Church, discipline is almost lost, and its loss weakens the testimony of the Church, and gives a false sense of security to the wrongdoer. The Church has no right to tolerate evil on the ground of broad-mindedness. If there is a definite evil within the Church, the Church is called upon to exercise discipline, and put outside her fellowship those guilty of the sin. The history of the Church shows that the Church pure is the Church powerful; and the Church patronized and tolerant towards evil is the Church puerile and paralyzed. There is great necessity for the exercise of discipline.

But we must ever be careful that our discipline is in the spirit of Christ. Christ died for the heathen man and the publican. Do not let him go. Follow him, attempt to lead him back; and if presently, under the very dominion of Satan, he comes to the hour of knowing the folly and the emptiness of the destroying power of the carnal, it may be that his spirit life will be delivered, and he may be received again. We shall find later that this man was repentant, and Paul told them he was to be received again.

ii. Disputes	vi. 1–11
a. The Principle	1
b. The Arguments	2–11
1. " Or know ye not "	2–8
The Fitness of the Saints for Judgment	
Stated	2–4a
Enforced	4b–8
2. " Or know ye not "	9, 10
The Unfitness of the Unbeliever for Judgment	
Inheritance of Kingdom of God Impossible	
Self-evident Deduction	
3. How the Saints were Made Fit	
Washed	11
Sanctified	
Justified	

I CORINTHIANS vi. 1–11

IN our study of this letter we now come to that part which has a very definite local background and colour. The Corinthian conditions were such as to create many of the difficulties with which the apostle was now dealing. Therefore that local colour must be kept in mind. That however does not interfere with the value of any part of the letter, because here we see the great apostle, led and guided by the Holy Spirit of God, dealing with local matters in the light of eternal and universal truth. It is with these principles we are particularly concerned.

Of this paragraph (1–11) it is peculiarly true that it had a Corinthian application. It is equally true that it reveals important and abiding truths for the Church of God at all times. Glancing first at the local, the setting is between the case of gross immorality within the church with which the apostle had dealt in the previous chapter, showing that there was need for discipline in the interest of the church, in its testimony and witness, and teaching concerning impurity of conduct generally. At the close of chapter five Paul dealt with the whole subject of immorality. The case of incest with which the apostle had dealt had in all probability given rise in the law courts to certain cases, and it is possible that this case had become a *cause célèbre*, and there had been a noted trial, though there is no proof of this. The patent fact is that disputes among members of the church were being submitted to heathen tribunals, and with that the apostle was dealing. Those within the church were submitting disputes between members of the church to the heathen courts that existed in Corinth. In dealing with that local condition he reveals these eternal principles.

We may divide the paragraph thus : First of all, there is a challenging enquiry (1). That is immediately followed by arguments against their action (2-10). Then in the closing verse (11) is a remarkable description of the fitness of the saints for the exercise of judgment, showing the wrongness of the position occupied, in view of what they were doing. Those children of God, sons of the Most High, these members of the Christian Church were perfectly equipped for doing the very thing they were asking to be done by outside, heathen, pagan tribunals.

It is a challenging word with which the apostle starts, "Dare any of you?" Have you the courage? We see at once it is a question almost of amazement on his part, as though the apostle, on the human level, could not understand their doing it. How dare you do it? Having a matter against a neighbour, dare any of you go to law before the unrighteous, and not before the saints? It is a challenge. The implication is that to do any such thing would be to violate the very principles of their life, and he says, Dare you do it? Have you the courage? Their action was a violation of the very genius and value of their life as Christians. To take the matter of disputes within the church outside the church and ask the arbitrament of heathen tribunals was to violate the very principles of the Church's life. The emphasis in that opening statement is on "you." "Dare any of *you?*" That must be interpreted by going back to the beginning of the letter, and seeing to whom it was addressed, the church in Corinth, those called saints, set apart in the name of Christ, and those who had been put by God into fellowship with Jesus Christ. "Dare any of *you?*" Whatever other people may do, dare you do it?

The translation "against his neighbour" is a little misleading. What is meant by "neighbour"? If is meant anyone who lives near you, that you have association with in social or commercial life, in ordinary life, that is not the point here. That is not the meaning, the meaning is "another." That is what the apostle really wrote, "Dare any of you, having a matter against another," that is, another of you. The whole consideration is bounded by the fact of the church, its fellowship with Christ, and consequently its fellowship within its own borders. Dare any of you, on that account, having some dispute with another of you, go to law before the unrighteous? The question is one between one saint and another, and the apostle shows that the submitting of such disputes to the unrighteous, or the unjust, those *adikos*, those who are foreigners to the great truth of the fundamental principles, is wrong. These the apostle indicates are incapable of final and correct discrimination. Dare *you* go to them? Dare you people, inside this Christian fellowship, take the disputes within the borders of the fellowship, and carry them into the pagan atmosphere, and present the cause to pagan judgment? Dare you do it? That is the challenging question.

Now to show how unnecessary it was for them to do it he turned to the arguments (2-10). There are three facts concerning the saints. Verse 2, " Know ye not that the saints shall judge the world? " That is the first fact. The second is close to it, and is correlative. Verse 3, " Know ye not that we shall judge angels? " Again in verse 9, he asks the question, " Or know ye not that the unrighteous shall not inherit the Kingdom of God? " He asks, Do you not know these things? The implication is that if they did not know them, certainly they did not know them in such a way as to produce any effect, or they would never have dared to go to heathen tribunals.

Why should they not go? " Know ye not " thrice repeated. There are the arguments. What does he remind them of? What are the facts?

First, Do you not know that we shall judge the world? The saints to judge the world? Yes, in the fullest sense. In that fullest sense, carry on the thought beyond the present moment to the final Judgment Seat, and not merely to the Bema, the judgment seat of Christ before which the saints are to appear, but to the great white Throne of ultimate judgment. Carry the whole thought through to that. The apostle said, Do you not know the saints shall judge the world? That is the hour when the world will come to judgment before the great white Throne, face to face with God. That tremendous, ultimate fact in all human life is fearfully lost sight of today. Men and women are rushing on, with no thought of the ultimate. " It is appointed unto men once to die, and after this cometh judgment." All it stands for is being forgotten. We are only glancing at it here, for it is involved. The saints shall judge the world, says the apostle, but that judgment seat is to be occupied by the Son of God, by the Lamb. He is the Judge before Whom humanity shall appear, as God is in Him judging the world, and that means that the ultimate association of the saints is with Christ.

Is there any statement in the apostolic writings in certain senses which has a more definite and tremendous implication of the union of the saints with their Lord? They shall judge the world. This is one element of the significance of what Paul wrote to Timothy when he said, " If we endure, we shall also reign with Him." The one activity of reigning is judgment. To gather up in a statement. In the final judgment of men He will associate with Himself redeemed humanity. We shall judge the world. God has put us into fellowship with Him, and that fellowship has brought us pardon, and that brings us peace, and that fellowship ultimately is to be one in which we share with Him in His final judgment. We shall judge the world, and yet the people who are appointed, said the apostle, to that as the ultimate, were taking their own disagreements out into the pagan atmosphere, and before heathen tribunals, and asking for judgment there. "Know ye not that the saints shall judge the world?"

Again, "Know ye not that we shall judge angels?" That is but a wider application of what is already said, that because He will have final and ultimate authority, not only over humanity, but over all created beings, including angels, He will be the Judge of angels as well as of men. He will associate with Himself in that tremendous judgment His own, His redeemed, the saints. We shall judge angels as well as men.

Then that third statement, "Know ye not that the unrighteous shall not inherit the Kingdom of God?" "Unrighteous," it is the same word *adikos*, that he used when he spoke of the unrighteous tribunals at the beginning, "going to law before the unrighteous." The same word is now used. What does that statement mean, "The Kingdom of God?" In that fact is found the ultimate seat of all judgment, and the ultimate assurance of unquestioned justice. These tribunals to which these people were going did not know anything about it. They cannot inherit it. They are not living in contact with the principles of eternal justice. Yet these Christians were going to them to decide some dispute among them. Those are the arguments against the action which the apostle here and now condemned.

In the next verse (5) the apostle dropped into satirical language. "Is it so, that there cannot be found among you one wise man?" They had been boasting in wisdom, and were puffed up. He has pricked the bubble of their pride before, and now goes back to it again. Is that the case, that you cannot find in that fellowship one able to judge and arbitrate and adjudicate among you? If not, there is another alternative. "Why not rather take wrong? why not rather be defrauded?" Why not rather suffer, why not rather submit? That is their very sense. Why not rather take wrong? Why not rather be defrauded? Rather than what? Than take the disputes to these heathen tribunals, where disputes cannot be dealt with because they cannot inherit that Kingdom of God, the very principle of which is strict, impartial, eternal judgment and justice. If you have not got one wise man you had better stay where you are, suffer your wrong, and be defrauded. That is tremendous. Rather suffer injustice than seek for justice before a wrong court.

We come next to the closing words. The apostle gives that fearful list of evil things. Corinth was full of every one, and many of them had invaded the church, as we shall see later on. He says, "Such were some of you." You lived among those conditions. You gave yourselves up to those practices. Mark the sharp "But." "But ye were washed, but ye were sanctified, but ye were justified in the name of the Lord Jesus Christ, and in the Spirit of our God." There is a revelation of the secret power resident in the church for the exercise of jurisdiction for disputes if they arose among them. Ye were washed, quite literally. That first tense is a little different from the rest, "Ye washed yourselves, ye were sanctified, ye were justified." "Ye washed yourselves," and the reference is to belief in the Lord Jesus Christ by which there came cleansing. Being cleansed you are set apart and separated from the world, and from the society in which you are bound to live. You are in the world, you have to stay there, but you are separate from it. You were washed, separated, and were justified. Whatever it means evangelically, it is there; but let us keep in the realm of this power of judgment and jurisdiction. You were justified. You have entered into an inheritance, the Kingdom of God. You have had the sentence passed upon you which is in accordance with eternal justice by faith. You are justified, and therefore in that Kingdom you are in touch with the ultimate Throne and authority for strict truth and impartial justice. That is your fitness. You were filthy, you were some of those who are doing these very things; but you were washed, and being washed, you were set apart to your Lord, and being set apart, you are justified. You yourselves have received the sentence of acquittal by eternal justice, that He might be just and the Justifier of him that believeth in Jesus—Paul's words in another connection. That being so, you are ready and prepared, in proportion as you live in right relationship with these things. Of course it must be taken for granted that with the cleansing that came to you, when you were washed, you were sanctified and justified within your own soul, and have the consciousness of the eternal justice of God working within you. By these things you are prepared. Dare any of you, having a matter against another, go outside the holy fellowship of the washed and sanctified and justified to have disputes settled?

The Corinthian colour is very evident all through this, but the principles abide. This has to do wholly with disputes within the Church. I do not hesitate to say even today that if there should be a member of the Christian Church who takes action before the courts of law of the country against another member of the Christian Church, he is violating these great principles. That does not mean we are not to use the courts of our country under any conditions whatever. That is not true. It is well for us to remember that our courts of justice are very different from those in that pagan world where Paul exercised his ministry, and where the Church first existed. With pride we can say our courts are characterized by marvellous justice and equity. There may be miscarriages of justice ever and anon, but for the sake of humanity at large the work they are doing is wonderful work. But there is no reason why, if I have a dispute with you, I should go before an earthly court. The Church ought to be able to deal with it. But do not forget, the man who wrote this letter appealed to earthly courts. He appealed to Cæsar, and claimed his Roman citizenship under certain conditions; and at the last, when secondary officers were trafficking with his liberty, he used the great talismanic word, "I appeal unto Cæsar." As to whether he got justice, that is another matter. I do not press that; but he used his right in the interest of his earthly citizenship. But disputes between Christian people ought, as then, now and always to be capable of solution within the borders of the Church. That is the great teaching as to principle of this paragraph.

```
     iii. Desecration                                              vi. 12-20
        a. Statement of Principles                                    12
           1. All Things Lawful
           2. Limitations. Expedient
              No Mastery
        b. Application to Prevalent Impurity                        13-20
           1. The Body for the Lord, and the Lord for the Body     13, 14
           2. The Body. Member of Christ                           15-18
           3. The Body a Temple of the Spirit                      19, 20
```

I CORINTHIANS vi. 12-20

THE apostle is still dealing with defections from morality. We now turn to the continuation of that chapter, and find that he now dealt with the general subject. Having dealt with the particular case of the actual wrongdoing of one man, information of which had been sent to him from the household of Chloe, now he dealt with that subject, a painful and difficult one.

It is important to remember that we must keep in mind the Corinthian background, the fact that these people constituted the Church of God in Corinth. The whole trouble can be summarized by saying that the spirit of the city had infected the church. That is always a peril. The Church's business is not to catch the spirit of the age, but to correct it. When the Church of God knows its own business, and is living in accordance with its own mighty laws of life, she is a perpetual rebuke to the things that are merely of the passing and ephemeral age. Yet one must have the background in mind here. A good deal can be accounted for only by that fact. If the background be lost, the first reason of the apostolic writing is gone. While the background is peculiarly Corinthian, the questions are all universal, and the great thing we have to look for in this section is not so much the Corinthian necessity—though that of course must be seen—but the principles revealed by the apostle as he dealt with these Corinthian details.

This is an amazing letter. In the course of my teaching ministry, from Dan to Beersheba in this country and across the water, when people have spoken to me of the failure of the Corinthian Church, or of churches, while the fact of failure is there, I do not think I have ever come across anything in church life that can be compared with the dreadful condition of things in Corinth. Some of them had sunk to a low level, and the rest were tolerant of it within the church. That must be remembered.

As Paul turned to this general subject, it became very clear that immorality was positively prevalent within the church, the evil which Paul speaks of as fornication. That is made even clearer in his second letter. There he says very distinctly (xii. 20) of church members, "Many . . . have sinned . . . and repented not of the uncleanness, and fornication, and lasciviousness which they committed." That is the Corinthian background that we must bear in mind.

There are two matters to be considered: first, the Corinthian background. It must be remembered, whatever Paul has to say on this subject, this sin was a common one in Corinth, in the city. Moreover, not only was it a common sin, it was not counted sin at all by the Corinthian philosophers and teachers. They did not look upon sexual things as sin at all. Corinth was at the time one of the great centres of the worship of Venus, a description of which is not to be named among saints. This sin with which Paul was dealing in this particular section of his letter was part of the worship of Venus.

Christian people were there. If the first matter is the Corinthian background, the second fact is Paul's abiding sense of the wonder and glory of the Church. Reading all his writings, one is more and more impressed with that fact, the marvel and wonder of the Church ideally. Paul had that in mind here. While not suggesting that Paul was not concerned with individual sin and moral delinquency, he was more concerned with the effect that the toleration of such sin had within the church—blasting that church, and hindering it in its life, and preventing it fulfilling its high function.

Turning to the paragraph itself, it falls quite naturally into two parts: first of all, a statement of principles. That is the supreme value of the paragraph. Secondly, an application to this particular subject.

The statement of principles is contained in this opening verse, "All things are lawful to me," twice repeated. The first principle is liberty.

Paul says it here twice, and again in the tenth chapter, verse 23, he enunciates that principle again in application to another subject, that of meats offered to idols. Get the simple principle itself. "All things are lawful for me." The apostle meant *all things*, that every essential gift and power of human life is lawful to the Christian. The statement of liberty is a revelation of the naturalness of the Christian life. He insists upon it. These people knew perfectly well what was in his mind. This he made clearer in the following paragraph, and clearer yet in the one beyond that. But for the moment he is thinking within the realm of sex. "All things are lawful for me." The Christian is not called upon to deny the activity of any natural power or function. That is the first principle, and it is a tremendous truth. "All things are lawful." The remarkable thing here is that he was quoting something that was being said by the Corinthian leaders and teachers, that their philosophers were saying. That was the doctrine of the Epicureans. "All things are lawful." Do not put rein or restraint at all, just express yourself. Experience and expression, that was Epicureanism. Paul says, Being a Christian does not mean the stultification of any natural power he has.

"All things are lawful for me." But wait. If the first principle shows the naturalness of the Christian life, the second principle for Christians shows the supernaturalness of it, that all natural things are to be under the control of the spiritual and the supernatural. It is interesting to notice how he puts this. First, "All things are not expedient." What is meant by "expedient"? We say expedient means politic, all things are lawful but they are not politic; or sometimes we mean they are not convenient. But the Greek verb here means something far more than that. It is the verb *sumphero*, which means bearing together. Immediately we see that, there is a light shining on this. All things are lawful for me, but I am not living alone. I cannot live alone. No man lives to himself. I have relationships with other people, and there are things which might be perfectly lawful for me, that will not help my fellowship with my fellow Christian. That is why they are not expedient. What may be perfectly right for Paul may be absolutely impossible for Paul for the sake of others. All things are not expedient. All things are not things that tend to the possibility of bearing together, "bearing one another's burdens," to quote from another letter. There is a limitation, which is peculiarly Christian. It is found nowhere else in the religions of the world. It certainly will not be found among these Greek philosophers under whose influence the Corinthian Christians were living. We have crystallized the thought of life in a somewhat vulgar phrase, and yet suffer it: "Each for himself, and the devil take the hindmost." What about others? Oh, that is not thought of. I may observe, in passing, in that idea of life the devil usually takes the foremost, not the hindmost. But, again, that is a Christian conviction, and it grows out of Christianity. It is not expedient. These are the things that reveal one's relationship with, and responsibility for, other people than oneself. All things are lawful; but things one could do, one cannot do. Why not? Because they are not expedient. They are not bearing together with other people in their responsibility.

Then the second limitation, which swings back from the relative to the personal. "I will not be brought under the power of any." The lawful things may gain a mastery over me. Lawful things may become my law, and when they do that they are ruining me. "I will not be brought under the power of any." The word there for power is not *dunamis*, but *exousiazo*, authority. There are here two alternatives. First of all, liberty: "All things are lawful for me." No natural power is to be stultified in Christian experience, but all natural powers are to be limited, are to be held in restraint. There are limitations. There are restrictions, and they are twofold. First, my relationship with others, all things are not expedient; and, secondly, the effect upon me, "I will not be brought under the power of any," so as to become a slave to it, and to deny my one and only Lord and Master, to Whom all such things are for evermore to be submitted. Such are the great principles.

The application is self-evident. Paul proceeds to give an illustration first of all, and then dismisses it. It is an illustration of functions. "Meats for the belly, and the belly for meats." That is a true function. Meats need the belly. The belly needs meats for the maintenance of physical life, but they are quite secondary. "God shall bring to nought both it and them," both the belly and meats. They are passing and transient. They are not abiding. But the body is not for fornication, but for the Lord; and the Lord for the body." In applying this, Paul speaks of the body, not of the flesh. That distinction has been made before. The flesh is used consistently in the New Testament to describe that attitude of life which is submitted wholly to the material and the carnal. The body refers to something which is a Divine creation. The word *soma*, translated body, means soundness. The apostle is referring to the body as a sound whole, ideally. Notice in this paragraph three things he declares about the body. First, "The body is ... for the Lord; and the Lord for the body." Presently, "Your bodies are members of Christ." Finally, "Your body is a temple of the Holy Spirit." How that illuminates all the dark background! How it sheds its light upon Christian life!

The body, that is, considered ideally, the *soma*, the whole, wholesome, complete, the healthy body itself, is for the Lord, and the Lord for the body. Paul has used an illustration by contrast, and shown how that illustration refers to transient things which God will destroy. But now he is dealing with the body of the Christian soul, and shows it is not transient but permanent, for he shows God will raise it up, the body for the Lord, His instrument, for the working of His will, for the doing of all the things that are in accordance with His will, lawful things in themselves, and more lawful as they are submitted to His Lordship, and are used wholly and only under His conrtol. Notice, he not only says the body is for the Lord, but the Lord is for the body, supplying all its needs under His government, so that there is nothing that is proper and natural in the functions of the body that is not under the control of the Lord. "The body is for the Lord, and the Lord for the body."

Then Paul summarized everything in a tremendous statement, best left without note or comment. "Your bodies are members of Christ." "He that is joined to the Lord is one spirit," one spirit with Him. All the functions and powers were under the control of that Spirit under Whose control He lived a human life, and while all things were lawful for Him, in the interest of His mighty mission, there were things not expedient, and He never granted the desire for that which was lawful, or allowed it to have the mastery of Him; and we are one with Him. "Your bodies are members of Christ."

We come then to the final statement, which is of course inclusive of everything. "Your body is a temple of the Holy Spirit." Temple, *naos*, sanctuary, the inner sanctuary. We saw in iii. 16 that he spoke of the Church, and said it was a temple of God, a sanctuary of God. It is the same word, the actual dwelling-place of the Holy Ghost. You have received that Holy Spirit from God. You are not your own any more. You cannot order your own ways and goings and actions. You have been "bought with a price," therefore "glorify God in your body."

This positive consideration supplies the negative application. The body is naturally a Divine creation. We remember the word of the psalmist, who said, we are "fearfully and wonderfully made." Have we ever carefully pondered that tremendous 139th psalm?

> "Thine eyes did see mine unperfect substance,
> And in Thy book were all my members written,
> Which day by day were fashioned,
> When as yet there was none of them."

The body is a great thing, a marvellous thing. What marvellous inventions we have had in the scientific world! One is not complaining. One is thankful for them, not thankful when they are prostituted to damnable uses, as they are today, but thankful for them. But in all scientific discovery nothing yet has been discovered comparable to the human hand. We are fearfully and wonderfully made. All the functions of the body are lawful, but that body by redemption is a sanctuary, indwelt by God by the Holy Ghost; therefore it is related to others. There are things that are expedient, and things that are not expedient; but supremely the body is to be mastered in all its thoughts, in all its duties, in all its practices, in all its exercises of natural functions, by the mastery of that one Lord.

III. *Difficulties* — vii–xi
  i. Concerning Marriage — vii
    a. The General Question — 1–9
      Apostolic Advice
        1. Celibacy Good — 1
        2. Marriage Necessary — 2–5
        3. Marriage Not Obligatory — 6
        4. Decision with the Individual — 7–9
    b. As to the Married — 10–24
      1. The Charge of the Lord — 10, 11
      2. The Apostolic Ordination — 12–17
      3. The Principle Illustrated — 18–24

I CORINTHIANS vii. 1–24

WE now come to the third and last movement in the corrective section of this letter, which deals with the carnalities that existed in the church at Corinth and oftentimes have persisted through the history of the Church of God. The apostle previously had dealt with the divisions which had been reported to him by the household of Chloe, and that at some length. He also had dealt with the one case of serious moral dereliction, well known, of personal wrongdoing. The great trouble was not in the fact of the wrong of one person living in incest, but that the church was tolerating it, which toleration was harming the church.

Now he began to answer this letter to him. It is an interesting fact that this letter was really an answer to one he had received from them, and that when he began to write, he did not immediately take up the subjects on which they had written. He first devoted six chapters to other subjects before dealing with those they had named. Notice how the chapter begins: "Now concerning the things whereof ye wrote." Evidently they had written on subjects causing wondering and questionings among the members of the church, many of them who desired to fulfil their true function. They were troubled by certain conditions of life. The four chapters (vii–xi) may be summarized. The first subject concerned marriage (vii). The next concerned things sacrificed to idols (viii–xi. 1). The third subject concerned women (xi. 2–16), and the last was concerning the Lord's Supper (xi. 17–34a). The end of verse 34 suggests how glad Paul was when he reached that point, as he said, "And the rest will I set in order whensoever I come." He was tired of having to deal with these things of correction, and was eager to get on to the more powerful matters, as he said at the beginning of chapter twelve, "And now concerning the spiritualities."

Here we commence this subject of marriage. Note in this seventh chapter certain statements. Verse 6, "But this I say by way of permission, not of commandment." Verse 10, "I give charge, yea not I, but the Lord." Verse 12, "But to the rest say I, not the Lord." Verse 25, "Now concerning virgins I have no commandment of the Lord; but I give my judgment." Then at the end of verse 40, "After my judgment; and I think that I also have the Spirit of God." That is a very interesting gathering together of sentences from this chapter in Paul's letter. There is nothing like that anywhere else in his writings, a clear distinction in his mind which he maintains all through, and draws attention to the fact. He is careful to draw this distinction between the specific instructions of the Lord, and those instructions which had no such specific command on record. That does not invalidate the apostolic teaching, but he is careful to show the difference between the things directly spoken of the Lord, and the things which may be deduced, and which he deduces as having been granted to him, as he says, believing as he does, that he has the mind of the Spirit. It is an interesting case of the exercise on the part of the apostle of the sacred office of the scribe.

We read of the scribes in the time of our Lord. They were in opposition to Him. That office of the scribe was a Divinely recognized office, though not ordained. The office emerged in the time of Ezra, who was a great scribe. They were the moral interpreters. They interpreted and applied the law. We might say that many of them in the time of our Lord misapplied and misinterpreted it. But that was their function, and our Lord recognized their position when He said, "The scribes and the Pharisees sit on Moses' seat; all things therefore whatsover they bid you, these do and observe." It is especially interesting that our Lord called His disciples scribes. "Have ye understood these things?" He said to them after He had given them the parables of the Kingdom. They replied, "Yea." And He said unto them, "Therefore every scribe who hath been made a disciple to the Kingdom of heaven is like unto a man that is a householder, which bringeth out of his treasure things new and old." That was the office of the scribe. When our Lord gave His interpretation of the Church in the sixteenth chapter of Matthew and again in the eighteenth, He used two phrases which were peculiar phrases of the office of the scribe, loosing and binding. That simply means, what is binding is that which is obligatory, from which there can be no appeal. What is loosed is that which is optional; it is a matter for personal decision.

Now all through here, Paul was binding and loosing. He was declaring the things absolutely obligatory, and those are the things that have the word of Jesus Himself behind them. The other things are optional. There is a point where they will have to use their own judgment. He can give his judgment and opinion, and he does that; and that constitutes the reason of this remarkable section.

Again, bear in mind the Corinthian background. We must not merely see the Church ideally, but the church existing in that city, and must keep in mind the conditions obtaining in that city. There is no question whatever that this particular section on marriage occupying the whole of this seventh chapter has things in it that seem strange to us, and almost irrelevant to the day in which we live. While remembering the local background, if applications vary, the principles that are revealed are of abiding force; and it is to those principles we want to direct our attention especially.

In these twenty-four verses we have two movements: first of all, a general one, and then one as to the married life in itself and those who are married.

First of all, a general question concerning marriage. Paul says some things here which are inclined to make us stop and think, almost to stagger us and make us wonder. He is answering these people who had written to him. He is exercising the office of the scribe. Notice the limitations of marriage. No attempt is made here to state the Christian doctrine of marriage in its fulness and completeness. That must be sought elsewhere, and will be found if we study his Ephesian and Colossian letters, and those to Timothy. There we have specific instructions on the marriage relationship. Here it looks as though Paul considered the marriage state a little lower than the state of celibacy. However, he cannot be interpreted in that way, for do not forget that when he was writing to Timothy he spoke of "forbidding to marry" as a "doctrine of demons." If one is tempted to feel he was undervaluing the marriage relationship, and suggesting Christian people were better free from it, there is a reason for what he was saying. All the teaching here is in answer to questions arising out of conduct in Corinth. There impurity in sexual matters was rampant, and evidently the question had arisen among these Christian people as to whether, in view of these evil conditions, it were not good to remain unmarried. That is the plain question, in the plain language of our own time, that they had written and asked. In view of all these conditions, would it not be safer to remain unmarried?

Paul first declared that it was a good thing not to be married. He did not say a better thing, but a good thing. In other words he declared that celibacy was a perfectly proper thing under certain conditions, and under certain facts concerning the man or the woman, as the case may be. It is not evil. There may have been there, as there are those in the world still, who think there is something wrong if someone is not married. Oh, no, he said, it is perfectly right. There is nothing evil in celibacy. We remember that remarkable passage in the teaching of our Lord (Matt. xix), showing that celibacy may be a very fine thing under certain conditions. They had come to Him with certain questions, and He said, "All men cannot receive this saying, but they to whom it is given. For there are eunuchs, which were so born from their mother's womb; and there are eunuchs, which were made eunuchs by men, and there are eunuchs, which made themselves eunuchs for the Kingdom of heaven's sake. He that is able to receive it, let him receive it." There is a recognition of the fact that celibacy may be a high and holy thing in the interest of the Kingdom of heaven, and Paul emphasized that here at the very beginning.

Our Lord uttered those words in reply to a question about divorce, and immediately following, they brought little children to Him, and He said, "Suffer the little children to come unto Me." The subjects are all linked up in the most remarkable way in the account of the ministry of Christ. So Paul is emphasizing what our Lord had said, that celibacy may be good.

Then Paul went on and showed that there are conditions of human life and experience in which marriage was found to be necessary. Then he insists upon monogamy, one man, one woman. That is a basic thing in the Christian attitude. He showed that within that marriage relationship there are mutual responsibilities, the husband for the wife, and the wife for the husband. The whole sacred fact is held up there, that there is to be no defrauding on either side. It is a wonderful little passage.

He next showed that marriage is not obligatory. One is not bound to marry. Finally, therefore, the decision has to be with the individual. In a sense we today do not need these instructions, and yet remember the Corinthian conditions and the principles revealed concerning the marriage relationship.

He wrote then to those who were married, who had entered into the marriage relationship, and he laid upon them the charge of the Lord, not his own opinion. There is to be no separation, or if there be separation, then there is to be no remarriage. Again we refer to the words of our Lord Himself, which are perfectly explicit on this subject. When they came to Him about divorce, as Mark records it, they said Moses suffered them a bill of divorcement, appealing to Moses the law giver as authority; and He said this sifting thing to them, Yes, Moses allowed you a bill of divorcement because of your unbelief, but " from the beginning!" They were testing marriage by Moses. Marriage as a sanction went far out beyond Moses and his time, or later, even though that was a Divinely given law. "From the beginning." He made them male and female, and there is to be no separation, but the qualification of that is found in the Sermon on the Mount, when He said save for the cause of fornication. I am not entering into recent discussions on this subject. I have the greatest respect for those who do not at all agree with my position on this matter. There is only one real ground for divorce, and that is the ground of infidelity within the marriage relationship. We have modified our laws within recent years, much to the detriment of our high standards of morality, which will be proven in the process of years. Do not forget that it is the guilty party that is not allowed, by the law of Christ, to be married again. Here I differ from very many. Some of my friends in the ministry will not marry a divorced person. I will, within the limit. If the man is not guilty, and has to divorce his woman; if the woman is not guilty, but has to divorce her man, then I will marry him, or her; but not the guilty party.

Paul says something here very striking, that the apostolic admonition as to believers is that they are not to separate from unbelieving husbands, or *vice versa,* as the case may be. The remarkable declaration is they are to remain together for the sake of the children. I do not think there is anything so tragic in divorce as the position to which children are brought. Recently one of the most bitterly caustic things came to my notice, of two little children, a boy and a girl. Their father and mother were separated, living apart. I do not know if there had been any divorce, but they were separated, and the children were in the custody of the woman. The children had been evacuated, and were talking together when others were around. One of the children said to the other, "You know, Daddy is coming to see us today," and the other said, "Would it not be awful if Daddy and Mother came the same day!" I think that is a terrible story. Poor children! I always feel that that is the most tragic element in divorce, not the sin of the man or the woman, as the case may be, that is tragic enough, but that they should separate. Oh, those children! What chances are they going to have? One reason for not breaking up the family is the children. Paul brings this up in an aside.

But if the unbeliever in such a union goes, then the believer is not under bondage. The believer is set free by the act of the unbeliever; but the believer is never to be active in bringing about separation.

What is the principle here? Paul ends with it. Abide in your calling with God. Then he goes off to illustrate. Circumcision or uncircumcision are of no moment; nor bondage or freedom. Those are simple questions of ritual for the person. Stay with God in your calling, whatever that calling may be.

So the whole question of marriage is lifted on to the highest level. It is seen to be a perfectly lawful, natural, and beautiful thing. It is seen to be a Divine ordinance, but it is always to be treated in that way. If peradventure there be man or woman who in the interest of the Kingdom of God remains single, and who lives the celibate life, let such man or woman not look down on the married, or the married look down in contempt upon the single. The local colour is here, but the principles are abiding and eternal.

   c. Unmarried Daughters of Christian Parents

Apostolic Judgment	vii. 25–40
1. No Commandment, but Spiritual Judgment	25 & 40b
2. The Principles	26–35
Celibacy Good, by Reason of Present Distress	26
Nevertheless Freedom	27, 28
The Governing Principle	29–31
The Advantages of Celibacy	32–35
3. The Applications	36–40
Circumstances Must Decide	
The Balance in Favour of Celibacy	

I CORINTHIANS vii. 25–40

As we saw in the previous study, in the first twenty-four verses of this chapter the apostle has now turned to questions arising out of their letter to him. The first subject on which they had written was that of marriage. He had first discussed the subject generally, and then the Christian position of those married. He now turns to a correlated subject concerning which they had evidently inquired, namely, the position of the unmarried daughters of Christian parents. Here again, in view of the prevalent and rampant impurity in sexual matters obtaining in Corinth, the question had arisen as to whether it were not better for Christian young women to remain unmarried. That was undoubtedly in the mind of those who sent the question to Paul, to which question he now replied.

There are one or two preliminary notes to make on this subject. The word "virgin" here occurs, which is the Greek word *parthenos*, which simply means a maiden, and always an unmarried maiden. The translation here in the Revised Version is "virgin daughter," the word daughter being supplied to make sense. Notice again how this subject is bounded. The opening verse reads, "Now concerning virgins I have no commandment of the Lord; but I give my judgment, as one that hath obtained mercy of the Lord to be faithful." He is careful to point out that he has no commandment of the Lord, but he gives his own judgment. The word "judgment" would be more helpfully rendered opinion. I give my own opinion. Notice the remarkable suggestion there. That presupposes Paul had an intimate knowledge of the commandments of the Lord. One might speculate on the questions of dating and authorship, which would be most interesting, as to whether we are right in saying that these Corinthian letters were written before the Gospels. That is a view held very strongly today. I do not know about that, but if the Gospels had not been written by this time, if none of them had been written—and that I am not prepared to admit—then by ear, and by the testimony of such as Luke described as those who were "eye-witnesses and ministers of the Word," Paul knew what our Lord had definitely commanded.

As he approached this subject of the unmarried daughters, he declared he had no commandment of the Lord. As we go through our Gospels we find out how true it is, so far as the Gospels do record the teaching of Jesus. They record the teaching of Jesus with absolute fulness so far as humanity is concerned. There is nothing that has a bearing on this particular aspect of the subject. Paul here starts by saying so. Concerning virgins, concerning maidens, I have no commandment of the Lord; but I give you my opinion. He is careful to tell us that his opinion is not merely one of his own thinking, but the result of the fact that he had obtained mercy, his opinion illuminated by the fact of mercy. The word "mercy" there means the kindness of the Lord, and his obtaining mercy to be faithful, that is, to be trustworthy. On the basis of that Divine reception of grace, he has formed an opinion, and he gives it.

At the end of the chapter, verse 40, he says, "She is happier if she abide as she is, after my judgment." Again the same word, after my opinion, "and I think that I also have the Spirit of God." This reference is very interesting, it being the only passage in which he seems to differentiate between his opinion on certain bases and the direct and specific will and teaching of his Lord. Those are the boundaries of our subject.

He then replies, which reply consists first of a statement of general principles (26-35). Then he makes certain particular applications in the remainder of the chapter (36-40).

With regard to the general principles, notice carefully what he says, "I think therefore." That is a repetition. Do not forget the basis of his thinking. "I think therefore that this is good by reason of the present distress." The method is that of applying to the immediate the light of the ultimate, of the things they were living in the midst of, to eternal and abiding things. That is an expressive phrase, "the present distress." All he is saying now is the result of his thinking, because of "the present distress." Other expositors must decide exactly what he meant. I cannot. I do think that he was referring to local conditions. There are those who think Paul meant by "the present distress," the whole period of the Church's history to the time of the Advent. Perhaps that is so in a certain sense; but I do not think that was all. I think he was referring to the pressure of circumstances in the midst of which the church was living at Corinth, "the present distress." He was thinking of that. He was recognizing the difficulty of their life. Of course it was difficult. Is it any easier to-day? There are different forces at work, but if we could only analyze them we should find the same underlying causes pressing in upon the life of Christian souls. We can describe a definite event as "the present distress," the present period, that is of necessary constraint, when everything is under constraint, the pressure of the surrounding forces of evil. I think he was thinking of Corinth principally.

What was Paul's first judgment? "I think . . . this is good by reason of the present distress, that it is good for a man to be as he is." He did not say anything about maidens now. The Corinthians had written to Paul about unmarried daughters. The principle applies to the daughter and the man as well, and so he began not with the maiden, but with the man. Then he addressed the man. "Art thou bound unto a wife? seek not to be loosed. Art thou loosed from a wife? seek not a wife. But and if thou marry, thou hast not sinned." Then he goes back to the maiden, "And if a virgin marry, she hath not sinned. Yet such shall have tribulation in the flesh; and I would spare you." All that is needed for the exposition of that passage is a correct emphasis. It is a great gift if one can so read the Scriptures as that they carry their own message.

What is all this about? First of all, the fact that marriage is perfectly proper, and that celibacy is perfectly proper. There must be no attempt to dissolve the marriage relationship in the interest of the

Kingdom of God. But, according to his thought of the present distress, if someone, a man or a maiden, had not entered into the marriage relationship it may be better for them to remain celibate. That was his view. That was his thought. That was his conviction at the time.

Next comes this wonderful little paragraph flashing its light back upon the things already said. "But this I say, brethren, the time is shortened." He had told them what he thought about these matters immediately, but here was the revelation of the reason of his own thinking. "The time is shortened," and shortened in such a manner, "that henceforth both those that have wives may be as though they had none; and those that weep, as though they wept not; and those that rejoice, as though they rejoiced not; and those that buy, as though they possessed not; and those that use the world, as not abusing it; for the fashion of this world passeth away." What a remarkable grouping of things here, beginning with that sentence, "The time is shortened." The Old Version has "The time is short." That is to say, we are living in a time when everything is pressed into narrowness. You remember those lines that speak of the fact that we live in an age when

"Every hour
Must sweat, its sixty minutes to the death."

That is what Paul meant, "The time is shortened." We are living in a time that has the characteristic of pressure, of urgency, of immediacy. "The time is shortened."

Then he enumerated five things, all of them necessary, all of them inevitable, all of them the common experience of men in this world—marriage, sorrow, joy, commerce, and the world in its entirety. Paul says the distress of the present time has shortened the time. The present distress has rendered every moment of vital importance, and, in view of this, it is good that all these things, not improper, but proper, should be treated as secondary. They are to be treated as non-existent. Do not apply that only to marriage. Apply it to sorrow, apply it to joy, apply it to commerce, apply it to the world at large. All these things are to be treated from the standpoint of the shortness of the time and the pressure of life upon those who are desiring to witness for Jesus Christ.

Then Paul went on to tell them that he would have them freed from care, and that in order that they may have care on the highest level. What is that? "The things of the Lord." All this may seem to be very severe, and it is. Who will deny it? It does not mean that marriage is improper. It does not mean that sorrow is to be treated as though it were non-existent in the sense of becoming callous and hard.

It does not mean for a moment that joy is to be subdued and silenced, and all songs are to perish from the life. It does not mean there is to be no buying and no selling. It does not mean that the world is not to be used. Oh, no, but all our attitudes towards all these inevitable things are to be qualified by our relationship to the Lord Himself. It can be bluntly put. If the marriage relationship is going to interfere with our relationship to the Lord, then we are to treat it as nonexistent. If sorrow threatens to come between us and our duty, it is to be trampled under foot. If joy seems to threaten us in our loyalty, it is to be denied. If our commerce interferes with our relationship to our Lord, we are to buy, and yet as though we did not possess the purchase when we get it. Then taking the whole world, the whole material realm in which we all live, if the world becomes master, and if instead of using it, we allow it to use us, then we are abusing it, and that is what Paul is forbidding.

In view of all these things, his judgment for the time being, for the then present distress, was that celibacy had its advantages. Evidently that weighed on his mind very largely, for he was anxious that they should have care on the highest level, without distraction. There is our test. Marriage may be a distraction. Sorrow may become a distraction. Joy may become a distraction, or commerce, or the world. Then we are to turn our backs upon all these things. He has lifted the subject on to the very highest level. He has no commandment of the Lord, but he is giving his opinion.

When he turned to the particular application, notice that he declared distinctly that as to whether the maiden should marry or not—and he includes the man as well, for there is no use talking about the marriage of the maiden unless a man is in view—this must be a matter of personal conviction, and must be decided personally by circumstances. Paul's judgment at the time was that the balance was certainly in favour of freedom from the marriage relationship. That was his judgment, and that in the light of what he called "the present distress."

In the light of this teaching let the sons and daughters of the King settle the question of marriage always under the limitation of their own relationship to the King, consenting or refusing as such action will help or hinder the realization of His purposes. I leave that statement in that way, but it bears a good deal of thinking about. The subject might be illustrated in almost agonizing ways. Oh, the wreckage and ruin that has been wrought when a Godly young woman has joined her life to someone not under the mastery of the King. It is quite true the other way. How many a man has been wrecked and ruined, and some of them in the ministry, because they had become enamoured of a woman whose loyalty to Christ was not their loyalty to Christ. The whole thing is expressed by Paul elsewhere, " Be ye not unequally yoked together with unbelievers." I think that ought to be borne in mind by all Christian young womanhood and manhood. The matter is to be decided when we are alone, in the light of the interest of the Kingdom of heaven.

Thus the most sacred and beautiful things of human life are seen to be conditioned within the government of the Lord. To go outside that government, now to concentrate everything upon the real subject, in marriage, we are violating our vows and imperilling our influence, and perchance laying up in store sorrow upon sorrow for those who are to come. So whereas the Corinthian colour is here, the eternal principles have immediate application.

```
ii. Concerning Things Sacrificed to Idols              viii-xi. 1
    a. The Principles Stated                               viii
        1. The Subject                                       1a
            " Things Sacrificed to Idols "
        2. The Contrasted Principles                       1b-3
            The Admission. " Knowledge "                    1b
            The Contrast                                    1c
                Knowledge Puffeth Up
                Love Edifieth
            Illustration                                    2, 3
                The Insufficiency of Knowledge              2
                The Sufficiency of Love                     3
        3. The Subject in the Light of the Principle       4-13
            In the Light of Knowledge                       4-6
            In the Light of Love                           7-13
```

I CORINTHIANS viii

THE apostle now turned to the second subject about which the Corinthians had written to him, that, namely, of things sacrificed to idols. This section runs on and includes the first verse of chapter eleven. The whole of that section is really the outcome of their inquiry. Let it be recognized at once that this is not the only subject dealt with in that section, for Paul turns aside to deal with other matters, always throwing light upon this one subject, by emphasizing the great principles that were to govern these people in Corinth.

The question was of vital importance in Corinth, involving as it did the supreme question of the influence of the Christian community in a pagan city. That must be borne in mind. All through the letter we have seen the Corinthian background, and that is specially so here. At first it would appear as though this subject had no relevancy whatever to us; but it still has direct meaning for missionaries where the same actual question arises. Talking to Miss Mildred Cable not long ago, this question came up quite incidentally, and her reply interested me as she said this was the actual situation in China, whether the Christian community ought to purchase meat from the shambles where the carcasses of sacrifices were on sale. She said, " We have distinctly to say, No, it must not be done, and for similar reasons." This actual question, Shall meat that has been offered in sacrifice, that part of it which is afterwards on sale, be eaten by Christians? That was the question the Corinthians had asked. Here, as always, the apostle dealt with the local situation in the light of principles, and this is the supreme value for us. Whereas this subject of meats sacrificed to idols may have no meaning for us, the principles the apostle enunciated are binding.

Take the whole section (viii–xi. 1). In chapter eight the principles are stated which are to govern Christians. Then Paul turned aside, still dealing with those principles, but in another application. In ix–x. 13 he illustrated those principles in other realms. Then in x. 14–xi. 1 he applied those principles. That is a survey of the whole section.

Take chapter eight, in which the principles are stated. In the first part of the first verse the subject is stated. Then, beginning in the middle of verse one, to the third verse, Paul declared two principles of action, and showed the contrast between them. From verses 4–13, he showed how these principles should be applied.

"Now concerning things sacrificed to idols." The principles apply over a far wider realm. There were certain portions of sacrifices offered in the great pagan temples that were reserved and put on sale for food. We remember in Hebrew peace offerings, and so in Greek sacrifices, that was done. A study of the Mosaic books will show of the offerings brought, some portions were retained for the food of the priests, and the rest, offered to God, was consumed by fire. So the two things in the offerings of the Hebrew economy. In Corinth this was even more marked. There were certain portions reserved and offered to the gods, and very often in the Greek rites that meant offering to the priests, and they were sacred. Then the part of the carcass not so used in distinct sacrificial worship was put on sale, and anyone could buy and eat such meat for food. In that way it was offered at a lower rate of exchange, consequently people bought it more readily, for human nature is the same all down the ages. That was the condition of affairs in Corinth.

Now the question arising was this, whether purchasing and using such meats by Christians involved them in compromise with the idols that were worshipped. Here is meat. Part of it had been sacrificed on the heathen altar of idolatry and the worship of false gods and the rest, still belonging to the carcass, may be eaten. If we eat that meat, which is eaten by Corinth, part of which has been an idol sacrifice, are we in any way compromising our position? Are we involving ourselves in the practice of idolatry? As we think about this we see that the question was more than an interesting one. It revealed two things, that in writing to Paul to ask this they first manifested a great tenderness of conscience. They were not sure, and they wanted to be sure. They were anxious not to compromise their witness in that pagan city in any way. So they submitted the question to apostolic authority. The other simple fact is that, showing they did ask the question, there was a divergence of opinion. There were those who said it did not matter at all, that it did not compromise them at all, that they could take the meat and eat. But there were others who said in effect, We are not so sure. Let us write and ask the apostle, and so the letter came. That was the subject and the reason for it.

How did Paul deal with it? He started with a remarkable statement in the second part of the first verse. "We know that we all have knowledge." We know, we Christian people, who are believers in Christ Jesus, who have been made members of Christ Jesus, who are among the saints, who call upon the name of our Lord Jesus Christ, "we know that we all have knowledge." That does not mean they knew everything, but it does mean this, entrance into relationship with Christ has brought us a clear shining light upon all subjects. We have the knowledge.

He went on to show one application of that knowledge. Does that not remind us of the words of our Lord Himself, "I am the light of the world; he that followeth Me shall not walk in the darkness, but shall have the light of life." One great ineffable blessing that comes to those who have the light is that they have knowledge at their disposal, to which they may appeal, and all that knowledge is centred in Him. So Paul started by saying, "We know that we all have knowledge."

Yet it seems to me when he wrote that, he saw the abuse of this great fact, for he immediately drew a sharp contrast, which is arresting as we find it stated here. "If any man thinketh that he knoweth anything, he knoweth not yet as he ought to know." We have knowledge, but if there is a man who thinks he really knows completely and finally, he has not the first element of knowledge, nor this consciousness of the things he does not know, and needs to have interpreted.

Then Paul went on. "Concerning therefore the eating of things sacrificed to idols, we know that no idol is anything in the world." That is one thing we know. We are quite sure of it. Go back to the first verse here. He had said, "We know that we all have knowledge," and then there comes a contrast. "Knowledge puffeth up, but love edifieth." If we know that we all have knowledge, do not forget that knowledge alone puffeth up, but love edifieth. Knowledge puffeth up, that is, inflates, that is, makes proud. Knowledge of itself has a tendency always to make the intellectual proud and conceited. Paul distinctly said so here. If that is all, if we are only being mastered by the fact that we know, our knowledge may make us proud, puff us up, and the puffed-up intellect is incapable of true discernment and judgment. "Knowledge puffeth up." The contrast here is between "puffeth up," and "edifieth." "Puffeth up" is inflation, and anything puffed up is liable to collapse, to burst. But "love edifieth," buildeth up. The contrast is between the powerful result of knowledge and the collapse that may follow the interpretation of mere knowledge, and the lasting effect when love enters into the calculation. That is a remarkable contrast. What Paul intended here was to show the insufficiency of knowledge for those who were perplexed about things sacrificed to idols, or any other matter. If they have no more than knowledge, they are incapable of judgment, for knowledge alone will make them conceited. But if love is there, love is concerned, not with personal advantage, but with others. It builds up.

He then went on and illustrated. They had knowledge, and they knew there were no idols. Here is meat sacrificed to idols. It is absurd, for there are no idols. There are many gods as such, but there are none. There is no reality in them. We know that we all have knowledge of that. Therefore there can be no meaning in things sacrificed to what does not exist. Therefore it does not matter. We can eat this meat. Men can go out to the temple and offer part of the sacrifice, and the part is offered for food; but what they did in offering was foolishness, because there are no such things as idols. There is one God. Consequently we can do as we like; we can eat.

But wait. Love thinks of someone else, of that man who is watching these Christians, and he does not know, as they know, that those idols are non-existent. He believes, in some sense, that they are real, to whom sacrifices must be offered. He watches the Christians going and purchasing the food, and they are placing a stumbling-block, by their eating, in the way of that man. Love comes in and says, If you act upon the basis of knowledge, and you know there is no reality in the business, that is the acting of knowledge; but love says, someone is watching. There is a man here who has not your knowledge that idols are non-existent, and when he sees you partaking of part of the sacrifices, you seem to him to be owning the reality of the sacrifice and of the gods to whom these sacrifices are offered. Love will therefore come in as a corrective to knowledge and balance it.

To turn to the application of the principles. The action of the Christian will not be based merely upon knowledge the Christian has, but upon the love which the Christian also must have. So the principles are applied. Our action based upon our knowledge may not be understood by the man outside, and his superstition may be strengthened by what seems to him to be the reality of idol sacrifices. That summarizes the teaching.

Do not forget Paul says here that this man may be tempted to look upon with contempt the man to whom you feel yourself superior because you have the knowledge, that is the man for whom Christ died. It is wonderful the introduction of that tremendous statement here. To put a stumbling-block in the way of that man is to sin against Christ Himself.

So the great teaching here is that there must be the mastery of love in the exercise of our judgment. Knowledge may go astray. Knowledge may lead us to do things which in themselves may not be wrong to us, but which may be causing the weak brother for whom Christ died, the unenlightened man, the man who has not received the knowledge that has come to us, it may cause him to misunderstand and stumble.

So the ultimate victory of love in the forming of a judgment is the foregoing of a right, and perhaps that is the supreme thing. Oh, yes, we may have a perfect right to eat these things. We know there is nothing in these temples and idols and sacrifices, and because of our knowledge we have a perfect right to eat. But wait a minute, love will suggest that we forego the right, and refrain from eating, if by so doing we may be helping the man who lacks our knowledge. Nothing can be clearer than this teaching.

This, however, must be said. Use has been made of this statement of Paul in this application, " Wherefore, if meat maketh my brother to stumble, I will eat no flesh for evermore, while the world standeth." I have heard unjustifiable and unwarranted use made of that statement. We must remember this must be interpreted by a justifiable effect of conscience on our action, and no further. I do not think any particular word of application is necessary. It must be proved that an example of ours ever made anyone to stumble, or offend in that particular matter. That applies in a good many ways. Some people make use of it when there is no excuse for their action, when it is not based upon our action.

But there is something else lying behind it. For instance, I do not suppose anyone would dream of saying, If clothes maketh my brother to stumble . . . You finish it! One has to be careful to use the sanctification of knowledge, mastered by love. If there are acts that really make others to offend, though, from the standpoint of knowledge, one may have perfect liberty to do those acts, one has not perfect liberty through the love-mastered life.

Paul then went on to apply the principles in another realm, and then came back to the application again to the sacrifice to idols.

```
    b. The Principles Illustrated                    ix–x. 13
        1. The Limits of Liberty                         ix
            Apostolic Rights                           1–14
                The Official Rights                     1–3
                The Rights of Maintenance              4–14
                    Stated                              4–6
                    Argued                             7–14
            Apostolic Restraint                       15–23
            " But "
                    The Facts                        15–18
                    The Method                       19–23
            Apostolic Appeal                          24–27
                The Race.  " So Run "
                The Games. " So Fight I "
```

I CORINTHIANS ix

This portion constitutes a part of Paul's answer to the question the Corinthians had raised concerning things sacrificed to idols. There does not seem to be very much in this passage on the subject, but as we proceed we see the reason for that omission. In the last analysis, the whole question must be considered in the light of Christian liberty and its limitations. Paul dealt with that matter in chapter six, saying there, " All things are lawful for me; but not all things are expedient. All things are lawful for me; but I will not be brought under the power of any." Then in chapter ten, verse 23, " All things are lawful; but all things are not expedient. All things are lawful; but all things edify not. Let no man seek his own, but each his neighbour's good." He goes on, " Whatsoever is sold in the shambles, eat." He is still in that region of things sacrificed to idols. The passages show that the whole question raised now about things sacrificed to idols there in Corinth, and all similar questions of conscience arising in the minds of Christian people, must be considered in the light of Christian liberty and its limitations. Liberty is limited. That is one of the characteristics of our liberty. " All things are lawful for me; but not all things are expedient. All things are lawful for me; but I will not be brought under the power of any." There is the whole matter.

In this whole section we have seen that Paul stated the principles in chapter eight. He next illustrated the principles (ix–x. 13). Then the principles were applied (x. 14–xi. 1). This teaching grew out of the Corinthian question as to what they should do in the case of things sacrificed to idols.

Beginning here with the ninth chapter, Paul illustrated these principles in other directions, but the principles abide. We shall find he came back to the actual subject under discussion. Notice the fifteenth verse, " But." That marks the second half of the chapter. There was something else to be said. The chapter is not complete. In the first fourteen verses there are certain things interesting and arresting. They are wholly concerned with the apostle's rights. Liberty is here, " all things are lawful "; " but! " He dealt with his rights. In the second part of the chapter we see what he does with his rights. There is a good deal to be said.

Take that first part (1–14). It is a very remarkable passage concerning his rights. He dealt with two rights that he claimed, first his official rights as an apostle. That is in a very few sentences, but they are tremendously full of meaning. Then he dealt with his right to maintenance by the Church of God, the right he had to expect the Church should care for him in all his carnal affairs, and the right every preacher of the Gospel has a right to expect.

In the first three verses Paul dealt with his official rights, and that in a remarkable way. We have seen the principles of action in chapter eight. They were that knowledge must be conditioned in love. Now he is going to illustrate that principle, not in application to things sacrificed to idols, but the same principle as it obtains in his own case, and in the case of the Christian ministry. Evidently there was opposition to him in Corinth. He had spoken of divisions, some saying they were of Paul, some of Apollos, others of Cephas, and so on; and there is no question but that there was definite opposition to him, and to his claim of apostleship. He went aside here, not from principle, but he took the opportunity to apply the principle to answer those who called in question his authority as an apostle. Take the third verse, " My defence to them that examine me is this . . ." Do not rob that sentence of its full meaning. He was using, evidently with intention, the actual words of the courts of law. " Defence " is such a word, it is apologia; and " examine " is also such a word, definitely used in a court of law. When Paul said, " My defence to them that examine me," he was putting himself in the place of someone charged with something. He is on defence, and he is making his answer to those charging him, or examining him. It is legal terminology, the actual words of the law courts, with which they were all familiar. So he said, If you would examine me, here is my defence, what I have to say in answer; here is my apologia. He here uses the word apology in the true sense. He was not admitting he was wrong. He was claiming he was right. Paul was not apologizing in our sense of the word. Paul was declaring that which cleared him of the charges they were making against him, " My defence is this . . ."

It is perfectly evident, as we read Paul's letters, how constantly he fought and argued in defence of his right as an apostle. He says he was an apostle, not of the will of men, or of the flesh, but of God. I do not think Paul was ever *persona grata* in official Jerusalem. I think they were always a little suspicious of him, which is a great comfort to some of us. There was always some little question about his regularity. Paul combatted that attitude, not for the sake of the glory that is in apostleship as an office, but because his authority, being the authority of the apostle, was being questioned, was likely to weaken their faith and wrong the church, and so wrong the whole city of Corinth in the testimony the church was called upon to bear. So he was on his defence, and was answering those who were examining him.

What about this examination? What does he say? First notice that the translation is in the form of questions. This again suggests he was answering them. As though they were saying, Paul, you are not free to express your opinion. You are not really an apostle, because you have never seen Jesus. Do not miss this. Go back to the first chapter of the Acts, that wonderful chapter. The Lord had gone as to bodily presence, and He had charged His disciples to do nothing until they were empowered by the coming of the Holy Ghost. They got together, and " Peter stood up in the midst of the brethren and said (and there was a multitude of persons gathered together, about an hundred and twenty), Brethren." Peter was going to make a speech, and to point out the necessity for filling the gap. We know the story. " It was needful that the Scripture should be fulfilled." Judas had fallen out, and a gap had been created, and it was important that the gap should be filled at once. So they got to work to fill it. Oh, if someone could have said, Man, Simon, you have no right to do anything. You have been told to wait until you have power. But it is very important that this gap should be filled. It was quite a powerful speech he made. He went on to tell the company what had been the characteristics of the men elected. " Of the men therefore which have companied with us all the time that the Lord Jesus went in and out among us, beginning from the baptism of John, unto the day that He was received up from us, of these must one become a witness with us of His resurrection." He was absolutely wrong and mistaken. On the basis of the belief that one must be elected who had been with Jesus all the time from John's baptism to the time of His ascension they made their first blunder when they elected Matthias as an apostle.

He was never chosen of God to the office. After his election it is interesting to see how he passes out of sight. They cast lots, and resorted to a pagan, or semi-pagan, way of deciding an election. An old writer said,

> "The lot is cast into the lap;
> But the whole disposing thereof is of the Lord."

So they went on doing it and using lots. Do not forget the Church must not do it.

Paul is saying here, "Am I not free? am I not an apostle? have I not seen Jesus our Lord? are not ye my work in the Lord?" Here is a series of questions, but all to be answered in one particular way. "Am I not free? am I not an apostle?" that is, one exercising delegated authority? Jesus chose that name for the twelve. He named them apostles. We are distinctly told that as He had called them, separated them to be with Him, ultimately to send them forth, He called them apostles. It is a great word. Yes, it meant messengers, but first it meant separated, and then sent forth. "Am I not an apostle?" Have I not been separated? Am I not authoritatively sent forth? A delegated authority he is claiming. "Am I not free?" that is, free within the limits of his delegated authority?

Then comes his question, "Have I not seen Jesus our Lord?" He did not answer that here. He leaves it, a question, which they had been asking. He says, "Have I not seen Jesus our Lord?" We can answer it for him. Go through the story and we find he had actually seen Jesus. He saw Jesus on the way to Damascus. He saw Jesus in this very city of Corinth when he was in the house of Titus Justus, when Jesus told him to stay there, because He had much people in the city. He saw Jesus again in the prison in the Roman dungeon, when the Lord appeared to him and said to him, "Be of good cheer; for as thou hast testified concerning Me at Jerusalem, so must thou bear witness also at Rome." Oh, yes, Paul had seen Him. These men were still hemmed in by material thought, to those who had actually seen Him in the days of earthly limitation in the body. Paul had definitely seen Him, and if that be a qualification for apostleship, then Paul could claim to be an apostle. He did not seem to fulfil the requirement, because their understanding of conditions was false.

Then Paul dwelt upon that statement, "Are not ye my work in the Lord?" Look at the church of which you are members. The Corinthian church is in view for the moment, the church which under God, and under the guidance of the Spirit of God, Paul had founded, had planted. "Paul planted, Apollos watered, and God gave the increase." But Paul had planted it. "Are not ye my work in the

Lord?" What they were, in position and privilege, was guarantee of his apostleship. He was free, under delegated authority. He had seen the Lord, and how wondrously he had seen Him. Moreover, these Corinthians proved it. They were his work in the Lord.

He went on, "If to others I am not an apostle, yet at least I am to you; for the seal of mine apostleship are ye in the Lord." Notice the word "seal," the insignia of authority derived. Pilate had sealed the tomb of Jesus, had placed the seal of authority upon it. It was no good. But that is what the seal meant, authority; and Paul here declared the Corinthians were the seal of his authority. So he stated and defended his apostolic rights.

He then went on, "Have we no right to eat and to drink?" Have we no right to lead about a wife that is a believer, even as the rest of the apostles, and the brethren of the Lord, and Cephas? Or I only and Barnabas, have we not a right to forbear working?" He is rather giving away something to which he comes later on. Yet he says he need not have worked. He had the right to forbear working as the other apostles did. Notice his claim here, to summarize. He claims the right of his fellow-apostles, and all this in the ministry of the Gospel, for he names Barnabas, who never was an apostle. He claimed that they had a right to accept and had to be maintained on the material level by those whom they served in the spiritual realm. That is the whole argument here. The force of stating it comes when we get to the latter part of the chapter. Here he states his right in this regard, the right to eat and drink, that is, to be supported by the church itself.

Have we not a right to lead about a wife that is a believer, a sister, that is, a Christian? It is an old question, was Paul married? At any rate, he said he had a right to be. Was he? I do not know, but I am certain he had been married. In Farrar's *Life of St. Paul* (i. 92) he maintained strongly that he was a married man, or had been. While the case is not proven, I believe he was a widower. When Stephen was committed to martyrdom, Paul said he gave his vote. That meant he was a member of the Sanhedrim, and no one was a member of the Sanhedrim except married men. Whether he was married or not, he said he had the right to be married. He had a perfect right to lead about a wife. I rather like that expression "to lead about a wife." He said, All the others were doing it. Here were his rights, the rights of his official apostleship; and now he claimed the right to be maintained by the church.

He then used five illustrative arguments, which are interesting. It is a common practice that if a man toils he expects to share in the result of his toil. The soldier, the vine-dresser, the shepherd; but more than that, it is according to the law of Moses, in God's care for the oxen. He had care for the oxen, but he showed that had a deeper meaning in the interest of those toiling for gain. And the reason for it, "If we sowed unto you spiritual things, is it a great matter if we shall reap your carnal things?"

In the twelfth verse is the next illustration. "If others partake of this right over you, do not we yet more? Nevertheless we did not use this right." He is getting to what he will say more fully later on in this chapter. He had the perfect right to maintenance. His official right was that it was the law of the temple. The final finding is in the fourteenth verse, "Even so did the Lord ordain that they which proclaim the Gospel should live of the Gospel."

As to the application of this study, concerning the question asked, he was not turning aside from the great principles he had laid down. The principles were that we have rights; but, secondly, that they may be conditioned by the mastery of love. So far we have simply looked at the rights. It is important, but it does introduce us to the next word in verse 15, "But." He went on to show his relation to those rights. This second right of maintenance he surrenders. The right of apostleship nothing will persuade him to surrender. We shall see this whole principle is there—liberty, freedom, the rights of the believer; but in their exercise they must be qualified by some higher law, the law of love; and the law of love is never self-centred. It is always proceeding to forego in the interest of outsiders.

Continuing, Paul's answer to the Corinthian question concerning things sacrificed to idols, in the eighth chapter he had contrasted two principles of action, those of knowledge and love, showing that the Christian must ever condition his knowledge by his love. Then he had turned aside to illustrate the operation of such principles in the case of his apostleship, the necessity for the mastery of knowledge by love. In our previous paragraph we considered his rights as an apostle. There is no doubt that his apostleship was called in question by certain of those in Corinth.

Having thus shown his rights in the first part of this chapter, Paul began his second part of the chapter, with a "but." When I was a boy at school they used to teach grammar, and we had to learn definitions of the different parts of speech. I was taught that "but" was a disjunctive conjunction. It is a good definition. Our schoolmaster explained it by saying, You see the railway lines, and the point where a train turns off at a switch on to another line, and it goes on its journey. That is a disjunctive conjunction. We have been travelling along a certain line, now we are going off on to another line. Continuing the subject, Paul turned to another aspect. That makes the word here "but" dynamic and forceful. All he had said of his rights as an apostle was true. All he had said about the rights of maintenance as an apostle in the ministry of the Gospel was true. But! Now he had something else to say, and in the rest of this chapter the subject is that of his attitude toward his rights, in obedience to the principle already laid down in chapter eight. Simply to act on the basis of knowledge may make one conceited, proud, and arrogant; but love conditioning knowledge will build up and edify. That is the principle.

In effect, Paul said here, I want to apply that principle to my own apostleship, the principle that knowledge must be qualified by love. I want you to see how it works out in my case. He referred to both the rights already declared, those of his apostleship and of his right and others to be maintained by the Christian Church. He now dealt with them, however, in the reverse order; first, he dealt with his rights of maintenance, and then with his right of apostleship.

His rights of maintenance are found in verses 15 and 18, and then his rights of his apostleship are in verses 16 and 17, and then in verses 19 to 27.

Verse 15, "But I have used none of these things; and I write not these things that it may be so done in my case." Then in verse 18, "That, when I preach the Gospel, I may make the Gospel without charge." In those two sentences is a revelation of what he had to say about his rights as to his maintenance. What was his attitude? What did he do about them? It is important to remember that he had been perfectly clear, and he had argued it, that those who preach the Gospel should live of the Gospel, that they ought to have no care about the worldly things at all, that they ought to be taken care of. What about himself? He said, So far as the rights of maintenance are concerned, I have surrendered them. He had given them up, he had not claimed them. As to the past, "I have used none of these things." I have not taken from you the things necessary for my material life. Of course in other places we learn that he wrought with his own hands as a tent-maker. What he had a perfect right to expect he had not had, and he had not expected. He had not asked for it. He had surrendered his rights. Take that as a brief statement of what the apostle had to say concerning the rights of maintenance.

He then told them the reason. In the fifteenth verse, "It were good for me rather to die, than that any man should make my glorying void." That is why for these Corinthians. It was not always so. There were others who sent to him and cared for him. He did not want it from Corinth. One reason was that he would rather die than have any man make his glorying void. What was his glorying? We shall find that as we go a little further on. But look at the eighteenth verse. "What then is my reward? That, when I preach the Gospel,

I may make the Gospel without charge, so as not to use to the full my right in the Gospel." He gave up the right he had in the Gospel to claim sustenance, that the Gospel might not be hindered. That was the case with the Corinthians. Here is the illustration. Again it does not apply everywhere. It did not apply to Paul everywhere. But here was a case where there was criticism, and those who did not believe in his apostleship. Then he said, I owe you nothing, I have made use of none of these things that are my right. I am not writing to you for you to make up wherein you have failed, but my purpose is that I may continue to glory in my Gospel, and that the Gospel may have its full power, and shall not be hindered by anything of that kind.

He then turned, in the second place, to the rights of his apostleship. The whole thing may be summarized by saying he showed that the rights of his apostleship are those created by his Gospel. It was the Gospel for which Paul was careful, and about which he was thinking. What a wonderful word it is! There is no need to interpret it. It has become so commonplace. It is so central to all the Christian fact and message. It is the Gospel, good news; and when we find out what the good news is, the Cross is in it, redemption is in it, all the purposes of the Divine grace made accessible to the needy and broken heart of man. That is all true. It is this Gospel about which Paul was thinking. It is wonderful to trace through Paul's epistles, those we are certain he wrote, and to find this fact of the Gospel is referred to no less than eighty-three times. Once he wrote, " My Gospel," in writing to the Romans. This was a burden upon his heart for evermore, his sense of the deposit committed to him, entrusted to him, and of his consequent responsibility for that deposit. In this very chapter the word " Gospel " occurs nine times. It is running all the way through the Gospel, his sense of the supreme importance of his deposit.

I have used that word deposit quite resolutely. In writing to Timothy, Paul said, " I know Whom I have believed, and I am persuaded that He is able to guard." Guard what? It is almost always quoted as we find it in the translation, " He is able to guard that which I have committed to Him against that day." To translate from the standpoint of the work of the translator, without any prejudice, or reading into it what they think Paul meant—a peril to every translator and every true expositor of the Word is constantly praying he may be delivered from saying what he thinks the writer meant—Paul says here, " I know Whom I have believed, and I am persuaded He is able to guard my deposit against that day." That may be the same thing, but it may be quite different. " My deposit," that which I put into the bank. " My deposit," that which I commit to Him. But there is another meaning. It may not mean what I have committed to Him, but what

He has committed to me. I think that is undoubtedly what the apostle meant. Take the context. He was writing to Timothy about his charge, about the things for which he was responsible, and he said to Timothy, speaking to him personally, " I know Him Whom I have believed, and I am persuaded that He is able to take care of the deposit that He has left with me." Paul had a deposit entrusted to him. He was responsible to Christ for it, but, finally, He will care for it. It is a great thing to know that, for every preacher to know that. Sometimes we waste a good deal of time trying to take care of God's truth, forgetting God takes care of His own truth. Our business is to proclaim it in the right way. We do not need to defend the truth. I am persuaded He is able to guard my deposit.

What was his deposit? Listen to him once more, and again in another letter, familiar to all. " I am debtor both to Greeks and to barbarians," to the learned and the unlearned. I am debtor. I owe them something. I have something I have on trust for them. What was it? The Gospel. His right in the Gospel is here, the secondary right of being maintained in material things by Christian people. He insisted upon it as a right; but he gave up that right. He was not claiming it.

Now to summarize. What he was not going to give up were his rights in the Gospel. He could give up his rights of maintenance, but not in the Gospel. That is what he now argued at length. He said, Necessity is laid upon me, constraint, something from which there is no escape, constraint laid upon me, imposed upon me. I am mastered by this thing. I cannot get away from it. Necessity is laid upon me to preach this Gospel. I cannot escape from it. I can do without your material gifts. I am willing to waive my right there, but not in the necessity that is laid upon me.

Then that illuminative word, if I fail there, what then? " Woe is unto me, if I preach not the Gospel." We should understand that " woe " is not really punishment, that he is suggesting that he will be punished if he fail. It is rather a sense of agony in his own soul if he break down and fail. The word " woe " there means " alas," alas to me. I cannot help it. Necessity is laid upon me, imposed upon me. I am constrained. I am tied up. I am bound up. It is part and parcel of my very life and nature. Alas, if I fail here. Alas, if I preach not the Gospel. No, no, he said, there are rights I cannot give up, they are the rights of my apostleship, and the whole of them are found in the Gospel, and the necessity for publishing it.

There is the real secret of readiness for, or preparation for what we term today quite rightly, the work of the Christian ministry. I have said sometimes, and have been misunderstood, when a young man comes to me and says, I think I should like to enter the Christian ministry, I always reply, Are you sure? And if he replies, I am not, then I always say, For God's sake keep out. No man has any right to think he has a call to the ministry unless he knows it, and is certain. He may not be able to explain the reason, or the necessity, but the sense—it would be an appalling catastrophe if he did not have it. It is the Gospel, and these are rights, Paul's right as a messenger, an apostle, a teacher of that Gospel. These cannot be given up.

Then at verse 19 he speaks of the method by which he is carrying this out. He has come in bondage to all. What for? In order to gain. Always in order to gain, the winning of men for Jesus Christ, the winning for this Gospel, the gain of human lives, and the bringing of them under the mastery of the Gospel, loosing them from their bondage and its power, and bringing them into the glorious liberty of the children of God.

He says he became all things to all men. It is remarkable that he says to the Jew that he became as a Jew, that is, those under the law, as though he were under the law. To those without law he became as without the law. What is that, in the light of what he had already said about the stern necessity laid upon him to preach the Gospel, so that he thinks all things tragic if he fail? He cannot give it up. So far as that is remembered, then in this statement of Paul is the fact of adaptation to those with whom he comes into contact. He would take his place by the side of Jew or Gentile, and be as that one. Make no mistake. He is not free from law. He is under the law of God, the law of Christ, but always to gain. It is a great grace when a man can do that without any compromise to his Gospel. There is no compromise for the Gospel. Necessity is there, the imposition upon me of a deposit, and an agony if I fail the Gospel. The Gospel, yes, without compromise. If I sit down with a Jew, or hold communion with a Gentile, I become all things to all men. He became hail fellow well met to everyone. That did not mean he lowered the flag, or minimized the Gospel. Woe is me if I fail!

He then took two illustrations pertinent to Corinth, the great city of learning and luxury and of athleticism. They all knew the figure of the race course and the arena. He showed them a man in the race course. He said, So run that you may attain. Personally, I do not think Paul wrote the letter to the Hebrews. Some do. I think it was written under his influence, by Luke. Call to mind the word there, " Therefore let us also, seeing we are compassed about with so great a cloud of witnesses, lay aside every weight, and the sin in good standing around, and let us run with patience the race that is set before us, looking off unto Jesus." "So run," he says, "that you may attain." That is the duty of every Christian witness.

Then he went over to the arena, and looked at the games. He watched men boxing. That is what he really says here. He says, "Every man that striveth in the games is temperate in all things." "So run, as not uncertainly; so fight I." The marginal reading is, "So box I." That is the word, "boxing," fighting with fists. "So box I, as not beating the air." I make my blows tell. "I buffet my body," I bruise my body, very literally Paul says, I keep my body under, I give myself black eyes. I see to it all the material is held in complete subjection to the master passion of the declaration and revelation of the meaning of my Gospel.

Then that last word, "Lest by any means, after that I have preached to others, I myself should be rejected." The old version had it, "castaway," unapproved, that is, lest I should fail to fulfil the real meaning of my apostleship. That is the peril.

"Alas, if I preach not the Gospel." In the case of Paul's own apostleship is further demonstrated the fact that knowledge must be conditioned in love for others, that seeks to build up. The knowledge of his rights might have puffed him up, so that he would have become proud and arrogant, and that would have killed the power of his message. But his love qualified his message, making him ready to abandon his own rights on the material level, in order to maintain those on the higher level of the purpose of the Gospel, that love that ever sought to gain some.

```
    2. The Abuse of Liberty                                x. 1–13
        An Illustration                                    1–5
            Privileges of the Fathers                      1–4
            Failure of " Most of Them "                    5
        The Teaching                                       6–10
            The Destructive Use of Liberty
                Lust                                       6
                Idolatry                                   7
                Fornication                                8
                Unbelief                                   9
                Murmuring                                  10
        The Appeal                                         11–13
            The Value of the Illustration                  11
            The Need for Caution                           12
            The Inspiration of Courage                     13
```

I CORINTHIANS x. 1–13

STILL occupied with the principles enunciated in the eighth chapter, which principles cover the whole field of life for the Christian, the apostle now took an illustration from the history of Israel. He had illustrated in his own case his rights as an apostle, and the right he had to be maintained as a minister of the Gospel. Now he turned to the history of Israel, the opening word of this chapter, the word "for," connecting it with what he had just written as to the possibility of becoming rejected or a castaway. There is the closest link between that very solemn word in verse 27, in which he showed the possibility of being a preacher to others, a minister in holy things to others, and of being rejected, becoming a castaway, as the Old Version had, an appropriate word, which may mislead. It might appear to mean he would lose his soul; but it does not mean that, but that he might lose his apostleship.

To summarize everything in this study, his intention throughout is to show that privilege is no insurance against ultimate failure. He had been dealing with the tremendous privilege of his apostleship, the rights for which he was prepared to fight, not of maintenance, but the fact of his apostleship. Yet he saw he might be rejected, or become a castaway. How important it is that we should realize that! There is a terrible danger of trusting in our privileges, and in the fact that we are privileged people, forgetting that privilege always entails responsibility.

Paul took this remarkable illustration in a striking way as applicable to the whole nation of Israel. These thirteen verses may be described as an excursus, as they would say in academic halls, on the possible abuse of liberty. He has turned aside, though still in the same realm of ideas, though it has its bearing on the whole subject. Its theme is that it is possible to abuse liberty.

There are three movements here. The fact of liberty is illustrated (1–5) in the case of this nation. Then in verses 6–10, in a most searching paragraph, he shows how these people abused their liberty. Then in verses 11–13 he makes application of it to the people of God.

How remarkable a summing up this is of the way this nation was brought into liberty, out of slavery into freedom—the emancipation of the nation! Of course he was writing to Christians, to Greeks, to Gentiles, but he uses the illustration of his own life history and nation in writing to them. Notice in these four verses the recurrence of the word "all." "Our fathers were all under the cloud," "all passed through the sea," "all were baptized unto Moses in the cloud and in the sea," "did all eat the same spiritual meat," "did all drink the same spiritual drink."

Go back in the history found in detail in the Old Testament. He says they were all under the cloud, that is to say, they all were Divinely led and guided. That is the first note of privilege noted. Yet, in spite of that, we see in verses 5 to 9 the appalling failure; but they were all under the cloud, Divine guidance.

They all passed through the sea, that is, deliverance. Guidance by the cloud was in order to deliver, emancipate. Keep in mind what Paul certainly was doing, describing the condition of these people in slavery in Egypt. They were brought out, emancipated. They all passed through the sea.

Then that interesting way of stating it, They "were all baptized unto Moses," that is to say, they were all unified under the leadership of Moses, all constituting an assembly, just as in the Christian Church. Entry to the Church is by baptism, not water baptism, but the baptism of the Spirit, every man being made a member of the Church of God. Every man is a member of the Church when he is born again, baptized by the Spirit into the one Body. Paul will say that a little later on in this same letter. It is that unity and fellowship, and he uses the expression "baptized unto Moses," that is, to that whole Mosaic economy of which Moses, under God, was the leader. They were baptized to him in the cloud and the sea as they followed the guidance of the cloud; as they passed through, the waters were divided for them, and they became more than a wandering mob. They became a nation and a community. They were baptized into that great and wonderful fellowship. Mark their privileges.

Then there was the period in the wilderness. They all ate the same spiritual meat, the manna. That was given to them. They could not provide it. They knew nothing about its source, save that it came from God. They were fed materially with the supply that God gave them. And they "did all drink the same spiritual drink," and Paul very daringly said, the rock from which they drank was Christ. The very centre of their life was Christ, the Messiah, the coming One; consequently, the water that came from the rock was Christ. So that we may take the last two, spiritual meat and drink, and there we see Divine sustenance. Notice what those simple things reveal. Under the cloud, guidance; through the sea, Divine emancipation; baptized unto Moses, a Divinely created freedom, and a new community, joined together in that way. Divine sustenance, as they ate and drank, supernaturally provided food and drink. Mark the privileges of these people. That is what Paul is here emphasizing.

Paul was reminding them how that nation passed out of bondage into liberty and freedom. That was the difference. They had been slaves. They came out into the place of freedom. He was reminding the Corinthians how it all happened, their passing from bondage into liberty. Again, to repeat from another angle. Nothing was the result of their own effort. Everything depended upon the goings and doings of God. He provided the cloud, the deliverance, freedom, the meat and the drink, the privileges that were theirs. Everything was of God, and nothing of themselves. Everything was supernatural, the doings of God.

He now asked these Corinthians to take that as an illustration of a certain great principle. The first feeling may be that a people so privileged cannot fail. If indeed God undertook for them in this way to guide, to deliver, to constitute them a community on a new basis, and supplied their needs physically and spiritually and supernaturally, what a wondrous liberty it was into which they were brought by God!

We come then to verse 5, "Howbeit with most of them God was not well pleased; for they were overthrown in the wilderness." That "most of them" is an accurate expression. What did happen in the case of these people? How many of them were overthrown in the wilderness? Every last one of them except Joshua and Caleb, that is, of the people who came out of Egypt. Most of them, said Paul, fell in the wilderness, that is, all except two.

Why did they fall? We shall see why as we look at these verses 5 to 9. "Lust," idolatry, "fornication," unbelief, murmuring. Paul did not take them in the order in which they were manifested in the wilderness, as he has listed them.

Turn back to the record, to the central and specific illustrations, the things he named. First of all, lust. The story of that is in Numbers 11, the lust for something which was outside the Divine provision. It does not look a very serious thing, but read that chapter in Numbers and see how they lusted. They desired for something that was not provided for them by God. Oh, it is terrifically true that He gave them their desire. We remember something written in the Psalms that throws light upon that:

> "He gave them their request;
> But sent leanness into their souls."

That is a tremendous declaration. It is possible to desire something, and in the overruling of God He gives it to us in order to show us the folly of our desire. These people desired something outside the Divine provision. Why should they not have flesh and meat? The answer is simply this, it was not provided, but they desired it. How often we have desired things outside the Divine provision, in which there seemed to be nothing wrong, that seemed to be lawful; and there are times when God has allowed us to have the thing we have hankered after. Yes, they lusted and desired, and that was the beginning of defection. It always is. It is in that strange, mystic realm of desire. Is there any psychologist who has explained it in this day of psychology? I am not disrespectful to the said psychologists who think they know everything. Ask the psychologists to interpret desire. They may tell us about inhibitions and prohibitions, and yet that realm of desire is the supreme thing in human life; not the mental, save as it helps there; not the volitional, save as it touches the realm of responsibility; but that which underlies the thinking of the mind and the willing of the will—desire. It is always the beginning of deflection. What a remarkable illustration this is in the beginning of the Bible story, that of the fall, which, personally, I have not got rid of yet! How did the fall begin? Go back to the story and investigate. "When she saw that the tree was good for food, and that the tree was to be desired to make one wise"—desire for something outside the Divine provision. These people were the people of God, the people of liberty; and lust was the first thing to which Paul drew attention as being a violating of the law of liberty.

Then next we come to idolatry. That is a reference to the story in Exodus xxxii, one that we all know. Moses had gone into the mount, and the people got restless, and asked where he was. They did not know what had become of him. They made themselves a representation of God. Aaron received all their jewellery which they had brought with them out of Egypt, and he melted it down and constructed a calf. When he was interrogated he said that which stands out for evermore upon the page as a most revealing statement. He said that he put these things into the furnace, and, lo, "there came out this calf." It must have been a remarkable furnace! Oh, no, he meant it to come out. He tried to show it was an accident. No, it was an attempt to put something up to represent God. That was the beginning of all the trouble. It was not to be someone in the place of God, the breaking of the law of making a representation of God that was false. Paul tells us what they did, that they made a gesture of worship, and then they had a good time, they "sat down to eat and drink, and rose up to play." Idolatry, and these are the liberated people, failing to fulfil their responsibility, turning aside, contrary to the distinct command of God to make something to represent Him, which misrepresented Him.

When long years after there came that hour in the national life when the nation was rent asunder, we remember that story after the death of Solomon. They came and asked Rehoboam to grant certain privileges that Solomon had taken away from them, and he consulted with the young men, not the old men. If he had taken the advice of the old men there might not have been the trouble. That is not always so. The young fool, imagining that autocracy could be inherited, said, If my father chastised you with whips, I will chastise you with scorpions. The issue was Jeroboam's words, "To your tents, O Israel," and the nation was rent in twain; and Jeroboam led the movement in the north. What did he do? He repeated the sin of the golden calf. He set up an idol to represent God. He did not intend a substitute for God, but to assist the people in an understanding of God, and he put up a monstrous thing like this. So that, beginning in Exodus and again long centuries after, we see this nation, so guided and led, so delivered in the sea, was making substitutes for God.

Then the terrible word, fornication. Read the story in Numbers xxv. These people deflected from their true liberty, abusing it, failing to be true to it, formed acquaintance and marriages, and infinitely worse than marriages with the daughters of Moab, they committed fornication in conformity with the practices of Baal-peor. The lowered standard was even lower yet now. Yet these were the privileged people, these were the delivered people, the people brought out into glorious liberty by the action of God.

Next, unbelief. That story is in Numbers xxi specifically. They were impatient, discouraged, and they became blasphemers.

Then, earliest of all, murmuring, discontent, manifesting itself. What a list! What an appalling contrast is here between the description of the emancipation that set them at liberty and how they acted! What did it all mean? Privilege in itself was of no value. Abuse of liberty destroyed them. They had their liberty, but instead of living according to it, in the glorious freedom of the servants of God, they turned aside in all these terrible directions. Paul was showing from that great illustration, that liberty in itself is no guarantee, that privilege is no guarantee if responsibility is forgotten.

Turning to the application, Paul showed these things happened, and were written for us, that is, for those to whom he was writing and for all Christian souls "upon whom the ends of the ages are come." In this age, the consummation of the ages, this age to which all the others had been leading, we look back to some of those ages and see what happened. The people of privilege failed and were destroyed in the wilderness because of their failure, and that in spite of their privilege.

The central warning of course is found in the twelfth verse, "Let him that thinketh he standeth take heed lest he fall." It has many applications. Let him that thinketh he standeth, because of his privilege, be careful lest in spite of them he shall fall.

Then note the gracious words with which Paul ended this paragraph. We have our trials. We shall find the lure of these lower things in order to seduce us from loyalty, and that will destroy the liberty. "There hath no temptation taken you but such as man can bear," and "God is faithful, Who will not suffer you to be tempted above that ye are able." That does not mean to say God will not allow us to fall; but God will so arrange, and has arranged and has provided, that we need not fall. He "will not suffer you to be tempted above that ye are able; but will with the temptation make also the way of escape, that ye may be able to endure it." We shall have our temptations. We shall hear these seductive voices that call us to the false, but we need not yield to them, and that is true for every man. The way of escape is always there when we are confronted with temptation. Many years ago I heard Dr. Hutton say a thing that bit into my memory, which I have never forgotten. He said, "God always makes a way of escape, and sometimes, the way of escape is the King's highroad and a good pair of heels!" If the temptation is there, again and again, the best way for us is to run away, to put ourselves out of the reach of it. If we stay in the neighbourhood of the temptation we may lower the standard of our liberty, we may fall, even though we think we stand. There are moments when the true and courageous thing is not to face it and fight the temptation, but to turn round and run away. God always makes a way of escape.

So the whole teaching may be gathered up, not in the words of Paul, but in those of Peter. In his first letter, Peter says this, when writing to Christians, "As free, and not using your freedom for a cloak of wickedness, but as bond-servants of God." There are the limits and limitlessness of our liberty, bond-servants of God. Let us beware lest we take the liberty in which we boast as Christians, our liberty in Christ, and make even that liberty a cloak that hides evil things, wickedness. So Peter summarizes all that Paul has here illustrated.

c. The Principles Applied	x. 14–xi. 1
1. Definite Prohibition	x. 14–22
The Command	14
The Argument	15–22
Approach	15
Statement { Positive	16–20
Negative	21, 22
Conclusion	
2. Final Instructions	x. 23–xi. 1
The Principles	23, 24
The Specific Application	25–30
The Summary	x. 31–xi. 1
The Glory of God	31
The Good of Men	32
The Apostolic Example	x. 33–xi. 1

I CORINTHIANS x. 14–xi. 1

THE apostle now definitely returns to and completes the section of the letter which was an answer to the question the Corinthians had asked concerning the eating of things sacrificed to idols. We have seen that the apostle laid down governing principles (viii); and illustrated those principles in application to his apostleship (ix), and as revealed in the history of Israel (x. 1–13).

Liberty has its restrictions in the life of faith, in the life of all Christian people. Coming back to the specific subject in a remarkable way, he concludes it. Here we have first of all definite prohibition (x. 14–22); and then final instructions (x. 23–xi. 1).

The fourteenth verse is brief, but very suggestive. "Wherefore, my beloved, free from idolatry." "Wherefore" depends upon something already said. It marks a result. Whether "wherefore" or "therefore," the words have exactly the same significance. The injunction here is, "Flee from idolatry." Linking that with what immediately preceded it, we see how significant it is. Take the last part of the previous verse, "God is faithful, Who will not suffer you to be tempted above that ye are able; but will with the temptation make also the way of escape, that ye may be able to endure it. Wherefore, my beloved, flee from idolatry." The connection is seen at once. God makes the highway, the way of escape. See to it that we make use of it, and in this case the highway means flight. Do not linger in the neighbourhood of the lure; flee from it. In the previous part of this chapter, when concluding the sins that characterized this Israelitish nation, in the committal of which they forgot their responsibility, one was idolatry. Paul there gave the illustration of idolatry which is found in Exodus xxxii, when they made the golden calf and worshipped it, and then sat down to carousal, to eating and drinking. That was the illustration he had given of idolatry. He said, Flee from that, or anything of that kind.

What was idolatry then in that case? It was the making of a false representation of God. When they made the golden calf they were not intending to set up a new God. They were not violating the first of the commandments, but the second. They made something to help them to realize God, and the moment they had done it they had lowered the ideal of God. That golden thing in front of them did not represent God at all, but they worshipped it, they offered sacrifices in its presence, and then after they had done all that was necessary, they gave themselves up to carousal, to eating and drinking. That is to say, the idolatry that is referred to specifically here is that putting of something in the place of God, ostensibly to represent God, which does not represent Him, and to offer worship to something which was to degrade the whole concept of life. "Wherefore, my beloved, flee from idolatry." There is a way of escape.

Then the apostle went on. Notice how he approached them. "I speak unto wise men." Expositors are not agreed about that statement. Some think it was the language of great sarcasm. We remember that earlier he had laughed at their supposed wisdom. Some are inclined to think he was still ironical. I do not know, but I think he was granting that they had knowledge and understanding and wisdom, and so he appealed to that. "Judge ye what I say."

Then comes this very remarkable passage (16–20). To summarize the passage, he takes the great service of remembrance and proclamation as the symbol of relationship, to show them how far those who came to that service were removed from every other form of worship. He took the two things, the cup of blessing, and the bread. These were the elements in the memorial and proclamatory service. We are all familiar with that service. We may have different ideas as to how to observe it, but we agree as to its sanctity and beauty and value. The one word we cannot consent to use is the Mass, but we speak of it as the Lord's Supper, the service of Communion. We may speak of it as the Eucharist. Personally, I would always call that service by that name, the Eucharist, for to me it is a most fitting description. To translate the Greek word, the Eucharist is the giving of thanks, and that is what the Communion service is. It is the one service when we adore, and worship, and give thanks. We have no business to come to the Table of the Lord and confess our sins. That should have been done before we come. Sin ought to be dealt with, and set right before we come. Paul cited that service for a certain reason, which will emerge presently. "The cup of blessing which we bless, is it not a communion of the blood of Christ? The bread which we break, is it not a communion of the body of Christ?" We are at once helped by the word "communion." What is the word? We have had it in our earlier studies, though in our translation it does not appear in that form, but it is the same Greek word. We considered it where Paul declared the function of the Christian Church. "God is faithful, through Whom ye were called into the fellowship of His Son Jesus Christ our Lord." That is the word, fellowship, *koinonia*. To take that word and change it. "The cup of blessing which we bless, is it not a fellowship of the blood of Christ? The bread which we break, is it not a fellowship of the body of Christ? Seeing that we, who are many, are one bread, one body; for we all partake of the one bread."

Notice what Paul has done. He has reminded them of the central fact of worship, as it remains until this time, the most sacred act of worship in all the exercises of the Christian Church, whatever the form in which we observe it. What did he say about it?

First of all, the cup of blessing, what is it? It is the communion of the blood, that is to say, when we take that cup we are showing our fellowship in regard to our redemption. When we take that bread, it is the fellowship of the body of Christ, that is to say, when we take that bread we are showing our fellowship with the very life of Christ. The blood, redemption; the bread, life in all its fulness. He is saying to these people, When you come to the Table of the Lord, you break bread, and you take the cup. Do you understand what you are doing? You are expressing your fellowship with Jesus Christ. He took that tremendous illustration of the facts of Christian life and experience to use it in application to these matters.

All this is so characteristic of the deep things of the Christian faith. Nothing is small to the Christian. Nothing is unimportant. Nothing is really secondary, because all these things are affected by the tremendous facts of our relationship. Shall we eat things sacrificed to idols? Do not forget this, that we have a meal that is at the very centre of our worship, which whenever we eat and drink, we are showing our communion with the Body broken for us, with the Blood shed for us. These are the great things of our lives as Christians. Paul has said to them, Do not forget that.

In the light of that, see what we are able to do. In a remarkable way Paul showed that communion, fellowship, with evil spirits is impossible to those who know what communion is with Christ through His shed blood and His broken body. He shows it is impossible. "What say I then? that a thing sacrificed to idols is anything, or that an idol is anything? But I say, that the things which the Gentiles sacrifice, they sacrifice to demons, and not to God; and I would not that ye should have communion with demons. Ye cannot drink the cup of the Lord, and the cup of demons; ye cannot partake of the table of the Lord, and of the table of demons." If you do, what happens? You "provoke the Lord to jealousy." Paul made use of that tremendous word about God which comes over from the Old Testament, "Our God is a jealous God." It is a word that has in it exactly the same values as the word zealous, in application to certain conditions. It means that God is jealous of His honour, jealous of His rights; that when He puts a man or woman into the fellowship of Jesus Christ, and gives them the cup of blessing in the blood of Christ, and the broken bread in the body and very life of Christ, God expects something from them. If these people turn aside and worship at idolatrous altars, and conform to heathen practices, God is angry, and jealous for His honour.

So on the highest level Paul drew to a conclusion what he had to say on this specific subject in his final instructions. Here we have a final and lucid answer to the questions which the Corinthians asked. He recognized the principles. He repeated that some things were not expedient, although lawful. Expedient, *sumphere;* they were not things that were bearing someone else's burdens as well as their own. The things expedient were the things bearing together with others. Those things may be perfectly lawful to us in themselves, but they are not expedient. Again, some things are lawful, but they do not build up, edify. Now lawful things are not permitted when they are either not expedient or not edifying. There we come back to the principles laid down in chapter 8. And the test for the Christian is not to be found in self, or in advantage to self spiritually, but in others, and the effect that may be produced upon others.

In verses 25 to 30 Paul made specific application to Corinth. There a great part of the sacrifices offered to these idols, or demons, as Paul calls them, afterwards went back to the market-place, the shambles, the place where people bought meat for food. What were Christian people to do? He declared that things sold in the shambles might be bought and eaten, asking no question for conscience' sake. If they bought in the shambles, do not ask anything, "for the earth is the Lord's, and the fulness thereof." The meat bought is a Divine provision. That is one thing.

But Paul had not finished. He now went further, and declared if they went to a feast to which they were invited, given by those who were unbelievers, they could go, and if meat was set before them, and they did not define it at all, they were not to raise the question with the host, if he did not tell them it was sacrificed to idols, but they were to eat.

On the other hand—mark the subtlety of this, and the peril—if they were invited to a feast, and were distinctly told by their host, that the food had been offered to idols, then they were not to touch it or eat it, and that for conscience' sake, for the sake of the man who told them it had been sacrificed to idols. Then they were to refuse to partake.

The last movement begins at the 31st verse. How wonderfully he summarized everything. "Whether therefore ye eat, or drink, or whatsoever ye do, do all to the glory of God." The opening words, "Whether therefore," lean back upon all Paul had been saying. It goes back to the beginning as he reminded them of the central fact of their worship, in which they drank the cup marking redemption through blood, and ate of the bread, marking their living union with the eternal Lord. Because these things are so, whether you eat or drink, or whatsoever you do, do all to the glory of God. We do not do things to the glory of God when we are vaunting our liberty at the expense of our brother's wrong. We do things to the glory of God, when, as in the case of Paul, we give up certain of our rights in the interest of others. That is the first principle.

But there is another. "Give no occasion of stumbling, either to Jews, or to Greeks, or to the Church of God." There are the two principles of action. First, everything to the glory of God; secondly, putting no stumbling-block in the way of a brother man. The glory of God and the good of man—all life is to be conditioned by these things.

Then comes the final movement, when Paul, writing to these Corinthians, quotes his own example, "Even as I also please all men in all things." He had already told them he had become all things to all men to win some. "Even as I also please all men in all things, not seeking mine own profit, but the profit of the many, that they may be saved." That is the ultimate purpose and passion of the Christian's life. And then this final sentence, "Be ye imitators of me, even as I also am of Christ." It is a wonderful passage. He has now finished that subject, and passes on to another one, full of great interest and importance, and evidently also one that had been raised by the Corinthians.

iii. Concerning Women	xi. 2–16
a. The Apostolic Praise	2
b. The Relation Between Man and Woman	3–12
1. Inclusive Statement	3
2. The Case of the Man	4
3. The Case of the Woman	5–10
The Rabbinic Rule	5, 6
The Apostolic Answer	7–9
The Central Declaration	10
4. The Relation in the Lord	11–12
c. The Appeal. " Judge Ye "	13–15
d. The Dismissal	16

I CORINTHIANS xi. 2–16

In this paragraph it is specially necessary to discriminate between that which is local to the Corinthian church and condition, and that which is universal in its application to the whole Church of God. The apostle was still dealing with the things in the church that had hindered, and were hindering its fulfilment of its holy function of fellowship with Christ in the city of Corinth, and of its power.

There is no doubt that they had written to the apostle on the subject with which he now dealt, that of the behaviour of some of their women in the public assembly of the church, in praying and prophesying. Notice the first verse, " Now I praise you that ye remember me in all things, and hold fast the traditions, even as I delivered them to you." That warrants us in believing that they had written to him on this particular subject.

As we approach our consideration of the paragraph we must remember that this letter was sent first to the church in Corinth. The church was failing largely because she had compromised with the things in Corinth. She had allowed the spirit of Corinth to enter into her life, and there had been definite compromise. That accounts for what Paul had to set right, and the way in which he proceeded to do so.

Then the subject unquestionably is that of married men and women in the church. The relationship of the unmarried is not in view, except in a very indirect way. There were women in the church married, who were behaving in a certain way which had caused difficulty in the minds of others. About that Paul was now writing to them.

We take the paragraph and divide it first of all, and then follow the divisions very briefly. He first lays down a general principle (3), and it is vital to everything. Then he applies that principle to the Corinthian conditions (4–6). In verses 7–12 we have an interpretation of what he had said, and in verses 13–16 he ends with a warning.

The general principle is stated in these words, " I would have you know, that the head of every man is Christ; and the head of the woman is the man; and the head of Christ is God." Notice where he began and ended. It is a threefold statement. Here we have the pattern of relationship between man and woman, of course between husband and wife particularly. The word that stands out in that verse, at which we must look carefully without prejudice, is the word "head," "the head of every man," "the head of the woman," "the head of Christ." Some people are fond of that word "head" in this verse, and make good use of it. There are others who very much dislike it, and do not care to have it applied. I do not say to whom I am referring, whether men or women, or this or that division of the Church. I am little concerned with all these things. But the fact remains there are good Christian people who love that verse, especially the middle part of it.

What is the meaning of the word "head"? One thing only, government, authority. That is the simple and plain meaning of the word "head." Paul says, I would have you know that the authority of every man is Christ; that the authority of the woman is the man; and that the authority of Christ is God. No one of those phrases must be taken alone. They must be kept together. There is no escape from the simple meaning of the word, and its significance of government and authority in every case.

The question then arises at once, how are we to interpret the meaning of that fact of headship? Let us begin with the last stated, which is the highest of all. God is the Head of Christ. What do we know about Christ and God? We are on sacred, holy, and mysterious ground. We are in the presence of great facts that always baffle us finally, yet there are the facts revealed. God is equal with Christ, "I and the Father are one." God ever co-operates with Christ. "I am not alone, My Father is with Me." God is the Head of Christ. "My Father is greater than I." It is that last phrase that is full of mystery, and yet there it is. We must interpret the final statement of our Lord—and I have only quoted His statements, and that of definite purpose—by the others. "I and the Father are one." He was referring to His work. He was not leaving Him alone, "I am not alone, My Father is with Me," in all His service co-operating with Him, in all His mighty work. Then "My Father is greater than I." Keep these three facts in mind, and remember they interpret the meaning of headship, final authority; but the authority of the closest and most intimate fellowship and co-operation in being and in service.

So with Christ and man. So with Christ and every man who trusts in Him, and the word man there is generic. So of Christ and every believer the same thing may be said. I am one with my Lord. I am never alone. My Lord is ever with me, but my Lord is greater than

I. I am under the authority of One Who is always with me, and He is always working together with me.

So come down to the particular application. So it is with the man and the woman. Behind this of course is the marriage relationship. One cannot speak of an unmarried man or woman in these terms. It is of those who have entered into the marriage relationship. There may be certain ways in which there is an application to the unmarried, but generally here it is the thought of those married.

What is the great ideal, then, of this passage? First of all, it is the realization of the original purpose of God in creation. Paul here says so. The man was not created for the woman, but the woman was created for the man. Therefore in that creation they entered into a unity. Sometimes I am inclined to agree with the Roman Church, which teaches that marriage is a sacrament. There is such a sanctity in the whole matter, and that was the whole ideal of God at the very beginning. The woman was made for man, but man was never complete until woman was there. Go back to Genesis, and read the statement, "Male and female created He them; and blessed them, and called their name," not the Adamses, but "Adam." To say the Adamses is an admission of an inferiority, that was not there ideally.

Here again is exactly the same thing. To know the exact relationship between husband and wife as it is adumbrated through the whole of this passage, turn to the letter to the Ephesians, and in the fifth chapter the husband's authority is insisted upon, but it is the authority of self-sacrificing love. "Husbands, love your wives, even as Christ also loved the Church, and gave Himself up for it." Then we turn to the statement concerning the wife, "Wives be in subjection to your own husbands, as unto the Lord." That is to say, the wife's position is that of a glad and willing response to the authority, but it must be the authority of self-emptying love. That mystic relationship, almost of the nature of a sacrament, is very sacred. In that relationship the woman is under authority, but when we insist upon that authority, remember the nature of it. It is the authority that empties itself completely, in complete self-sacrifice, in the interest of the loved ones. Every true woman who realizes that ground of authority yields to it by the very fibre of her nature. I think that woman who feels she cannot do this is happy if she never marries. Once I asked a brilliant woman, a friend of mine, why she had never married, and I have never forgotten her answer. She looked at me, and her eyes flashed and brimmed as she said, "I have never found the man who really can master me." She has never married. There was the recognition of the inherent necessity of the case, and that is what Paul has brought out here. Those are the eternal principles revealed. That is the supreme matter and vital. All the other things are secondary.

Paul now turned to the church and began to apply the principle. Again he stated general principles. "Every man praying or prophesying having his head covered, dishonoured his Head. But every woman praying or prophesying with her head unveiled dishonoureth her head; for it is one and the same thing as if she were shaven." The man praying or prophesying while covered, dishonours his Head, which is Christ. The woman praying or prophesying uncovered, dishonours her head, and her head is her husband. "It is one and the same thing as if she were shaven." In the case of the man praying or prophesying, there is the double function, praying, speaking to God in the assembly, prophesying, that is, speaking to man on behalf of God. Praying is speaking to God on behalf of man. Prophesying is speaking to man on behalf of God. Paul says that every man doing that with his head covered dishonours his Head.

Now, the remarkable thing here is this: Paul was a Jew, and here he uttered language entirely antagonistic to Jewish custom and rabbinical teaching. He was seeing the glory of his inheritance in Christ, as a messenger of Christ. The rabbis had long been teaching, and it was still observed, and still is among those who are orthodox Jews, to veil the head, to wear what is called the tallith. The whole veiling of the head by these Jewish rabbinical teachers was due to a misunderstanding of something in their own history. To go to the second letter, in chapter three and verse thirteen, "We . . . are not as Moses, who put a veil upon his face, that the children of Israel should not look steadfastly on the end of that which was passing away. For until this very day at the reading of the old covenant the same veil remaineth unlifted; which veil is done away in Christ."

There Paul was referring to this custom of veiling the head by the rabbis. He says they did it undoubtedly because of the glory that shone on the head and face of Moses when he descended from the mount, that it should be veiled by Divine authority. Paul pointed out that Moses did not veil his face because of the glory, but veiled his face because the glory was fading and passing away, and he did not want them to see the fading of the glory. Yet on that misinterpretation of the historic event, the rabbis had taught the necessity for teachers and rabbis to put the veil on. In the second letter Paul distinctly taught that the veil is done away in Christ.

The man praying or prophesying, covered, dishonours his Head, his Lord and his Master, the One Who is in high authority over him. How does he dishonour Him? He has not recognized that the veil has been done away in Christ, and the glory is no fading glory, but a lasting one, the glory of His message. In Christ the veil is done away, both for praying, speech to God; and prophesying, speech to man.

Next, " every woman praying or prophesying with her head unveiled dishonoureth her head." The words used about her are exactly the same as those used of the man, a man praying or prophesying, and a woman praying or prophesying. The implication is that the woman has a right to pray and a right to prophesy. If it had not been so Paul would have stated it here. I am not dealing with statements in his other letters now. They all have their interpretation. Here we are face to face with the fact. Paul recognized the right of women to pray and prophesy, but certain habits on the part of those who do it must be corrected. We may be quite sure that the Holy Spirit does not contradict something taught in another part of Scripture, and the Holy Spirit was poured out, according to Joel, " that your sons and your daughters shall prophesy." That was fulfilled at Pentecost; and the daughters of Agabus prophesied. This is a big subject. If a woman has received the gift and heard the call, she has a perfect right to pray, preach, or prophesy. I do not think it is often so, but I know there have been glorious illustrations of that, and still are.

What then is the matter? This is peculiarly Corinthian. " Every woman praying or prophesying with her head unveiled dishonoureth her head." Why? Because " it is one and the same thing as if she were shaven. For if a woman is not veiled, let her also be shorn, but if it is a shame to a woman to be shorn or shaven, let her be veiled." Why was it a shame for a woman to be shorn, unveiled, or to be shaven? The answer is perfectly simple. The unveiled woman in Corinth was a prostitute. It was the sign of prostitution, and in the most flagrant cases not only was the woman unveiled, she was also shorn or shaven. Get the contemporary history of Corinth, and of Greek civilization, and it will be seen this is so. But these Christian women were saying, All things are lawful to me. We need not wear these veils, nor conform to these things. Paul replied, Yes, that is so, but you are in Corinth, and if you pray or prophesy in Corinth without the veil, you are adopting that which is the ultimate badge of prostitution, and if you appear like that, you are dishonouring your husband, you are dishonouring the head. Corinthian conditions are clearly in view. Therefore the requirement that the head must be veiled, or else the woman dishonoured her head, her husband, because the uncovered head in Corinthian conditions was the badge of prostitution.

Again verses 7 to 11, in the first part of the seventh verse notice how Paul set aside the rabbinical order altogether. The man is the image and glory of God. The woman is the glory of the man, the reflection of the glory of God, a relationship which does not mark inferiority, but grading for the full purpose of revelation. That is a tremendous theme. We cannot read the Bible without seeing that it reveals the Fatherhood and the Motherhood of God, that the two great facts lie within the mystery of humanity, and are resident within Deity. I have heard a good deal about man's sphere and woman's sphere, and some people speak of woman's sphere as a little derogatory or inferior. There is no warrant for that in the Bible. We talk about woman's sphere. She has not got a sphere. My dear sisters, if you speak of man's sphere, you are wrong. The two constitute the sphere. Man is a hemisphere, and woman is a hemisphere. When we have both, we have God unveiled in the mystery of humanity. That is all here, in the teaching. The Corinthian references all show it. The woman is veiled because of the angels. That is a remarkable little phrase, perhaps difficult to understand. My mind went over to Hebrews when pondering that, the opening chapter and verse 14, which says of the angels, "Are they not all liturgical spirits, sent forth," worshipping spirits? Also in Isaiah, in his vision of the Throne, they were sent forth to do service to the heirs of salvation. There is a recognition of the fact that what we used to sing in Sankey's hymn is quite true, "There are angels hovering round." They who know the true line of order, of authority, for their sakes let there be decency in the behaviour of these women in Corinth who are living in the midst of such corruption.

Paul finished by saying, "Judge ye among yourselves." There is a question of seemliness. He appeals to Nature and in man's usage. Do not the facts of life all around you show the truth of what he had been saying? Then that remarkable and revealing finish. If they want to quarrel about it, and raise a discussion on it, "we have no such custom, neither the churches of God."

As we study this passage, let us beware of the slavery of tradition. Beware lest we let something important in the long ago govern our thinking in the present time. Yet let us remember the possible importance of secondary things, because the Church is ever witnessing to the world.

iv. Concerning the Lord's Supper	xi. 17–34a
a. The Apostolic Praise Withheld	17a
b. The Corinthian Disorder	17b–22
1. Disorder in the Ecclesia	17b–19
Schisms	
Factions	
2. Disorder in Observance of Supper	20–22
c. The Institution of the Supper	23–27
1. Divine Authority and Manner	23–25
2. Value and Purpose Thereof	26, 27
d. Responsibilities for Preparation	28–34
v. Conclusion	xi. 34b

I CORINTHIANS xi. 17–34

THIS is a passage of vital importance, with a strange background. The apostle was still dealing with the failure in the Corinthian church which was interfering with her fulfilment of her sacred calling, that of being in fellowship with Jesus Christ. He now turned to matters concerning the great Supper of the Lord. We know nothing of the conditions here revealed in our experience today, concerning which the apostle gave stern correction.

Glancing first at local conditions. The New Testament references reveal the fact that the Holy Supper was at first observed at the close of a meal, which was an early Christian social gathering in connection with the fellowship, or the *koinonia*. At the beginning they called that first meal the agape, which, being translated, is a love feast, and the two were merged. In Acts ii. 46 we read, " Day by day, continuing steadfastly with one accord in the temple, and breaking bread at home, they did take their food with gladness and singleness of heart." We read the phrase, " breaking bread," and we think of it immediately as referring to the Lord's Supper. It does not mean that primarily, because the Supper constantly followed the social gathering of the church, which was intended to express their fellowship. There is no doubt in the statement in Acts, the reference was to the whole fact of the agape and the Eucharist. Whenever we observe the Supper, whether in the early morning, after a service of worship, or in the evening, it is the very centre of Christian worship. It is the highest exercise of Christian worship. We come to remember, to adore, to worship, and magnify Him. It is the Eucharist, the giving of thanks, that is the special service.

In the early days it is evident the agape and the Eucharist merged. They met for a social gathering, and then went on to the Lord's Supper. Although it cannot be dogmatically stated, we read in Luke that when our Lord joined Himself to two disciples on the way to Emmaus and came into the house, they offered Him hospitality, and He accepted it;

He sat down to eat with them at their social meal, and then He put out His hand and took bread and brake it. He followed the social meal, the agape, for those two troubled hearts, with the observance of the Eucharist, the Lord's Supper.

In process of time we find, going outside the Bible to Church history, that these two feasts became separate completely. In the early period of Church history are accounts of the observance of the agape, the love feast, and the social gathering of the Church, and before long, the agape passed away altogether, but the Eucharist remained, the Feast of holy remembrance, and it has remained all through her history. Today many do not know anything about the agape or love feast. Our friends in the Methodist Church in my boyhood's days observed love feasts. I have attended them with my father more than once, at which they did not take bread and wine; but a biscuit and water. That was the love feast or agape, which has now largely dropped out.

This, however, was the condition in Corinth. The worship of idols was closely associated with social life, and there would be a great feast, united with the worship of idols, and very often the flesh at those feasts was the flesh already sacrificed to idols. There was merged in pagan Corinth the two ideas of social life and worship in one. Now, the Christian Church was established in Corinth, and what happened undoubtedly was that the heathen practice had impinged upon the Christian practice, and they were doing very much in connection with their love feast and Holy Supper what the pagans were doing in connection with their worship and social life. That was the whole trouble. This introductory word sheds its light upon the matter concerning which Paul wrote.

In this paragraph we have first of all the apostolic rebuke (17a). Then we have a picture of the Corinthian disorder (17b–22). Then follows a great passage so full of august beauty and wondrous solemnity (23–27), in which Paul told these Corinthians of the institution of the Lord's Supper, and revealed to them the nature of that Supper very clearly. Then the paragraph ends with his solemn words about preparation for participation in the Supper (28–34).

The apostolic rebuke, "But in giving you this charge, I praise you not." In the second verse of this same chapter he had praised them, "I praise you that ye remember me in all things, and hold fast the traditions, even as I delivered them unto you." Now he is not praising them. There was something concerning which he had no word of praise. An arresting rebuke begins this paragraph. Why? They had not obeyed. Go on to verse 23 and we read, "For I received of the Lord that which also I delivered unto you." "Delivered," not " deliver." He had delivered to them something in the past, some instruction had already been given. He had already given them the very instructions he now repeated, to which instructions they had not been obedient. Praise therefore was impossible.

What were the Corinthian conditions? The first statement shows that their gathering together was "not for the betetr but for the worse." They were gathering together as a church, the ecclesia; not a building but the assembly of believers to whom the letter was addressed at the commencement. They had gathered together in the ways we have seen, for social fellowship, as marked by the agape, and for worship as marked by the Eucharist. These two had been observed one after the other. Now Paul said that the method of their gathering together was not for the better but for the worse. In other words, he told them it was harmful. It was a strong word that he used.

Then he showed what they were doing. Verse 18 reads, "For first of all, when ye come together in the church, I hear that divisions exist among you; and I partly believe it." He dealt first with an ecclesiastical breakdown (18. 19), and then, secondly, with ritual breakdown (20–22). He says that as the ecclesia gathered together in the two feasts, both of which were professedly to celebrate their fellowship and their unity, they were not entering into the fellowship, and they were disunited. There was a disruption of the ecclesia when they gathered together. Paul said "divisions," that is schisms, splits, sects, and to get the social idea there, Paul saw that in Corinth, they were separating themselves into sets. That is a modern word, but it has the same idea here. They were broken up. There were "heresies," that is, factions. It did not mean wrong doctrine, but, based on it, parties, the very parties he had referred to in the opening chapter when some said they were of Paul, and others of Apollos, or Cephas, or Christ. What, he said, is this, that when you gather together in these feasts, supposedly giving expression to your unity, you are not united, but broken up into sects, into sets, into parties. The word he used literally means splits. You are split up. We sing today in the Church of God,

> "We are not divided,
> All one body we."

Oh, that is blessedly true if we get down to the deep spiritual truth about the Body. That hymn was written by Baring Gould to show that the Church of England was one, and not disrupted like the poor dissenters. The remarkable thing is when he had written it, the Methodists and the Congregationalists and the Presbyterians and the Baptists and all the other *ists* were taking it and putting it in their hymn-books; and at the end of his life he said that hymn and its reception had taught him that it meant far more than he had intended when he wrote it.

> "We are not divided,
> All one body we."

But here was a local occasion, in this local church it was broken by sects and parties and splits and schisms and factions, and the very feast itself was interfered with.

We then come to the amazing portion. These people were observing the Lord's Supper in close connection with the agape, and were allowing the differences revealed in the agape to be manifest equally in the Eucharist. There was division all through. That is what Paul was emphatically saying here, that the social gathering is not the Supper of the Lord. He showed them there must be a distinct division between the two. Here we reach the part which we can hardly understand. We have seen assemblies split up, and people go away, and form another assembly, but these people did not go away. They stayed in, and by their habits and selfish action they were denying the fellowship. It was a revelation of a serious matter. That is what was going on in Corinth. There were poor members of that flock who went hungry; and then the appalling thing, which we cannot conceive, some of them in the midst of feasting gave way to drunkenness in the agape, and crossed over the line into the observance of the holy Feast bemused, befogged with drink. That we cannot quite understand. It was obtaining in Corinth, and it brought forth the apostle's sharp reminder. He said to them, Get away home for your social engagements. He divided between the two. "What? have you not houses to eat and to drink in? or despise ye the Church of God," disesteeming its value, treating it disrespectfully. I cannot praise you for this. "I praise you not."

We have not the same form of manifestation, but we are in danger of the same spirit within the ecclesia, within the assembly, which differentiates and divides and separates. Until we have this party and that sect, and the sense of *koinonia* in all its rich beauty, the real spirit is lost.

Then comes that which needs practically no exposition. Paul would correct the failure of observance by presenting the truth concerning the eating of the Supper of the Lord. That is what he now proceeded to do. "I received of the Lord that which also I delivered unto you." It is very definitely a past tense, both with regard to his authority, "I received of the Lord," and with regard to the fact that he had instructed them, "I delivered unto you." Take it in the reverse order. "I delivered unto you." The reference is to the past, that he had instructed them on all these subjects. But notice carefully here what Paul claimed, "I received of the Lord." There is only one honest way of interpreting that. Paul claimed he had it from the Lord Himself, a direct revelation concerning that memorable occasion when this holy Feast was instituted. I received it from the Lord. Go on to the fifteenth chapter, verse 3, in which he says, "For I delivered unto you first of all that which also I received, how that Christ died for our sins according to the Scriptures." There is another reference to the fact he had given them instructions. He had delivered to them things that he had received.

Undoubtedly this is an instance in which he claimed direct authority resulting from direct revelation. How constantly Paul had to defend, not himself, but his apostleship. One's mind goes to his letter to the Galatians in which he said, "For I make known to you, brethren, as touching the Gospel which was preached by me, that it is not after man. For neither did I receive it from man, nor was I taught it, but it came to me through revelation of Jesus Christ." We do not know exactly when or where the revelation came, but we remember those wonderful years when he went to Damascus, and on to Jerusalem. Do not forget between two verses in the Acts, two years have to be put in when he went away to Arabia, and who shall say what illumination he had then, and how far he was instructed, directly and personally? Then he went down to Tarsus, and he was there years before Barnabas found him. It was a long period in which it was possible he received things from the Lord. That was his authority.

He reminded them of the things he had declared to them. Paul was concerned about their habit of observing the Holy Supper. The Agape and the Eucharist were merged, and the observance of the first had invaded the second, and desecrated it, so that they had despised the Church of God by the way in which they had observed it.

Then come the words with which we are sacredly familiar. What had the Lord delivered to him? This:

"How that the Lord Jesus in the night in which He was betrayed took bread; and when He had given thanks He brake it, and said, This is My body, which is for you; this do in remembrance of Me. In like manner also the cup, after supper, saying, This cup is the new covenant, the new testament in My blood; this do, as oft as ye drink it, in remembrance of Me. For as often as ye eat this bread, and drink the cup, ye proclaim the Lord's death till He come."

No comment on that is needed. It is a wonderful picture of that dark night. If any emphasis is needed upon the suggestion of the overwhelming darkness of the night in which He was betrayed, when all the forces of hell were gathered together to destroy Him, He gave thanks. Oh, matchless wonder!

He told them to take that bread and eat, and to take the cup and drink it in remembrance of Him, and He told them distinctly that as they did so they proclaimed His death, heralded it until He should come.

> "Thus that dark betrayal night
> With the last advent we unite
> By one long chain of loving rite,
> Until He come."

The apostle has lifted the Holy Supper into its true place, and shown its sublimity and simplicity, the sacred rite of the night, and the shining of the light as Jesus gave thanks, and made them participants in His body and blood and His showing forth. Paul was correcting the false by a statement of the true, and how sublime it is!

In the last verses (28–34) Paul insisted upon the need for preparation. Take that preparation on which he insists, and ask if after such preparation there could have been such actions as characterized their agape and Eucharist at that time. "Let a man prove himself," that is, examine and test himself to approve. Do not come to the Table unless you have passed through that experience, and when you come, do not forget the qualification. We must come discerning the Body, not only the broken human frame, but the mystic body of His Church. Paul will say more of this in the chapters to come. Discern the Body for a correct estimate of it.

The reason for their failure is that many are weak, that is strengthless, many are sickly, or infirm, and many are asleep, that is dead. Because of their failure to come to the feast with due preparation, and observe it in its true way, these calamities of weakness and sickness and death have fallen upon them.

Then he urged the need for self-judgment, that is, deciding, condemning, and never resting until the judgment can be the acquittal of conscience. Such is the idea of the word.

So he comes to the final word to these Corinthians. When they come together for fellowship they are to wait for one another. Let there be decency and order in that matter; and if it is the matter of a social gathering merely, the home is the best place for it, not the place of assembly.

Then comes the final sentence in verse 34, "And the rest will I set in order whensoever I come." We have seen the divisions, the appalling and solemn revelation of fearful possibility of evil things within the church, divisions, derelictions from morality, discussions and difficulties, all the things that have harmed and hurt them. Evidently there were other things, too, needing attention, and Paul said in effect, I am not going to write about the others. I will deal with them when I come. That leads us to the second division of the letter.

```
B. Constructive. The Spiritualities                    xii–xv
    I. The Unifying Spirit                             xii. 1–31
       i. The Creation of Unity                        1–3
          a. The Contrast
          b. The Principle Implied                     3a
             The Lordship of Jesus
          c. The Power                                 3b
             "In the Holy Spirit"
```

I CORINTHIANS xii. 1–3

HAVING dismissed the first part of his letter in the words, "The rest will I set in order whensoever I come," the apostle now turned to another matter and method. He realized that there were other things in Corinth that were not as they ought to be, other phases of disorder that were affecting the life and testimony of the church in Corinth; but he had dealt with the things of supreme importance, those things concerning which he had obtained information, and those concerning which they had written to him.

The "whensoever" is striking. He had no definite plan, he did not know when he could see them, but he intended to do so, and then he would deal with the other matters. Keeping that statement in close connection with our present paragraph, we discover he began to deal with another matter. There was something else to say, another matter to be dealt with, closely related to what had gone before, and yet to be held in separation.

The first part of his letter was wholly corrective. From this point to the end, it is wholly constructive. The corrective section was intended to deal with the disorderliness caused by the carnalities of the church, which were preventing the fulfilment of her function, that of fellowship with the Lord Jesus Christ. That was her function in the city. They had broken down, the reason being that of their carnality. When he came to them, he could not speak to them as unto spiritual but as unto carnal. They were dominated by the carnal side of their nature, living in a city given over to the material; and later, Paul again said, "Ye are yet carnal," accounting for all these things of disorder, declension, and difficulty that had been marring their testimony and preventing the fulfilment of their function.

"Now," he said, "concerning the spiritualities." Having dealt with the things producing weakness in the church, he now turned to deal with the things of the church's true strength, the corrective of weakness, followed by the constructive of strength. So the great letter naturally falls into two parts. Let us consider this new beginning and survey the whole section, returning to what is the fundamental fact, declared in the three opening verses of the twelfth chapter.

Paul began here, "Now concerning." Concerning what? In the Revisions, it reads, "Now concerning spiritual gifts." We are at once arrested by the fact that the word "gifts" is printed in italics. Every student of literature knows that a word printed in italics here does not give emphasis to the word, which such italics often mean in other books. It means that the word is not in the Greek, but has been supplied by the translators to give sense. Very often it does that. It certainly has its use; but here I think the word "gifts" is most misleading. Take this as the ordinary commonplace English reader would, it is interesting to find, consulting varied translations of this verse, that sixteen of them have rendered the Greek phrase in that form, "Now concerning spiritual gifts." The translation committees, all scholars, and these individual men have all rendered it "spiritual gifts." That however does not satisfy me, and I am bold enough to say I believe they are all wrong. Translators are often like commentators. They go in flocks. They follow one another like sheep, and we can often quote the Divine passage about them, "All we like sheep have gone astray." This is not a vital matter, but it is important.

What is this word? It is one word in the Greek, *pneumatikon*, translated sixteen times "spiritual gifts." Dr. Scofield translates it "spiritual gifts," and then at the foot puts a note, and says, "Spiritual gifts" is wrong. I found one translation only in another way. That was Young's translation of the New Testament. He renders this, "Now concerning spiritual things." He has added a word, *things*, instead of *gifts*. This difference is important.

The word so translated by these sixteen different translators occurs twenty-six times in the New Testament. Three times only the word gift is put by the side of it. Paul was writing to the Romans (i. 11), and he said, "For I long to see you, that I may impart unto you some spiritual gift." Here the translators have not italicized the word *gift*. It is the same word, some spiritual thing, some spiritual matter.

Turn on from this passage (I Cor. xii. 1) and we find it again in xiv. 1. "Follow after love; yet desire earnestly spiritual gifts." Those are the only three occasions where the translators have put the word "gift" in, and in every case it is misleading, and better omitted.

What, then, is this word? Literally translated, the Greek word simply means spirituals. We do not employ that plural in English, and probably that is why this word gift or gifts has been supplied, in order to explain the word. But we do use another, which is its exact equivalent, spiritualities, which I should use here. Paul says, " Now concerning the spiritualities." The word indicates that which is ethereal rather than gross, that which is of the spirit rather than that of the physical; that is, spiritualities. Here the word is preceded in the Greek by the definite article, *ton*. So it is not " concerning spiritualities," but " Now concerning *the* spiritualities."

These translators may have felt everything he had to write about to the end is a gift. If that is what they meant, then they were right to put in this word. But the fact of the matter is that the subject of gifts is dealt with later, one of the spiritualities. Now Paul was summarizing on everything he had to say. Cursed with carnalities, the church needed a return to spiritualities, the things of the spirit, as against the things of the flesh. So this opening sentence is a remarkable one, " Now concerning the spiritualities."

In order that we may have clear thinking, let us survey the whole section. From chapter xii to xv. 57, he is dealing with spiritualities. There is another chapter (xvi), an illustrative passage. Taking the whole of this section, what are the things with which Paul deals which he named at the first, the spiritualities? There are three main matters that he dwelt upon; first of all the unifying Spirit of God (xii). At the conclusion of that chapter he says, " Desire earnestly the greater gifts. And a still more excellent way shew I unto you." He now showed them the spirituality and unfailing law of love, described and applied (xiii, xiv). Then he set all the Church's life and service in the light of the larger life, the resurrection (xv. 1–57). So we may summarize for purposes of study by saying the spiritualities with which the apostle is dealing are the unifying Spirit, secondly, the unfailing law of love; finally, the ultimate triumph, that is, of resurrection.

Verse 58 says, " Wherefore, my beloved brethren, be ye steadfast, unmovable, always abounding in the work of the Lord, forasmuch as ye know that your labour is not in vain in the Lord." That ends the section dealing with the spiritualities.

The things Paul had to set in order and correct were, first, divisions; secondly, derelictions from the pathway of duty and morality; and, thirdly, difficulties arising in the mind of the church. Divisions are made impossible by the unifying Spirit. The unfailing law of love makes derelictions impossible. Difficulties are all solved in the light of the ultimate life and the resurrection. So the spiritualities absolutely correct the carnalities.

Once more read the culminating words in this section, and then go back to the fundamental declaration of the whole epistle and put the two together. "God is faithful, through Whom ye were called into the fellowship of His Son Jesus Christ our Lord. . . . Wherefore, my beloved brethren, be ye steadfast, unmovable, always abounding in the work of the Lord." The fundamental affirmation is in that first chapter, and the final appeal leans back on that affirmation. Put into fellowship with Christ, be steadfast, unmovable, always abounding in that work. In order that they may be thus steadfast, they have to correct the carnalities, and live in the power of the spiritualities. So we see the sweep of the letter.

Look now at the first three verses of the twelfth chapter. Notice how Paul insisted upon the importance of knowledge. It is not the only place where Paul says this. "Now concerning the spiritualities, brethren, I would not have you ignorant." I would not have you not knowing, agnostic. That is the Greek word. Agnostic means exactly the same thing as ignoramus. Paul did not want them to be ignorant, unintelligent, uninformed.

Then he asked them to take a backward look, and all this to lead up to the culminating statement, "Ye know that when ye were Gentiles ye were led away unto those dumb idols, howsoever ye might be led." You have that experience. Go back and look at it. Mark the satirical dismissal, "those dumb idols," literally those voiceless gods, idols, images, shapes; those things you put into the place of God. "Mouths have they, but they speak not." We remember the psalmist's description. Look back, and remember them, "dumb idols." You were led away in your devotion to those dumb idols, "howsoever ye might be led." Paul did not go into that, he did not describe their life. He looked at the whole of that, in order to say this.

It is as though Paul said, I want you to know the basic fact of all your life and all the life of the church. He was writing to the church. "Wherefore I give you to understand, that no man speaking in the Spirit of God saith, Jesus is anathema," and then, finally, "And no man can say, Jesus is Lord, but in the Holy Spirit." Whatever follows in this section leans back upon that statement. He was emphasizing the central verity of the entity, which he called the Church of God, and the central verity is the absolute Lordship of Christ.

Notice what the apostle says here. That central verity can only be apprehended, appreciated, as the result of the ministry of the Holy Spirit. It is the Spirit, and the Spirit only, Who is able to interpret the deep conviction of the Lordship of Christ to the human soul. It is the Spirit and the Spirit only Who can so interpret that fact as to bring the human soul into the position of agreeing. It is quite an easy thing to say, He is my Lord; but is it true? He Himself in the days of His flesh said, "Many will say to Me in that day, Lord, Lord, did we not prophesy by Thy name, and by Thy name cast out demons, and by Thy name do many mighty works? And then will I profess unto them, I never knew you." We can take His name, and affirm the fact He is Lord, and sing with great lustiness:

> "All hail the power of Jesus' name,
> Let angels prostrate fall."

No, it is the conviction of the soul to which allegiance is given in all life that He is Lord, that He is Lord alone. That can come only by the interpretation of the Holy Spirit, but that is fundamental.

Paul went on from that point to show there are diversities of gifts; but that is the central fact of the Church's life, the Lordship of Christ. There are so many things there growing out of it. Have we a Gospel? Are we preaching it? What is the great central verity? The Cross? Oh no, the Lord, the sovereignty of Christ, rooted for human redemption in the Cross, but it is the sovereign Lord. Know ye not "that God hath made Him both Lord and Christ, this Jesus Whom ye crucified "—that is the central verity of the Church.

This is a whole section of the revelation of the wonder and glory of the Church. We may summarize now by saying that the Church consists of those gathered around the Lordship of Christ, interpreted by the Holy Spirit. The Spirit alone gives the interpretation of the essential Lordship of Christ, and the essential Lordship of His Being. He is very God, and also the active Lordship of Christ, the Lordship of His redemption. It is the Spirit of God in the soul of a man who brings that conviction, that commands the soul's obedience and allegiance.

So turning to the spiritualities, the apostle has laid down first of all in these brief and yet pregnant sentences what is the central verity of the Church's life, the Lordship of Christ, as interpreted by the Holy Spirit.

ii. The Administration of Unity   xii. 4–7

    a. Diversities
- 1. Gifts. Capacities for Service
- 2. Ministrations. Opportunities for Service
- 3. Workings. Equipment for Service

    b. Unification
- 1. The Same Spirit
- 2. The Same Lord
- 3. The Same God

    c. Consciousness
- 1. Personal. Manifestation "to each"
- 2. Purpose. "For the Bearing Together"

I CORINTHIANS xii. 4–7

IN dealing with the spiritualities in this constructive section of his letter, the apostle's first subject is that of the unity of the Christian Church. In many senses it is the most remarkable chapter in the New Testament in its presentation of the Church. The stewardship of the mystery of the Church was committed to Paul. He was the great interpreter. All his writings have that stamp upon them. He has much to say about the Church, but in this chapter in condensed form is a remarkable account of the Church of God.

Having stated the fundamental fact in the first three verses, that of the Lordship of Jesus, and the Spirit's revelation of that Lordship, he now corrects the divisions of the Church by the vision of the unity of the Church. We do not always realize that Lordship, or we remit it to the background of our thinking. The authority, the Lordship, the mastery of Jesus Christ is the central and fundamental thing. The whole fact of the Church is there. "Whom say ye that I am?" We remember that, and the ultimate answer, "Thou art the Christ, the Son of the living God." That was the great Petrine confession, the fact of the nature and office of the Lord as the Son of God, and the full and final authority, that is central to the life of the Church.

The Lordship of Christ is interpreted only in one way, by the Holy Spirit. It is quite possible to speak of Jesus as Lord, but not in the full sense of the word, not in the full sense of the term as it is interpreted by the Spirit. The Spirit of God interprets the Lordship of Christ in two ways, first of all, in His Person, in His Being, the Son of God, God the Son; secondly, in His redeeming work, and that the Spirit is always doing. We do not see the fact of His personality if we speak of Jesus merely as a human being, greatest of all, *facile princeps,* as Renan says, among the sons of men. But that is not all. He is God manifest in flesh. That is the rock basis of His Lordship, and His redeeming work gives Him through the crown of thorns the crown of the eternal glory. These things are central to the life of the Church.

Paul then proceeded from that point to a survey of the Church. The rest of this chapter is a condensed and remarkable and complete statement about the Church. First, there is a great summary of truth concerning the Church (4–7). In that summary Paul speaks of gifts, ministrations, workings. Then (8–11) he speaks of the gifts more particularly, and (12–27) of the ministrations, and (28–31) of the workings. This chapter is a most systematic and artistic piece of work, for nothing is more wonderful than to see the clear, sharp, full system of revelation. There is nothing that needs to be said about the Church that is not said in this chapter, so long as the Church is considered, as we saw at the beginning, in fellowship and co-operation with Christ in the world by the appointment of God Himself.

Look now at the summary. Notice the words that recur, " diversities," " diversities," " diversities," " the same," " the same," " the same." Notice the unifying mystery of the Deity, the Spirit, the Son, and the Father. That is the complete summary of truth concerning the Church. There is much more to say about that, but that is where we must start.

That word " diversities " arrests our attention, " diversities of gifts," " diversities of ministrations," " diversities of workings." I am not suggesting that the word " diversities " is inaccurate, but we may miss something. The word is not differences, or distinctions, but diaereses. That is the Greek word which Paul used. Our word diaeresis is a transliteration rather than a translation of Paul's word. That is an interesting word, suggesting a separation between that which is always joined together. That is a glorious paradox, yet that is what it is. There are certain words in the English language, for instance, " naïve." The ordinary English reader would pronounce it nave, but the two little dots over the *i* means that it must be pronounced as two syllables, though closely joined. There are diversities, diaereses in the Church of God. Oh, yes, there are differences, using that word if you like, distinctions if you please, diversities certainly. Those words are not inaccurate, only remember it is differences with a difference from our ordinary meaning, when we read " diversities," separation of one part from another that are always together.

In this company of Christian people surrounding the Lordship of Christ, to whom that fact is the pre-eminent fact in all their life and service, in that whole entity, that whole company, there are diaereses of gifts, of ministrations, of workings, miraculous powers, to be quite literal; powers is the word used there. Then in the Church we have these differences.

Gifts, what are they? Capacities for service, gifts. They are all gifts. I will put this as roughly and bluntly as I can. Personally, I am nothing in myself, and no use to God or man for the service of the Kingdom of God. If He in His infinite grace has allowed me to serve for half a century and more, my qualification has been in the gift or the gifts He has bestowed. Gifts are capacities for service.

Ministrations. It is a great word. What does it mean? It means government, administration, and it refers to opportunities for service. Gifts are capacities for service. Ministrations show the opportunities for service.

Workings are powers, equipment for service. Paul is looking at the whole Church, and is summarizing. There are diaereses of gifts, of ministrations, of workings, but the same Spirit, Lord, God. What a tremendous, significant, majestic, and awe-inspiring vision of the Church that gives to us; gifts, capacities for service; ministrations, opportunities for service; workings, powers for service; and the unity, the Spirit, the Lord, the Father God Himself. We must not divide those three into separate Personalities. It is one God he is showing us here. He is bestowing gifts through the Spirit, arranging the manner of service through His Son, the one Lord; but He Himself is the great power, the great dynamic, enabling those who have received the gifts to exercise them to His glory.

Paul ends that by showing the consciousness of this in the Church. " To each one is given the manifestation of the Spirit to profit withal." Whether it be the gifts bestowed, or the ministrations under which we exercise the gifts, or the powers in which we are enabled so to do, there is a measure for each individual, for " each one." That does not mean to say each one may have the same gift. Indeed, it means quite the opposite; but it does mean the gift comes to the individual, and the gift is bestowed upon the individual, not for the perfecting of his own life, but to " profit withal "; the great fellowship is there seen. Whatever gift is bestowed upon me, upon you, it is bestowed upon us personally and individually in order that in its use we may profit withal.

iii. The Realization of Unity	xii. 8–31
a. Gifts of the Spirit	8–11
Capacities for Service	
1. Diversities	8–10
2. Unification	11
b. Ministrations of the Lord	12–27
Opportunities for Service	
1. The Figure	12, 13
2. Diversities	14–24
"Not One Member, But Many"	14–19
"Many Members, But One Body"	20–24
3. Unification	25–27
No Schism	
A Common Experience	
The Body of Christ	
c. Workings of God	28–30
Equipment for Service	
1. Unification	28a
"God Hath Set"	
2. Diversities	28b–30
Compare xii. 31 and xiv. 1	

I CORINTHIANS xii. 8–31

STILL dealing with the unity of the Church (verses 8–31), the realization of her unity is considered. Gifts of the Spirit are capacities for service. "To one is given . . . and to another . . . to another . . . to another." Those words recur nine times. Paul now names some of the gifts. This list is not exhaustive. He has not professed to name all the gifts. Turn to other references in his writings, and it will be found there are other gifts not included here. This is an illustrative list of gifts bestowed upon the Church by the one Spirit. Glance at them.

First of all, "the word of wisdom." That is a gift, and that means direct insight into truth, a gift bestowed. Secondly, "the word of knowledge," and that means not so much direct insight into truth as that which results from investigation, a gift bestowed. All Christians do not have either of those gifts. They are bestowed within the Body, and for the good of the Body.

Third, "faith." That stands at the back of the first two. It is the vision of the invisible. Faith is the substance of things hoped for, the evidence of things not seen. By faith there was one who endured as seeing Him Who is invisible. Direct insight into truth; knowledge as the result of investigation; and that great gift of faith which is the vision of the invisible, without which there can be no direct insight into truth, and there can be no investigation of truth; but it is a separate gift, and there are those who receive it, and there are those who do not receive it.

Then "gifts of healing." That literally means making sick people well, a definite gift. Do not wonder why we have not that gift now. The answer is the Lord has not bestowed it now. In the course of my life I have known one or two persons who most certainly had bestowed on them the gift of positive healing. They would lay their hands upon the sick, and they were restored. I am not saying they said to the sick, If you can believe, you can be healed. That is not the gift of healing at all. The gift of healing is supernatural. I believe there are those in our own country today who have it, but it is not bestowed upon the rank and file. It is one of the gifts within the Body, making people well.

Then "workings of miracles," and the word is powers. Supernatural things, a gift enabling those who receive it to do things that are entirely supernatural. Yes, they were bestowed. They still may be.

"The gift of prophecy," that is, ability to make the will of God directly known. Prophecy does not mean foretelling, except as an element within it. It is forth-telling of truth, and there are those who have the gift of prophecy.

"Discernings of spirits," a most important gift, power to distinguish between the false and the true, a distinct gift. There are those who still possess it. There are those who do not.

Then these, "kinds of tongues," ecstatic utterances always. Wherever we read of "tongues" in the New Testament, it is ecstatic utterances, not for preaching, but for praise. On the day of Pentecost they all spake with other tongues, but that gift was not the gift of preaching, but for worship, for praise, for ecstatic utterance. The crowds were arrested because they heard in their own language "the wonderful works of God." That was the peculiar gift. I am not going to say it is never bestowed today. It was common in the early days of the Church, that gift of worship in tongues, which were ecstatic utterances.

Notice, closely connected with that, "interpretation of tongues." There were some with the gift of ecstatic utterance, not understood by the ordinary man and woman. Then there was someone with a gift to explain these very tongues.

This is not an exhaustive list. There are others. Study them, and it will be found that some gifts are not now bestowed upon the Christian Church. But notice how this all ends, "But all these worketh the one and the same Spirit, dividing to each one severally even as *He* will." We have no right to say we want such and such a gift. "As *He* will." If He bestows, let us recognize and use the gift. If He withhold, and does not bestow any particular gift, it is still within

His own will, and according to His infinite wisdom. We have not exhausted that, but we have glanced at these illustrations Paul gives of nine gifts. These are bestowed within the entity and company of the Church. Differentiation will be found all the way through. Another and another. Cannot we arrange for this? Never. "Severally even as *He* will." That is the great word. There are these diversities of gifts, these diaereses; and there is always an intimate relationship of one gift with another. You have one, and I have another, and someone else a third, a fourth, a fifth; and they are all intimately related. They are separated, but related; and the unifying principle, if principle is the right word (I would rather say the unifying personality), is the Personality of the Holy Spirit Who bestows gifts as He will.

Here the Church is being built, as we shall see more particularly as we go on, as a great organism, not an organization. I am not saying anything against organization, but I am quite certain we have been more anxious about organization than the organic oneness and wholeness and entity of the Church. Here the Church is seen as an organism. The gifts are diversified. They are never in conflict with one another, and they are all contributing to the fulfilment of function, not of the individual but of the Church. So you exercise your gift and I exercise mine, and as we exercise ours under the power of the Spirit, and under the administration of the Lord, then the Church is fulfilling its function as the great organism in the life of the world, and for the glory of God, based upon the bedrock of the absolute Lordship of Christ Jesus.

We have considered the gifts of the Spirit. Now we turn to the ministrations of the Lord. "There are diversities of ministrations," but it is "the same Lord." Ministrations, administration, direction, control for service of the gifts bestowed, as to the use to be made of them. All that is under the administration of the one Lord. First of all, consider the figure which the apostle employed here (12. 13). Then notice the diversities to which he referred (14-24). Then in verses 25-27 Paul showed the unification of these diversities in the figure employed.

We begin, then, with the figure. It is an old story, but I wonder how far we have taken time to think in the realm of the figure. A figure is valuable only as it conveys a thought of a fact too fine to be apprehended apart from the use of the figure. The figure is valuable in proportion as it really helps in understanding of the tremendous fact. Let us keep those two things in mind. Here Paul took the figure of the body. For the moment forget all the spiritual content and intent of the passage, and fix the mind upon the figure employed—the body.

Paul has used that figure in other letters, when writing to the Romans, the Ephesians, and the Colossians, the Church as the body of Christ. But here in this chapter Paul specialized, took time to look carefully at the figure. Notice the 12th verse, "For as the body is one, and hath many members, and all the members of the body, being many, are one body; so also is Christ." Missing out the remaining verses of the section for the moment, go to verse 27. "Now ye are the body of Christ, and severally members thereof." Those are the boundaries of this particular section. It opens and closes with references to the body as the figure of the truth upon which he was insisting.

Consider this marvellous figure of the body. I wonder how long it is since we sat down and thought about our body, what a marvellous thing it is. The word here all through this passage for the body is *soma*, the body as a sound whole. Between these verses 12 and 27 Paul used the word "body" sixteen times, in the whole paragraph eighteen times in all. There are those who think Paul suffered all through the years from some physical infirmity, and I think he did; but here he was looking at an ideal body, and he was conscious of the wonder and marvel of it. Think of the combination in it of the apparently cheap and actually sublime. Many years ago, when in Chicago, a scientist, Dr. Craig by name, a fine man, and a definite and devout Christian, was lecturing on the human body before the Medical Association of Chicago. He was showing that other things have to be taken into account when considering the body, that it could not be accounted for on the level of the material alone. He said,

"Consider the average 150 pound body of a man from its chemical aspect. It contains lime enough to whitewash a fair-sized chicken coop, sugar enough to fill a small shaker, iron enough to make a tenpenny nail, plus water. The total value of these ingredients is ninety-eight cents, or about sixty cents per hundredweight on the hoof!"

Roughly, in our country, about five shillings! What do you think about that? That is all we are worth by chemical analysis. Take the lime and the sugar, the iron, and take the water from the tap, and all we are worth is about five shillings in our money, and that is the body!

But everyone knows that is not all the truth about the body. Go back once more to the book of Psalms, and we may quote very familiar words:

"I will give thanks unto Thee; for I am fearfully
 and wonderfully made;
Wonderful are Thy works;
And that my soul knoweth right well.
My frame was not hidden from Thee,

> When I was made in secret,
> And curiously wrought in the lowest parts of the earth.
> Thine eyes did see mine unperfect substance,
> And in Thy book were all my members written,
> Which day by day were fashioned,
> When as yet there was none of them."

My frame, this mixture of lime and sugar and iron and water, was not hidden from Thee. I am fearfully and wonderfully made. We may talk about the lime, and the sugar, more of it in some than in others, and more iron in some of us than in others, and water; but we have not told the story of the body. Behind the fact of the physical there is a mysterious essence, fearfully and wonderfully made, curiously wrought in the lowest parts of the earth. All the members were known to one mind and one Master before they came into existence. That is the figure Paul used, the figure of the body. Its material substance is almost worthless, and yet it is the very stuff needed to make the most marvellous organism known. As the body, so is Christ. What a humbling statement, and yet what an ennobling conception! What are we worth? Nothing at all, save as we are wrought into the mystery of His life and of His body.

Paul says in one Spirit we were baptized, whether Jews or Greeks, whether bond or free, into Christ Himself. The worthless material is taken up and wrought into the mystery of Christ Himself by the very life of Christ, constituting His body, that is, the Church.

Having stated the figure, Paul went on to speak of the diversities. "For the body is not one member, but many." Keep that in mind, and then glance on to verse 20, " But now they are many members, but one body." It is the same principle stated from two different angles. Paul has brought out two tremendous facts. He is writing to the Corinthian church, and the whole Church, and his subject is that of the unity of the Church. As is the body, so is Christ. This paragraph does not need much interpretation. Keep the background of the Corinthian divisions in mind, and the tendency there is to have divisions in the Christian Church today. He is showing here first of all that there is to be no self-depreciation. That is what he means about the foot that says to the hand, it is not of the body, that it is so unworthy, that if it were the hand, it might belong to the body, and then the ear and the eye. He takes certain parts of the body referring to certain functions of the body. Because the ear shall say, I am not the eye, I lack its brilliance, I am not of the body. That is self-depreciation, and Paul says there must not be self-depreciation.

That is not the contradiction of the great Christian principle that we are to deny ourselves. Our Lord's teaching was that if we deny ourselves we shall find ourselves. Do not forget that. He that loseth his life shall find it, his own, his own personality; and whereas there must be under the Lordship of Christ the consciousness of self stricken to the death, smitten until it is out of sight, we have no right to go round saying, If I were only Mr. So and So I could do something in the Christian Church. If only I had that position; if only I had his brilliance, his position. Paul said nothing of that kind is to happen. The weakest and the apparently lowest of the body is equally important in the functioning of the whole body. There is to be no self-depreciation.

Then he went on, at verse 20, " Many members, but one body." The eye cannot say to the hand, I have no need of you; and mark this, neither the head to the feet, I have no need of you. If in the first movement he showed that in the body there was to be no self-depreciation, now he is showing there is to be no depreciation of others. No member of the body can say to another member of the body, I have no need of you. In order to the functioning of the body in its entirety, in order to the fulfilment of its purpose, and for the living of its life, the eye and the hand, the head and the foot are absolutely necessary.

At once there comes before us the picture of the body, co-operating and acting under the mastery of the head; and there is no member in your body that has any right to say, I am not important, I do not count; and there is not one that can say he or she is of no account. You and I are dependent upon every member in the body, in the functioning of that great Body of Christ.

Then how wonderful is Paul's statement when he says " God hath tempered the body together," and He has set the members. Our Lord said to His disciples at the very end, You have not chosen Me, but I have chosen you and appointed you that you should bear much fruit. The word rendered " appointed " in that passage is the same word rendered in the 28th verse, " set." The Authorized Version renders it " ordained." Both words have missed the force of the meaning. I have set you. It is not ordination or appointment. " God hath set some in the Church," " God hath tempered the body together," and has set the members as it pleased Him.

So with regard to this body of mine, taking the chemical analysis I have referred to, and holding it in the light of the Divine revelation, we see how this body, fearfully and wonderfully made, is a part of the Divine work, a result of the Divine work; and then lifting the figure, notice that God has tempered the body together as it pleased Him. That which is set in the body is set in the interest of the whole body. " If thine eye be single, thy whole body shall be full of light." The eye is the servant of the whole body, and so with all the members.

God has not only set the members in the body, He has tempered them all together, so that they co-operate one with another.

And the final fact is that of unification, that there may be no schism in the body. How important that is with regard to our own bodies. How much more important when we are thinking in the realm of the Spiritual Body of Christ! Himself the Head, His own people the members of His Body, and with the utmost reverence, almost with trembling, notice Paul says the Head cannot say to the feet, I have no need of you. Even in that mystic body Christ needs the weakest, those who from our stupid human standard may be looked upon as weakest and unimportant. Each is important to Him, and as vital to the interests of the accomplishment of His purpose in His mystical Body in the world as any part of the body.

What a marvellous picture this is! To use again the expression, the Church is looked upon here as an organism, rather than an organization. That is not to undervalue organization. It has its place. But organization should be the preparing of means through which the organism can operate peculiarly. Is there anything in the realm of Nature as an organism more wonderful than the human body? I think not. A tree is an organism, but it can never be compared to for wonder with the human body. Paul has taken the ultimate and most perfect organism in all the natural world and has made it the illustration of the unity of the Body of Christ. The great lesson to be learned is that there is to be no self-depreciation; and, secondly, no depreciation of others, and then there will be no split, rent, schism. So there is a common experience. If one suffers, all suffer. If one rejoices, all rejoice; Christ the Head, the Body His members.

The Church is viewed as the Body of the Lord, the Spirit creating the capacity, the Lord directing the activity, God supplying the power. All that in view of the true functioning of the Church. God is faithful through Whom we have been put into fellowship, oneness in life and service, with His Son Christ Jesus our Lord.

"There are diversities of gifts, but the same Spirit. And there are diversities of ministrations, and the same Lord." And now, "There are diversities [or diaereses] of workings, but the same God." "God hath set some in the Church," apostles, prophets, teachers, miracles, gifts of healing, helps, governments, kinds of tongues. These diversities of workings, equipment for service, different kinds of equipment, different forms of energy are manifested in the Church of God.

We start with the declaration of the apostle that all these things are under the government of God. "God hath set." A great word, occurring earlier in the eighteenth verse. "God hath set," not merely He has ordained, not merely He has appointed, but He has put the gift where it is, *tithemi,* that is what the word means. God has placed these gifts in the Church. There are apostles and prophets, and so on. God has put them. The Divine wisdom is found in the bestowment of gifts.

Then Paul illustrated the diversities of these energies for service. Again we have not an exhaustive list of gifts bestowed here. Some gifts are not mentioned at all. These are illustrations. Take them, however, as Paul names them here. He says " First, apostles." There are different opinions about this. Some read the word "first" as indicating rank, those who take first rank in the Church, and that secondly comes the rank of the prophet, and thirdly, the teachers. I do not so understand the value of the words "first, secondly, thirdly," there. I think it marks an historic sequence in the history of the Church in the world. First came the apostles; then secondly, prophets, and thirdly, teachers. The work of the apostle was supremely that of setting out the truth. The work of the prophet was that of proclaiming the truth to the outside world; and the work of the teacher came next historically, that of instructing those who had heard the proclamation of the Word as entrusted to the prophets, that they might grow in faith.

What does the word apostle mean? We are constantly told that apostle means one sent forth. While that is accurate, it is not adequate. That is not the first meaning of the word apostle. That is only a transliteration of the Greek word. It does mean that, but not first. The apostle is one first of all set apart, and therefore sent forth. Take the apostles as we know them in the ministry of our Lord and Saviour, they were first chosen by Him and set apart; then they were sent out by Him, but the setting apart preceded the setting out. Mark tells us remarkably that when Jesus chose the men, He chose them "that they might be with Him, and that He might send them forth." Those were the first in the history of Christianity.

Then came the prophets. The word means not one who foretells events, but one who fore-tells the will of God. The prophet goes with the message to the outside world. Note in this list the evangelist is not named. Evangelists have their place. This is not again a complete list. The prophets are here, and they go to forth-tell, second in the historic order.

Then the teachers, the *didaskaloi,* who instruct those who are disciples in the way of the Lord. They were separate gifts.

Then came miracles, powers. These were bestowed, were given by God. Next the gifts of healing, which means gifts enabling, in the name of the Lord, to produce definite cure of disease. Take those two. It may be said, Why has the Church lost them? We must ask God.

If it were necessary to bestow the gifts, He would do so. He bestows gifts as necessary. He sets them in the Church. Do not confuse the gift of healing with what men call faith healing. As a matter of fact, there is no such thing as faith healing. There have been, and I have known personally, those who had the gift of healing. The fact that gifts are not bestowed today is in the wisdom of God. He bestows as needful.

Then "helps." That is a lovely word here in the list of gifts, the power which God bestows on some. The word "help" means that, helpers, those who give relief in any direction. A few weeks ago I conducted a funeral service for a man who had been here many years. He showed people to their pews. I was tempted to say that was all he did. I do not like to put it that way. He was a help, and I drew attention to the fact that the gift of being a helper in the house of God is a gift, a Divinely bestowed gift, and it never ought to be exercised unless it is Divinely bestowed. I have seen people act as stewards who never ought to have done it. Let the stewards remember that it is a gift—"helps."

Then "governments." The word means those who steer, those who pilot, those who direct. It is a gift, and all have not that. God has set the gifts.

Then "kinds of tongues." That is a gift that seems not to be bestowed today, those ecstatic utterances that had no value unless there was someone to interpret. These were all gifts, illustrative. Paul was showing the different energies that are in the Church, and that they were all in the Church by the will and act of God.

Then he showed that they were distributed. "Are all apostles? are all prophets? are all teachers? are all workers of miracles? have all gifts of healings? do all speak with tongues? do all interpret?" He is showing at once that no one member possesses all the gifts, that they are distributed, and that by God Himself. It is God Who gave me the gift of the teacher. It is God Who gave my friend the gift of the helper. It is God Who has bestowed upon some in office here the gifts of directorship, different gifts, yet every gift to be exercised in the community, and to the perfect functioning of the whole Body. If a man have the gift of prophecy, it is in the interest of all the fellowship. That is the great doctrine of unity. Here God is seen as working.

The whole section ends as Paul says, "Desire earnestly the best gifts." What are the best gifts? The answer will be found if we go on to chapter fourteen. The best gifts are those most calculated to help someone else. That all comes out in the fourteenth chapter in a very beautiful way. He now says, "Desire earnestly the best gifts; and a still more excellent way, the most excellent way shew I unto you," the one law of life, mastering our attitude towards these gifts that God bestows. What is it? "Follow after love." He turns aside in chapter thirteen to show us what love is. Covet earnestly the best gifts as I shew you the most excellent way. He turns aside, and there is nothing in all literature quite equal, from that standpoint, to that thirteenth chapter. When he has shown what love is as to its values, its virtues, and its victories, in the fourteenth chapter Paul says, "Follow after love." Let that be the law, the unfailing law, that governs the members in the Church of Christ.

In this marvellous chapter we have seen the Church of God as an organism, for the fulfilment of purpose, its gifts bestowed by the Spirit, its ministrations under the Lordship of the Lord Himself; and its energy, its workings the result of the Divine action.

II. *The Unfailing Law*   xiii. xiv
  i. The Law. As Governing Principle   xiii
    a. Values   1–3
      1. The Strength of Service   1
      2. The Energy of Equipment   2
      3. The Dynamic of Devotion   3
    b. Virtues   4–7
      A Double Seven
    c. Victories   8–13
      1. "Love Never Faileth"   8a
      2. Demonstration by Comparison   8b–13
        a. Things That Pass   8b–12
        b. Things That Abide   13

I CORINTHIANS xiii

From the standpoint of literature this is one of the most remarkable passages that ever came from the pen of man. In the apostolic teaching, however, this whole chapter is a parenthesis, and of great importance and value in its relation to all his teaching.

We saw the close connection between the last verse of chapter xii and first clause of chapter xiv. "Desire earnestly the greater gifts. And the most excellent way shew I unto you. . . . Follow after love." The words, "Follow after love" contain the declaration of what is the most excellent way. We therefore see that this chapter xiii is a parenthesis. Paul is showing them directly how to follow after love. Now he takes time here in this thirteenth chapter to show what love really is.

The chapter is characterized by poetic beauty and scientific analysis. One is almost reluctant to deal with it by way of analysis. It seems almost irreverent to analyze it. Many will remember that classic little brochure on this chapter written by Henry Drummond, *The Greatest Thing in the World*, a marvellous little book.

Then comes this sense of difficulty. I have read the whole chapter over and over again myself alone. It is full of beauty, and yet marvellous in technique. One is almost reluctant to tear it to pieces, seeking to see it. I have often used an old figure of speech to deal with this subject of analyzing, that it is very much like the study of botany. I am thankful that in my youth I took a course in botany. I am no great botanist, but I remember the fascination of it all; but I had the feeling that when we hunted amid the bogs the butterwort nestling there, and got it up, we had to tear it to pieces to see its beauties, but we could never put it together again. To pick a flower to pieces is to kill it. To deal with this chapter from the standpoint of examination and analysis is like botanizing, only the one great comfort is, if I took a flower and pulled it to pieces, petal by petal, and peered into its hidden beauties, I could never put it together again; but if we analyze the chapter, the chapter will be there when we have finished, and we cannot do any real violence to it. So we will look at it in that way.

There are three movements in this chapter on love. First, Paul shows the values of love in the first three verses. Then, for lack of a better term, he shows the virtues of love in verses 4 to 7, ending everything with the victories of love (8–13). That is a suggested tearing to pieces that we may see the structure of the chapter.

Look first at these verses concerning the values of love. He shows that love is the strength of service in verse 1; then that love is the energy of equipment in verse 2; and that love is the dynamic of devotion in verse three. His whole argument is to show the values of love. He does so by declaring that all these wonderful things he names are utterly valueless when love is absent.

Look at these values. "If I speak with the tongues of men and of angels, but have not love [mark the satire of it], I am become sounding brass, or a clanging cymbal." One can hardly read that without giving an emphasis that reminds one of the roar of the tocsin, the clatter of the cymbal, the sound of brass. Paul says, If I speak with tongues of men and angels, what does it all amount to? Noise. That is all. I can make a noise if I am quite eloquent, but it is all noise, sounding brass or a clanging cymbal. But if there is no love behind my speech, then what am I? I am an instrument like brass or a cymbal, without personality; nothing, emptiness, void of power. Love is the power of speech, and if it is absent, though one have the eloquence of a man or of an angel, we are only making a noise. There is a fine satire in Paul's word. It is more eloquent than the one I have used. That is what it comes to, we are a big noise!

"If I have the gift of prophecy, and know all mysteries and all knowledge; and if I have all faith, so as to remove mountains, but have not love, I am nothing." The gift of prophecy, of forth-telling the things of God, mark it well; and the gift of knowledge, investigation that plumbs the mysteries, and I am able to do that; and more even, if I have faith that can remove mountains, and have not love, I am nothing.

Once more. "If I bestow all my goods to feed the poor," the uttermost of benevolence, the giving away of everything to feed the poor—a fine thing to do—if I do that, and if my conviction carries me so far that "I give my body to be burned, and have not love, it profiteth me nothing." One cannot add to that, or interpret that. All the things that seem to us to be so fine, the voice of eloquence, the gift of forth-telling the will of God, the ability to peer into the mysteries, and come to understand, even the ability to exercise faith so as to remove mountains, the activity that bestows everything in order to the feeding of the poor, and conviction that carries me so far as martyrdom—it is all nothing. It does not avail. The values of love!

Consequently, from that negative paragraph we draw the positive conclusion. What is it? That when love is the motive, in every case, all this becomes a power, and of value. If love is the motive of speech, if love is the motive for the forth-telling of the will of God; if love is that which investigates the mysteries in order to understand; if love is the power in faith, if love lies behind the act of benevolence; if love carries me to the martyr's death, then these things are of supreme value. But without it, they are noise, excitement, of no value at all.

One must run on to the fourteenth chapter, linking that with what Paul said at the close of the twelfth. In the fourteenth chapter we see what love does, and how all these things become of value, of real dynamic energy and force in proportion as there is love. So much for this statement concerning values.

We come next to the virtues of love, or we can change the word, and say Paul describes the fruitfulness of love. This is the central passage, and how wonderful it is! Notice that Paul here gives us a double seven. There are fourteen things he says here, but unquestionably there is a differentiation. Glance at them in this way. In the first seven we have a description of the effect of love upon the individual under the mastery of love. In the second seven the value of love is seen in its relationships. First, personal; then, relative.

Let us bear in mind, as we glance over the ground, that the individual is always seen, and love is acting in the individual in relation to others;

and when we look at the relative declarations, we see the outcome of love-mastered personality.

What does love do in the individual? In every case we see the individual who is love-mastered acting towards other people. "Love suffereth long, and is kind." Do not hurry over that. That is the distinguishing quality of love, not merely that it "suffereth long," but is being kind. Love never says, The third time pays for all, which means that one has borne this thing once, twice, and the third time is enough. Oh, no, love does not end with the third. Once Peter thought he had reached a great height when he had overreached that popular statement when he said, How often shall I forgive my brother, until seven times? That was wonderful, seven times! The Lord laughed at him, and with tender satire He looked at Peter, and said, I do not say seven times, but 490 at least, seventy times seven. "Love suffereth long, and is kind." That is the overplusage which is the characteristic of love.

There is a wonderful illustration in what Jacob said about one of his sons,

> "Joseph is a fruitful bough,
> A fruitful bough by a fountain;
> His branches run over the wall."

Something for the man next door, something for the outsider, a great poetic declaration: "Love suffereth long, and is kind."

What next? "Love envieth not." That is to say, the ear is never undervaluing itself because it is not the eye. The ear is rejoicing in the brilliance of the eye. It is not envying anything that someone else possesses.

"Love vaunteth not itself." The whole emphasis there is on the word "itself." That is very wonderful. Love that talks of loving is not love. If anyone is constantly protesting to me they love me I begin to have doubts in my own mind. It does not boast about itself. It is a great quality, that, in love.

Love "is not puffed up." That is the sweet reasonableness of love. It is not greedy. That is why it does not vaunt itself. The vaunting of itself is the direct outcome of pride. Love is not puffed up, it is not conceited.

Then comes this, "doth not behave itself unseemly." That has been translated in many ways. The simple meaning is this: love is always polite. Love is courteous. It is not rough and brusque and brutal. It does not go about saying ugly things, and saying they call a spade a spade. Love does not do that kind of thing.

Mark this, "seeketh not its own." Perhaps that is the profoundest word about the self-emptying capacity of love, "seeketh not its own."

Notice the next, "is not provoked." The Authorized Version reads "is not easily provoked." The Revised has omitted the word "easily," for it is not there. That word has been an excuse for many a man getting into a bad temper. No, "is not provoked," is not exasperated.

Those are all descriptions of what love does to the individual. All the way through it is the individual in his relationship to other people, but it is the individual.

Paul then turned and shows the relative effect of love. It is there in the first seven, but it is very patent in the last, "taketh not account of evil." To render that in a slightly different way, Love does not keep a ledger in which to enter up wrongs to be dealt with some day later on. That is what this means. Love does not enter them up, does not book them, "taketh not account of evil."

"Rejoiceth not in unrighteousness." That is the other side of the first. If you do not keep a ledger in which you enter up things of wrong, you rejoice not in unrighteousness. That is why you do not enter things up.

"But rejoiceth with the truth." That is the reason of its inability to be glad in the presence of evil, but happy in the presence of God and truth.

Then that wonderful little phrase, "beareth all things." Do not confuse it with another statement that comes later. "Beareth," the word here means that which excludes things. It is the idea of an umbrella that you put up and invite someone to its shelter from the beating rain. It is the roof put over the head. Love acts as a roof over other people, shielding them from the storm as it sweeps.

Then again, "believeth all things." That does not describe credulity at all. That is not the idea. But it is the absence of suspicion in the nature. What a great thing that is. Some people are always suspicious. Love-mastered people are never suspicious.

"Hopeth all things." That is the optimism of love in spite of all appearances. We hope for the best.

Then "endureth all things," that is, remains strong through all processes. So the double seven, and the virtues of love are revealed.

Paul now comes to the victories of love, and everything is contained really in the first sentence, "Love never faileth." Love never fadeth, never withers. There is no such thing as the sere and yellow leaf in love. Love is eternally young, eternally fresh. "Love never faileth."

Then he shows by comparison things that pass. Mark them, high things; they are not low things. Prophecies, tongues, knowledge.

"Love never faileth; but whether there be prophecies, they shall be done away; whether there be tongues, they shall cease." It is good to remember that. "Whether there be knowledge, it shall be done away," as the larger knowledge comes. The former and lesser knowledge is superseded. Paul is careful to show what he means. "For we know in part, and we prophesy in part; but when that which is perfect is come, that which is in part shall be done away."

Then he illustrated from the growth and development of personality, and that very beautifully, "When I was a child I spake as a child." "Now that I am become a man, I have put away childish things." Not childlike, but childish, which means quite another thing. We still watch the passing away of these high and wonderful things as they are superseded. "Now we see in a mirror, darkly; but then face to face; now I know in part, but then shall I know even as also I have been known."

Then the great climactic. "But now abideth faith, hope, love, these three." Oh, yes, they abide, they abide for all time, they abide for all eternity, in all their greatness. Faith will never end, because the finite mind even in the glory that lies beyond will always have in front of it something of infinite meaning of the knowledge and glory to investigate. Oh, yes, in heaven we shall live by faith. And hope certainly, that will abide, always yet wider horizons flung out before our astonished vision. We cannot quite understand that now, but the fact remains. And love, the greatest of these is love, for never forget that love is at once the strength of faith and the inspiration of hope. So that while those things will abide, love will abide, and forevermore pre-eminent.

So let us close our study with the first verse of chapter fourteen in the light of this interpretation. In the light of what Paul has written concerning the values, the virtues, and the victories of love, "follow after love." That is a remarkable word, "follow after." It is not an easy-going word. It is a strenuous word. It shows the necessity for dedication, consecration, effort, persistent vigil. "Follow after love." No, it is not easy. I remind you that the verb Paul used there is found in other of his writings. When he wrote the great autobiographical chapter in his letter to the Philippians, he used the word three times over, when he spoke of what he was, in dealing with the Church of God, "persecuting the Church." It is the same verb. Farther down in that same chapter he says, "I press on." The Authorized Version gave it, "follow after." It is the same verb. Until he comes to the 14th verse, when he says, "I press" toward the prize. "Persecuting," "press on," "press." Yes, but the inner meaning of the word is passionate devotion. Paul said, Before Jesus apprehended me on the Damascene road I persecuted the Church; now I persecute toward the prize. It is the same verb, "follow after." Bring all your consecrated powers to the business of attaining to this high, eternal gift, the gift of love, in its perfect mastery. "Follow after love."

ii. The Law at Work	xiv
a. General Instruction	1–3
1. Stated	1
2. Illustrated	2, 3
b. Argument	4–25
1. Desire to Prophecy for the Sake of the Church	4–19
2. Desire to Prophecy for the Sake of Strangers	20–25
c. Corinthian Application	26–40
1. General Principle	26
2. Particular Instruction	27–33a
(Parenthesis. Women	33b–35)
3. Final Words	36–40

I CORINTHIANS xiv

This fourteenth chapter is wholly concerned with the application of the principle which has been revealed in xii. 31–xiv. 1.

In chapter twelve the apostle had said there was one Spirit, one Lord, and one God, and he had enumerated the gifts of that one Spirit. Then he had insisted upon the unity of the Church, and closed the chapter by urging them to desire earnestly the greater gifts, and then said, "And the most excellent way shew I unto you." The next sentence, so far as argument and injunction are concerned, is the first sentence of chapter fourteen, "Follow after love." We have studied that marvellous thirteenth chapter with its interpretation of love. Paul was saying to Christian people in Corinth, and Christians everywhere that the true coveting, the true passion for desire, is love. That is the great truth.

In the twelfth chapter, in which he was naming the gifts of the Spirit, at verse ten, he says, "And to another prophecy . . . to another divers kinds of tongues; and to another the interpretation of tongues." Those three are named among others. Now all through this fourteenth chapter he dealt with the gift of prophecy, the gift of tongues, and the gift of interpretation of tongues.

We shall take a particular survey of this chapter in its revelation of this gift of tongues, and shall note the interrelationships. There are some senses in which this is not so necessary today to do what I am now proposing. But I cannot escape from the conviction that it may be a good thing to do. I have lived for thirteen years in the United

States, and there found certain teaching on this subject rampant. Indeed, there is a whole movement there, which is called the Tongues Movement. I am not questioning the sincerity of these people, and a manifestation of it can be found in this country too, here in London; a certain teaching by people who believe in all sincerity, but who are entirely misguided, who are misinterpreting this gift of tongues.

I want to take this revelation in this chapter, because it may be called quite accurately the basic passage on the subject of the gift of tongues. It is so clearly dealt with by the apostle that we ought not to be misled.

Where in the New Testament do we read about the gift of tongues? The mind goes properly to the first reference in the Acts of the Apostles. There we read that on the day of Pentecost the Spirit appeared, and took the form of fire, one fire, disparting and sitting, in the shape of tongues, upon the heads of the assembled people. Then we read that they were all filled with the Spirit, and they began to speak with other tongues as the Spirit gave them utterance.

Then we find in Mark's Gospel, in the last chapter, the gift of tongues named as among the things that signalized and signified the mission of the early Church. It is simply named (xvi. 17). There are no details.

Go on in the history in the Acts of the Apostles once more, to the tenth chapter, where we find the wonderful story of Peter in the house of Cornelius. When the Spirit fell it is said they received the gift of tongues. Go further, and in the nineteenth chapter, the account of Paul's coming to Ephesus, finding there a group of the disciples, evidently lacking something, he said to them, not as our translation had it, " Have ye received the Holy Ghost since ye believed? " but " Did ye receive the Holy Ghost when ye believed? " They said, " Nay, we did not so much as hear whether the Holy Ghost was given." They had been baptized into John's baptism. When Paul expounded the truth, and led them beyond the preaching of Apollos, who had led them to a certain stage, then we are told the Spirit fell upon them, and they received the gift of tongues. Those are the only references to the gift of tongues.

Go back to chapter thirteen, to our last study, and notice one thing, leaving out the context in verse 8, " Whether there be tongues, they shall cease." There is the vibrant, clear as crystal statement of the apostle that tongues should cease. That should be kept in mind as we go forward.

Yet there can be no question, that whatever it was, and whatever it meant, it was a positive gift. The gift of tongues was bestowed upon certain in the Church; upon the whole Church on the day of Pentecost, but after that not upon all. But it was a distinct gift, just as much as prophecy was, and the gift of interpretation was, or the gift of healing was.

When we inquire what this gift was, we have first to remember that the Greek word here used, *glossa,* referred in Greek thought and literature to words that were either obsolete or incomprehensible, and the word was always used to describe a certain form of speech which was born of great ecstasy, the speech that was the result of a catching up of the spiritual or mental side of the nature, and carrying it away into some region of dream and vision, but always of delight and of ecstasy. That is what the word meant. And there is no doubt that this is exactly what it meant here, in the gift of tongues. If the gift of tongues fell upon anyone, it bore them up into a realm of vision and light and glory and joy and ecstasy, and they poured out that which described things they saw.

We come back to this chapter. Notice what the apostle teaches here incidentally. In verse two we read this: " For he that speaketh in a tongue speaketh not unto men, but unto God." At verse 28 we read this: " But if there be no interpreter, let him keep silence in the Church; and let him speak to himself, and to God." That is the first great truth to be remembered, that the gift of tongues was for addressing God. It was not for addressing man. It was never given in order that men might preach. To put it quite simply, in our everyday language, it was given to men that they might praise. These voices, these tongues, were the utterances of ecstatic gladness, in adoration, and in praise. Tongues were given, and they were to be used in addressing God.

Notice another thing. Again I go to the second verse. " He that speaketh in a tongue speaketh not unto men, but unto God; *for no man understandeth."* Go to verse five. " I would have you all speak with tongues, but rather that ye should prophesy; and greater is he that prophesieth than he that speaketh with tongues, except he interpret." Mark that. The tongues need interpretation in order to be understood. Or again in verse 9, " So also ye, unless ye utter by the tongue speech easy to be understood, how shall it be known what is spoken? for ye will be speaking into the air."

We have now two great principles in looking at this gift of tongues. First of all, they were to be addressed to God. Secondly, definitely they were incomprehensible to men. No one could understand them. Outsiders could not understand. I go further and say, they could not themselves understand.

Go on to verse 14. " For if I pray in a tongue, my spirit prayeth but my understanding is unfruitful." If a man have the gift of tongues, he can use it in addressing God, but he does not understand it himself. What he is saying he does not understand.

In the next place notice this. The apostle is teaching that there must be interpretation if tongues be used; and he distinctly says that. "Wherefore let him that speaketh in a tongue pray that he may interpret."

Once more, in gathering out the central statements, I go to verse 28. "But if there be no interpreter, let him keep silence in the Church; and let him speak to himself, and to God."

That gathers up the great teaching. Ponder it well. The gift of tongues was a gift of the Spirit. If I am asked why we do not have it now, I do not know. Someone may get it, may receive the gift of tongues. But supposing it is given, remember these simple things. First of all, it is to be used in addressing God and not men. Secondly, it will be quite incomprehensible to the men who do hear. As a matter of fact, the one so gifted will be borne up in an ecstasy, and will utter things not understood by himself or herself. Further, if used in public the gift of tongues demands interpretation, and the tremendous declaration is made that if interpretation is not there, the gift is not to be exercised in the presence of others, but is to be exercised when the recipient is alone with God. I maintain that the teaching is perfectly simple and clear, and is not to be forgotten.

Having come closely into contact with the movement that is designated the Tongues Movement, I have never yet found it fulfilling these conditions. There are people who profess to have the gift of tongues, and one could not possibly understand what they were saying. But the apostle also said if there was no interpreter, the gift was not to be exercised in public but only when alone with God.

All that is very mystical in a certain way. We may ask, What was the value of this gift? There is no doubt that at the very beginning it was a sign to the outsider; but even to the outsider it needed interpretation to carry the message. Go back to the story in Acts 2. We find two or three simple things. The miracle was that of hearing "Every man heard them speaking in his own language." What did they hear? They were uttering forth "the mighty works of God." In other words, they were uttering words that expressed the wonder of the things God had wrought, and the greatness of God, and the glory of God; and I have no doubt, the grace of God.

We ask, How did these people know? Notice carefully that in that gift at Pentecost there was the mingling of two things, and the supreme wonder is that what then was uttered was understood, but it led to inquiry. That was what it was intended to do. When they heard this, they were amazed, and they said, "What meaneth this?" Note two things. First of all, they were conscious in their own languages of a company of men praising God, sounding in high ecstasy the praises of the Most High; but they were led to inquire, What does this mean? And interpretation immediately followed. Peter, standing up, said, "Be this known unto you this is that which hath been spoken by the prophet Joel." Then he went on quoting. Then he began again the second division of his discourse, "Jesus of Nazareth, a Man approved of God unto you . . . He hath shed forth this, which ye see and hear." The gift of tongues was a miracle, in which men heard in their own language the praises of God. Inquiry resulted from it, because it was a sign puzzling them, "What meaneth this?" And Peter answered. Two brief sentences cover the ground. "This is that which hath been spoken by the prophet Joel." "He hath poured forth this." No, that company at Pentecost were not preaching. They were not declaring the evangel. They were uttering the praises of God, and interpretation followed, so that we have a wonderful picture of men understanding those men speaking in differing tongues as they celebrated the greatness of God; and when the apostle Peter became the interpreter, there was the interpretation of tongues, as he gave the reason for all their gladness and all their praise.

Bear one other thing in mind. This gift of tongues was possessed by Paul. Indeed, he says he spoke with tongues more than any of them. It was a real gift. We call to mind Paul's story of an occasion upon which he was caught up to the third heaven, and heard unspeakable words that it was not lawful to utter. That was a great spiritual vision of high ecstasy. I think it was there and then, among other occasions, when the gift of tongues was upon him. Yet he could not interpret, and therefore he was forever silent about what he heard, whatever the gift. It may still be granted, but I have never known of cases. I have known a great number of cases of people who have confessed or declared that they had received it. I have seen them as in some wild, half-hysterical condition they poured out words without sense and meaning. All I have to say is that they were distinctly disobeying the definite instruction not to employ the gift when there was no interpreter. While it was a definite gift, Paul did say in this chapter we have already taken (xiii. 8) that tongues "shall cease."

Ever and anon in the history of the Christian Church we have had a recrudescence of it, and many strange things have happened. While not denying that it may be bestowed, it must not be exercised before men unless someone is there who has the gift of understanding and of interpretation. Here are the great laws that govern its exercise.

Glance at the first three verses of this chapter. The supreme matter is, "Follow after love." Three of the gifts are in view: prophecy, the gift of tongues, and the gift of interpretation, and the interrelationship is seen throughout this chapter. The supreme matter is love. Why do we want this gift or that? Why do we want to be possessed of this gift of the Spirit, whether prophecy, or of tongues, or the interpretation of tongues? Let us answer the question in the loneliness of our own souls. If there is any other desire than love it is false. Love is the most excellent way. "Follow after love."

So to re-emphasize in a word what he said at the close of the twelfth chapter, Covet earnestly the best gifts. He then put into contrast these two gifts, tongues and prophesying. Notice what he says about these two gifts in those first three verses. To speak with tongues is entirely valueless to other people. It may be of value to the one possessing it. It may minister to spiritual strength, that very experience of high ecstatic utterance, but it is not helping anyone else. Paul did not deny the value of the gift, but he pointed out what it lacked.

But he that prophesies "speaketh unto men," those three great words, "edification, and comfort, and consolation." A man can speak in a tongue. It has its value to him perchance, but it is quite useless to the people round about him, for they do not understand. But if a man is exercising the gift of prophesying, he is helping to build up, and not only for "edification," which is building up, but "comfort," that is, consolation; and "consolation," that is comfort by companionship. It is the other man who is in view.

We desire a gift, what for? James has a great passage on that subject. "Ye ask and receive not, because ye ask amiss, that ye may spend it on your pleasures," your own desires, "your lusts" is the old word. We ask from God that which will minister to ourselves spiritually. That is not the true principle. The true principle of desiring gifts is that we may possess them for the sake of others, and that is why prophesying is the greater thing, which we are to seek, rather than tongues, which may be granted but which must be used in accordance with Divine instructions.

In this paragraph (verses 4–25) Paul is still dealing with the great subject of the law of love in relation to gifts, and here three gifts are in view, prophesying, tongues, and interpretation. While the law of love refers to every gift named in the twelfth chapter, as we saw, here three special gifts are dealt with.

We have also seen that in the first three verses the general principle was stated. This general principle the apostle now proceeded to apply and illustrate. The section may be divided: first, a general statement in verses 4 and 5; and then, from 6–25, arguments illustrating and applying that general principle.

This general statement is clear and simple. It is really a repetition of the principle stated in the first three verses of the chapter, but now with a particular application. Notice the two gifts referred to here, tongues and prophesying. As we have seen, the gift of tongues was always the gift of ecstatic utterance, never the gift for preaching to the outside world. It was always a spiritual experience finding expression in ecstasy and utterance. The other gift was prophecy, and that meant speaking forth to others. Each of these is named as a gift of the Spirit. To some the Spirit gave the gift of prophesying. Upon some He bestowed the gift of tongues, which also was a gift of the Spirit. We must be careful we do not undervalue that in our thinking, for it was a distinct gift of the Spirit. We must never forget that the Holy Spirit has one and only one sacred work to do. It is a related truth. To quote words from our Lord, "He shall not speak from Himself . . . He shall take of Mine, and shall declare it unto you." "He shall glorify Me." The work of the Spirit is that of glorifying Christ. I believe many godly people, His own children, are confused in their thinking. Many have said to me, I am praying for the coming of the Spirit into my life. If we are Christian that is a very foolish prayer, because that which makes us Christian is that the Spirit has come into our lives. Then they say, But we mean the fulness of the Spirit. That is a very different matter. People tell me they have sought it, and not obtained it. When one questions them as to the signs of the coming of the Spirit, they confess that they hoped there would be some definite experience, some entering of power into the life, an illumination and consciousness of the Spirit.

Now the Spirit never comes to create a consciousness of Himself. He comes to create the consciousness of Christ. Many Christian people are very conscious of Christ, and yet have not seen that is the very evidence of the work of the Spirit. That is the sign.

Both the gift of tongues and the gift of prophesying are gifts of the Spirit. It is the Spirit Who has bestowed, and the central value of the gifts is the glorifying of the Christ Himself. Notice, the apostle here speaks of a common factor, something that happens as the result of the reception of each of these gifts, that of edifying. "He that speaketh in a tongue edifieth himself." "He that prophesieth edifieth the Church." The gift is for the building up. It is bestowed in order that in its use it may serve for building up, growth, development. Whether the gift of tongues or the gift of prophesying, that is the common value of each.

But the important thing is to notice the distinction. If there is a common factor in building up, yet "He that speaketh in a tongue edifieth *himself;* but he that prophesieth edifieth *the Church.*" Neither of the gifts is wrong; both of them are right, and valuable; but notice the difference. If men or women have the gift of tongues they break out into glad ecstatic praise, as they did on the Day of Pentecost, for what the people heard was these people speaking of the wonderful works of God, magnifying Him in His government and glory and grace. That is what they were doing. They were singing. The wonder of the day of Pentecost was that the people understood their different languages, but the tongues was something more than a difference in language. It was an ecstatic expression, and it tended to edify. Now if a man have this gift, the apostle said it was good. Let him use it. There is nothing wrong in it, but do not forget, when it is exercised they are building themselves up, edifying their own souls, gaining from the exercise of ecstatic praise strength in their own personality. It is a great gift.

But prophesying, speaking forth, delivering the message is not merely blessing the man who is using the gift, but is intended to bless those who listen to him. There is the clear distinction. Prophecy therefore, Paul said, is a greater gift. Why? Because it builds up the body, builds up the Church, helps to build up that whole instrument of Christ which is His spiritual Body. Tongues, yes, they are perfectly right, only if one is going to use the gift of tongues so that others hear it he must be careful that someone also has the gift of interpretation. "I would have you all speak with tongues," said the apostle. He is careful not to undervalue the gift; but there is something greater than speaking with tongues. "Greater is he that prophesieth than he that speaketh with tongues, except he interpret." If the gift of tongues is exercised in the presence of others, you must also be able to explain to them what has been said. If that cannot be done, as we have seen, the gift is not to be exercised publicly.

We see at once the operation here of the law of love. "Covet earnestly the greater gifts. And the most excellent way shew I unto you." We know which is the best when we are mastered by love, and love is never self-centred. If we are seeking a gift in order to build up our own life, it may be bestowed upon us, but it is a secondary thing. But the gift of real value is the gift that, when exercised, reaches and blesses others.

Paul now went on and illustrated this. His arguments move in two sections. From verses 6-19 he showed the greatness of the gift of prophecy as compared with the gift of tongues within the Church. Then from verses 20-25 he showed the greatness of prophecy in the assembly in its influence upon the outsider, the unbeliever, who comes into the assembly. There are the two outlooks here.

He puts himself in front of them, and says, "If I come unto you speaking with tongues." It is interesting that Paul said he spoke with tongues more than any of them. There is no question that he obeyed the revelation made to them, and if he spoke with tongues he did so when he was alone, unless some other was there who could interpret. But even if he could speak with tongues, there was no value in it in the gathering of other men and women.

Then he uses four words: "Unless I speak to you either by way of revelation, or of knowledge, or of prophesying, or of teaching." Those are great words. "Revelation" is *apokalupsis,* unless I come with a revelation; with "knowledge," *gnosis,* pure knowledge; "prophesying," that is *propheteis,* the uttering forth of the will of God, and with "teaching," that is, simply teaching. All these four things mean making plain. Paul said if he came to them with tongues, he did not come with any of these things, therefore all his coming was worthless so far as they were concerned. It may have been of value to the apostle, but he would not exercise the gift in the presence of others.

Then he took a musical illustration, which need not be elaborated. He speaks of the pipe, the harp, and the trumpet, and the necessity for giving a certain sound. The trumpet must give a blast of certainty, or it will not call men to arms. Paul was illustrating and showing the necessity for a voice that has significance. That is the whole point. There may be ecstatic utterance, but unless it has interpretation, significance, it has no value. So tongues without interpretation are valueless. Therefore Paul told them to pray for the gift of interpretation. If the gift of tongues be granted, pray for the gift also of interpretation.

What then? In the presence of all these things "I will pray with the spirit," that is, ecstasy; and "with the understanding," that is, interpretation. "I will sing with the spirit," that is, ecstasy; and "with the understanding also," that is, interpretation. Therefore pray for this gift. He summarizes by reference to himself when he says he would rather speak five words with his understanding than ten thousand words in a tongue. Think of that—five words: "It is Christ that died." That is an illustration from Paul's own writings. He would rather say that to others definitely, positively, with the gift of prophecy, than he would go on pouring out in ecstatic utterance, even though ten thousand words passed his lips. They are of no value in comparison with the five words spoken with the gift of prophecy. That is all within the assembly.

The key in verses 20–25 is found in verse 23. Paul was taking the wider outlook. There might come, as there did come, as there do come into the assemblies of Christian people in their worship, those who were and are unbelievers, those who were unlearned, those who were ignorant, not knowing about these things. Such must be kept in mind. It is not personal building up, as in tongues. It is not the building up of the Church that does come by prophesying. But there will come those unbelieving men, those unlearned men, those ignorant men, who know nothing of the spiritual verities. What about such men? Notice how Paul began. See the background. He was writing to these Corinthians. He said to them, Do not be children, that is, do not be immature in your mind. He said, Be not children, but be babes. Those are different words. That takes you further back than the children. In malice be babes, but in mind be men. The background here is that something was creeping into the church at Corinth of boastfulness in the possession of certain gifts, that was creating the spirit of rupture and envy. Be babes in that regard, but be men, full grown and developed. That is the meaning of the word; be fully developed.

He then went on. What about these tongues? He said they are a sign to the unbeliever. It was so at Pentecost. But if the only gift exercised when that stranger comes in is the gift of tongues, what will the stranger say? He will say, You are all mad. Granted an assembly of the Church, and all of them happening to be speaking with tongues, and no one is prophesying, or interpreting, this stranger would say they were mad. That is what they said on the Day of Pentecost. They said they were drunk, which comes to the same thing. There was the necessity for Peter's sermon, which was an interpretation of the things that made them think those men were mad or drunk.

Paul said in effect, Keep your eye on that unbelieving man, that unlearned man, that ignorant man that knows nothing. If no one is speaking except with tongues, not understood, he will not only be unable to understand, he will count you as mad. But if you are all speaking with the prophetic gift, that is to say, one after another is bearing testimony to the power of the Gospel, that man will be reproved, he will be convicted, and he will go down before God, and will acknowledge God is with you, that there is reality in all your professions in proportion as you are able to reach him intelligently. The great thought all the way through this passage is intelligibility, something that can be understood. Here is something we cannot understand. One is borne up in a great ecstasy. I doubt that I have ever had the gift of tongues. I do not know. When I read of Paul's experience, when he was caught up to the third heaven, I have never known anything like that. Oh, in other ways, perhaps so. But while I was there, all I could do was to utter adoration, without interpretation. Yes, I gain by that. But my brother does not. My sister sitting by me, a member of the Church, cannot understand. It is valuable to me, to build me up, but it is of no value to others. That is supremely true, of course, when we think of the outsider coming into the assembly. To me that is the most arresting thought in that second part of the paragraph. If one shall come in, an unbeliever, an unlearned man, a man who does not believe, who is ignorant, there should be something for him. Therefore let the gift be exercised, one that reaches him and brings conviction to him, and brings him to the place of surrender to God Himself.

To summarize the teaching of this passage, we learn that gifts are for service. Every gift the Spirit bestows constitutes equipment in some form for service for others. The very holding and possession and exercise of a gift is of value personally, but we must test its value by the influence it exerts upon others. Consequently, love is the true law of desire. Covet the best gifts, and the most excellent way is, " Follow after love."

Paul has been dealing with gifts bestowed upon the Church, upon varied individuals in that fellowship. He has laid down the fact that the one unfailing law, governing life and service and the use of gifts, is the law of love. As we have seen, love is never conscious of itself, does not boast of itself, is always self-emptying, pouring itself out in the interest of others. He has made comparison between the use of two gifts bestowed. The great principle is applicable to all others. These gifts were well known, the gift of prophesying, and the gift of tongues. He dealt with these in their interrelationship, showing how each indeed is a gift, and how it is to be used, and that the master principle of the use of gifts is love. This means that a gift is to be desired and used in the interest of others, and not in the interest of the one who possesses it. That is true of prophesying and of tongues.

Through all this teaching, though the letter is to the Church of God universal, the catholic Church in the true sense of that word, there is the individual background of the Corinthian church. Therefore, there may be much that is not particularly interesting to us here. The underlying principles apply to all the churches, consequently there is great value in much found in this letter. There is a sense in which this chapter is peculiarly Corinthian, but the principles are of universal application.

In this closing paragraph (verses 26-40) Paul is still dealing with the unfailing law of love, which ends with this chapter. We find, first, general principles governing certain Christian gatherings (26). Then particular instructions concerning those selfsame gatherings (27-33). Next we find instructions concerning the activity of women in such gatherings (34, 35); and the whole section closes with general instructions (36-40).

Those Christian gatherings referred to by the apostle here were not gatherings for public witness to the outside world. They were not gatherings of the church that she might deliver her message to the outsider. There were such gatherings, but these are not in mind here. Rather they were the gatherings of the church, to use a word with which we are familiar, for fellowship. Notice the type of gathering referred to, one in which people come together with differing gifts. One comes with a psalm, that is, a song of praise. Another comes with a teaching, that is, some exposition or explanation of truth. Yet another in the assembly comes with a revelation, a declaration of the inner meaning of some mystery. Yet another in that gathering comes with a tongue, and we have seen that a tongue was a rapturous outburst of praise to God. And another in that same assembly has come with an interpretation, or has the gift of interpretation, most likely directly after the other one has exercised the gift of tongues. How different it all is! It is a meeting for fellowship.

While we know the word, how many know the experience of it? Meetings for fellowship have largely dropped out from the practices of the Christian Church. In such a meeting we approximate the true idea. There is no preaching. The members come for fellowship, and one has one thing, another, something else. We have had such meetings at Westminster which we call meetings for fellowship and discussion. There is no preparation, but there is a sense of the presence of the Spirit, and obedience to the guidance of the Spirit to speak, to sing, to pray, or to ask questions. That is a true fellowship meeting. Undoubtedly that is the kind of meeting Paul had in view. That very list of things shows it, though the list is not exhaustive. It is an interesting meeting, and I do not know of any gathering peculiar to the Church likely to be of greater value.

Notice, Paul says, "Let all things be done unto edifying." If you have a song of praise you are to announce it, but it is to be in the interest of all who are there, for building up. If you have a teaching, a revelation, a tongue, you are not to exercise the gift to glorify yourself as having that gift. No, it must be exercised in the interest of those who are round about you. That is fellowship. It is the communication, which is a good translation of the word fellowship, the root idea of the word being that of having all things in common. In the fellowship meeting everything is to be done in the interest of all, and that is Paul's last great word, "Let all things be done unto edifying." The edifying of the individual, of the Church itself; the building up of individual character resulting from this mutual interrelationship, and a sharing of things through these gifts possessed. It is a great picture of fellowship.

When Paul was writing to the Ephesians, in chapter four he described the Church in that masterly, magnificent, exhaustive passage, "One Lord, one faith, one baptism; one God and Father of all, Who is over all, and through all, and in all." Then he goes on, "Unto each one of us was the grace given," each one having a gift from the Head of the

Church; and he goes on down in that passage until he says that what is given to each one is given in order that the Church may be perfected "unto the work of ministering, unto the building up of the body of Christ; till we all attain unto the unity of the faith, and of the knowledge of the Son of God, unto a full-grown man, unto the measure of the stature of the fulness of Christ." The measure of the stature of the fulness of Christ has never been, can never be, in any one soul. That fulness can be realized only in the whole Church of God in its completeness. But to each one the gift, and the ultimate meaning of the gift is the perfection of the whole corporate Body of the Church.

That surely was in Paul's mind here. They were a little company, comparatively, there in Corinth of Christians, with the vast hosts of the saints of God; but the true value of all gifts wherever they are gathered together is this, that those coming are not acting under impulse, but under the guidance of the Spirit. Everything therefore is to be done for edifying, for the strengthening of each, and the final perfecting of the Church.

Paul then made particular application in the next verses (27–33). He went back to this question of tongues, one evidently very much in evidence there in Corinth, and causing a great deal of trouble. He says, "If any man speaketh in a tongue, let it be by two, or at the most three, and that in turn." The gift is not improper, and it may be a great gift, but it is the use that matters. Surely that is very mechanical and important. They are not to exercise the gift all together, but in turn, and then one is to interpret. "But if there be no interpreter, let him keep silence in the Church; and let him speak to himself, and to God."

He went on, "And let the prophets speak by two or three." There are those who come with some interpretation, with some speaking forth of the thought of God in the fellowship meeting. Let such speak by two or three, "and let the others discern." They are not to receive, or to believe what is said. "Let them discern." I like the marginal reading, "let them discriminate."

"But if a revelation be made to another sitting by, let the first keep silence." Paul is arranging for an orderly interruption in the fellowship meeting. Someone is exercising a gift of tongues, or of interpretation, or exercising the gift of prophecy; and suddenly a revelation is made to someone sitting by, some insight into truth. That is a perfectly proper interruption, providing that it is a revelation. "For ye all can prophesy one by one, that all may learn, and all may be comforted; and the spirits of the prophets are subject to the prophets; for God is not a God of confusion, but of peace; as in all the churches of the saints."

It is perfectly evident that the apostle has in mind these particular meetings. Although the corrective part of his letter is finished at the end of the eleventh chapter and he is now dealing with the constructive part, with the spiritualities, the undercurrent of discord and strife in that church is again seen. There were things there that ought not to be, and with these he was dealing. There was a recognition of disorder and strife obtaining in that church. Therefore he was careful to lay down these instructions for the conduct of such a meeting.

The next two verses have been mischievously twisted and contorted by many excellent people. Mark the emphasis here. " Let the women keep silence in the churches." I recognize what has often been claimed, that there is here an apparent contradiction of Paul's instruction in an earlier chapter (xi. 5). Paul there recognized the right of a woman to pray or prophesy, and gave instructions how she was to do so in the city of Corinth. However there is no contradiction, when we remember the Corinthian background. It is evident, when we read the instruction in chapter eleven, that there were certain women in the church in Corinth who were claiming their emancipation in an unwise manner, where the uncovered head was the sign of prostitution. Women there were claiming they were emancipated from all custom, and they were speaking and praying with heads uncovered. Therefore Paul gave instructions that their heads were to be covered.

Does that still obtain? I do not think so. That was Corinth. But the principle obtains. There must be no emancipation from general custom that may be misunderstood by the outside world. That was the prohibition in chapter eleven. Here however it is evident that these women were exercising a freedom harmfully, and everything depends on what the apostle meant by speaking. " Let the women keep silence in the churches; for it is not permitted unto them to speak," and again, " If they would learn anything, let them ask their own husbands at home; for it is shameful for a woman to speak in the church."

What is meant by speaking? Prophesying? Not necessarily. Quite simply and technically, this Greek verb translated here " to speak," the verb *laleo,* occurs over three hundred times in the New Testament, and in the most remarkable variety of applications; but the context is always necessary if we are to understand what is meant by this verb. It may mean, and so it is used to mean, talking, questioning, arguing, protesting, chattering. Paul might have written with equal accuracy, Let a man keep silence in the churches, for it is not permitted unto men to chatter, to argue. Let them be in subjection, as also saith the law, and let them discuss the subject at home.

What was Paul warning these people against? Undoubtedly there were arguments in those meetings for fellowship, and women were taking a very definite part in those arguments, questioning, protesting, trying to show their ability, and their freedom, and doing it in an improper way, and creating confusion, where there should have been peace and quietness. Someone may quote from another letter of Paul, "I permit not a woman to teach, nor to have dominion over a man." Again, Paul was writing then in view of local conditions. He might have written, I suffer not a man to teach by usurping authority; for that is the meaning of the passage. Here was a meeting for fellowship being broken in upon by certain women claiming liberty to speak with head uncovered. The apostle said that kind of thing must cease. They were not to be permitted to do that kind of thing. If they would learn, that is, if they really want to come to understand, such disputations in the church are out of place, and are not to be permitted. They are proper in the home. Let them ask, let them inquire, let them hold communion with their husbands in the fellowship of the home; but that kind of thing is not to be done in the church.

Evidently there were women in Corinth given to careless and contentious talk, and that is what Paul was prohibiting. Certainly he was not saying that a woman had no right to pray or to prophesy in the Church, because he had already given instructions as to how, and under what conditions she was to do it. No, something else had crept into that fellowship meeting, the attitude taken by the women who were indulging in contentious, strident speech. Such were to keep silence there, and to remit the questions and discussions to the quietness and fellowship of the home.

Paul went on to give general instructions. The 36th verse is very arresting. Again the Corinthian background is seen. "What? was it from you that the word of God went forth? or came it unto you alone?" Paul sees the arrogant position taken up by the Corinthian church, as though they were claiming they were the originators of the word of God.

Then, finally, "If any man thinketh himself to be a prophet, or spiritual, let him take knowledge of the things which I write." Mark here Paul's definiteness, that the things he wrote were "the commandment of the Lord." "But if any man is ignorant, let him be ignorant," so it reads. I prefer the other rendering, "let him be ignored." If a man is not amenable, and does not bow to these instructions, then let him alone.

So everything closes, "Wherefore, my brethren, desire earnestly to prophesy, and forbid not to speak with tongues. But let all things be done decently and in order." Two great words are used there: "decently," decorously, with beauty; "in order," with arrangement.

The Church is to guard against any method which is so purely spasmodic that it lacks decorousness and arrangement. Go back to the earlier word. "God is not a God of confusion, but of peace."

So ends the section dealing with the unfailing law of love. Love has been defined marvellously in that thirteenth chapter. It has been illustrated in the application to prophecy and to tongues. This law of love has the widest application, though Paul here has dealt only with three gifts. Whatever gift is ours is bestowed individually, but it is to be exercised only under the inspiration and power of love, and love never breaks down, "love never faileth." That is the unfailing law which, being obeyed, will put an end to all moral shortcomings and derelictions in the Church such as Paul had had to rebuke in the earlier part of his letter.

III. *The Ultimate Triumph* — xv. 1–57

  i. The Gospel of Christ's Resurrection — 1–11
    a. Its Preaching and Effect — i, 2
    b. Its Essential Notes — 3, 4
    c. Its Demonstration — 5–11

  ii. The Importance of Christ's Resurrection — 12–34
    a. In Regard to Our Salvation — 12–19
    b. In Regard to the Programme of God — 20–28
    c. In Regard to Present Conduct — 29–34

I CORINTHIANS xv. 1–34

WE have already studied two of the spiritualities, that of the unifying Spirit, in order to correct divisions; and, secondly, the unfailing law of love, in order to correct all the difficulties that had arisen in the church because of failure in moral life. At this point we come to the final movement in the spiritualities, that of the ultimate triumph, for the correction of all difficulties during the little while of our earthly sojourn.

The glory of our Christianity is that it never views life as being complete in this world. It always has its eyes lifted to the morning, and gazes out upon the eternities, recognizing that we belong to eternity as well as to time. So now the apostle deals with that great subject of the resurrection. Let us gain the full significance of that—the resurrection, that ultimate triumph of Christ, and ultimately of His people; that triumph in the light of which we may put all the difficulties of this little while. I have twice used that phrase, this "little while." The longest span of human life is but a little as compared with the eternity that stretches out beyond; and there, in eternity, is the full meaning of life, in the will of God, through the redemption in Christ Jesus.

So having dealt with the unifying Spirit, constituting the body of Christ, and with the unfailing law of love governing the actions of all members of that body, the apostle now comes to this great subject of the resurrection.

Everything in this whole chapter deals with it. Keeping in mind the Corinthian background, that whereas the letter was sent to the universal Church, it was first of all sent to this particular church in Corinth, that church in that pagan city, the whole reason why this great section is found is unquestionably discovered in the twelfth verse of the chapter, "How say some of you that there is no resurrection?" Notice that is a general statement. They were not saying Christ did not rise. That was involved; but they were taking the general statement, saying, There is no resurrection from the dead. To this we come in our next study, but that was the reason for the letter, because in that church in Corinth there were those who were denying the fact of resurrection, and, of course, in doing so were denying the fact of the resurrection of Christ and of their own ultimate resurrection.

In beginning to deal with the subject of the resurrection in the abstract, Paul comes to the concrete, with the one great central, final, unequivocal proof of resurrection, and that is the resurrection of Christ. These first eleven verses of the chapter deal wholly with that subject. He comes on to the subject of resurrection in the abstract in a marvellous manner, in one of the most wonderful passages in all literature. Now however he begins with the resurrection of Christ. We therefore centre attention upon these eleven verses.

What is the proof of the resurrection of Christ? That is the question about which he is writing to these Corinthians. How is it proven? There are three proofs, and we divide the paragraph quite naturally into three parts. In the first two verses he shows that the Gospel believed on is the proof of the resurrection. Then he quoted very remarkably the testimony of Scripture (3, 4). Finally, he declares the demonstration of the fact by naming the witnesses to the reality of the fact (5-11).

The Gospel. He says, "Now I make known unto you the Gospel which I preached unto you." Notice the past tense, "I preached unto you, which also ye received, wherein also ye stand, by which also ye were saved; I make known, I say, in what words I preached it unto you, if ye hold it fast, except ye believed in vain." He says he had made known to them the Gospel. He names it in those verses, and he says it is the Gospel he preached, that he had preached when he went to Corinth, and while he was there.

We may ask at once, What did he mean? What were the terms of the Gospel? That is revealed immediately in the following verses. Consequently, the next two verses are needed to reveal its content. "For I delivered unto you [keep the connection here with the first two verses] first of all that which also I received, how that Christ died for our sins according to the Scriptures; and that He was buried; and that He hath been raised on the third day according to the Scriptures." We remit now the phrase "according to the Scriptures," at which we shall look presently more particularly. There is the Gospel.

What had he preached? Christ died, Christ was buried, Christ rose, was raised, as he said. That is the Gospel. To me it is always an arresting fact that the apostle wrote, "and was buried." That made impossible the idea that Christ simply vanished and disappeared. Oh, no, he said, They put Him in His tomb. The death was a fact, and was evident, a fact that they put Him in the tomb. "He was buried," and He rose. The Gospel is that He died for our sins. That was the whole Gospel. He "died for our sins," and they buried Him; and He was raised from the dead. That is the whole message of our Gospel. He died. But that is not the last word, until we interpret the death by the fact of the resurrection, "He was raised." That is the Gospel he preached. How marvellously he has reduced it to the simplest terms! I make it known to you now that which I have already made known to you, that which I delivered to you. That is the Gospel.

What about it, Paul? I preached it. You received it. He leaves it there; and the supreme proof of the Gospel, of the value of the death, interpreted by the resurrection, is in the experience of the men who heard it, received it, and lived by it. Paul says here, "I preached, ye received . . . ye stand . . . ye are saved." "I preached . . . ye received." I always thank God for that expression in the first chapter of John's Gospel, which interprets that word "ye received." People say, What do you mean by receiving the Lord Jesus Christ? "He came unto His own, and they that were His own received Him not. But as many as received Him, to them gave He the right to become children of God, even to them that believe on His name." There is the interpretation of receiving the Lord Jesus, believing on His name. Paul preached the Gospel, the death and the resurrection of our Lord. They received it, and believed it, that is, they believed on Him; and the result was "ye stand, and are saved." Their saved condition and their standing are the demonstration of the truth of the Gospel that Jesus not only died, but that He rose again.

It is to me a matter of very great importance that we find here, as so constantly in the Scriptures, and in experience, that the final proof of the resurrection is not documentary, it is not even evidential, as proven by witnesses, although we have that here; but the final proof is the living experience of the Christian soul. That can be put in a wider way. If I am asked today what is the proof of the resurrection of Jesus, the actual resurrection of the One Who died and was buried, the proof is the Christian Church. That is a simple thing to state, and to understand. Not His teaching, not His miracles, not His dying, account for the Christian Church, but all these interpreted by His resurrection. There would have been no Church unless He had risen. The disciples were scattered like chaff before the wind. They were gathered by the resurrection; and that marvellous host running all down the centuries, that host of people saved because they stand in that Gospel which they received, is the great proof of the resurrection. That was the first line of proof.

We come then to those verses already read. What is arresting here is that Paul twice used the words, "according to the Scriptures." What Scriptures? There was no New Testament then. He was not referring to what we call our New Testament. He was referring to those Scriptures which he knew so well, which his son in the faith, Timothy, had known from a babe, that were able to make him wise unto salvation. Paul was referring to our Old Testament, for Paul had no other Scriptures. There may have been some of the Gospels in circulation, though it is doubtful that any were in wide circulation then. No, these were the Hebrew Scriptures of his boyhood, the Scriptures of the Jew. He quoted them twice over, and it is remarkable how often Paul quoted them. Going through his letters, we find he refers to "the Scriptures" fourteen times, and he always quoted them as authoritative, never once calling them in question as to authority.

That may lead to a little speculation or imagining. I can see Paul travelling among the Gentiles, going through Greek cities where they had no Bible, taking these Scriptures, and basing upon them the great Christian message which he had to deliver, so that when he wrote to these people he could refer to the Scriptures as authoritative. They must have heard him often in Corinth, and seen him taking some parchment, some part of the Old Testament, unrolling it, and showing how it had found fulfilment in his Lord and Master. It is very beautiful to see he quoted the Scriptures and referred to them.

What did he mean by saying that the Scriptures foretold the death of Christ and His resurrection? Think on a big scale. There is no text in the Bible but that needs the whole Bible to interpret it. Take the whole Bible, and there was a general testimony of expectation. The first gleam of light came from God to the mother in the Garden, spoken rather in her hearing to the arch enemy of the race. The woman's seed shall bruise thy head, and thou shalt bruise his heel. Poetic, infinite in suggestiveness. There is a day of triumph coming, said that ancient promise, but it will be triumph through travail. Go on and take your way through all the writings, psalms, prophets, and teachers in the Old Testament, and see how constantly that expectation of deliverance is seen to be wrought out through travail that proceeds to triumph. Read the 22nd psalm, read the 53rd chapter of Isaiah, read the opening sentences in the 6th chapter of Hosea. In every one we see the same thing.

Take the 53rd chapter of Isaiah. It is the coming triumph of the Servant of the Lord through travail, death, and yet resurrection; triumph coming after travail. Paul says, That is the Gospel I preached to you, that had been the hope and expectation of the writers of the past. According to the Scriptures He died. According to the Scriptures He rose, and these Scriptures thus became evidence of the truth of the resurrection, especially in the light of the Gospel and its effect produced upon the lives of those to whom Paul was writing. That was the second line of proof.

Come to the third, the witnesses. Paul has not exhausted the list, but has taken representative names. He actually appeared, the risen Christ, Jesus Who died, and was buried, and rose. He was seen after the death, after the burial, after the resurrection, He was seen alive. He was seen of Cephas. Read the post-resurrection stories of the appearances of Jesus. Peter was one of the very first to see Him. The women, some of them were the first, and to them the angel said, "Go, tell His disciples, and Peter." Peter went to see Him, and they had a private interview. When the two came back from walking to Emmaus, and the disciples greeted them, they said, "The Lord is risen indeed, and hath appeared unto Simon." Paul quoted him, the man who began his letter, which Paul had not seen then, "Blessed be the God and Father of our Lord Jesus Christ, Who according to His great mercy begat us again unto a living hope by the resurrection of Jesus Christ from the dead."

Then Paul named the twelve twice. We know the story of how He appeared to them on two occasions in the Gospel narratives. Paul next says He appeared "to above five hundred brethren at once," of whom the great majority remained until that day. We ask, Have we any account of that in the Gospels? While one cannot be dogmatic, I think we have. He said to the women to tell His disciples to go into Galilee, where they should see Him. There was a journey for those women and those whom they told, away up in Galilee; and I think as they went the news spread, scores and hundreds, five hundred disciples of Jesus, perhaps frightened by the Cross, gathered to Him, and five hundred of them saw Him. It must have been a marvellous gathering. Paul has given illustrations of the demonstration of the fact of His resurrection by the attestation of those who actually saw Him after He had risen. He names James, but we have no account of that appearing to him, as He had appeared to Cephas, and as the twelve saw Him.

Then he says, "last of all . . . to me also." There is Paul's definite claim that he had seen Jesus after His resurrection. We all know that matchless story. If there is one great individual proof of the resurrection, standing out from among the rest, it is Paul. Paul saw Him, who certainly did not expect to see Him, who certainly was amazed beyond measure when he did see Him; and not only was the vision unexpected and amazing, it was absolutely revolutionary. The man's whole life was changed by the vision of the risen Lord. It is interesting to remember that after he had been to Damascus, he went into Arabia, and was there two years, probably three. What was he doing? He was under the shadow of Mount Sinai, from whence the law had come, reconsidering it all in the light of the resurrection of the Christ. Then he went back to Jerusalem for a transitory visit, and then he passed away to Tarsus, and was there ten years before he began his preaching, before he began his great apostolic ministry; but it was that appearing that had inspired it; "He appeared to me also."

It is very beautiful what it had done for him. Jesus had produced in him an appalling sense of the failure and wickedness of the past. "Last of all, as unto one born out of due time, He appeared to me also. For I am the least of the apostles, that am not meet to be called an apostle, because I persecuted the Church of God." He is looking back at it. Oh, the terror of it! Of course, he had watched Stephen's death, and when he was going down, armed with the high priest's letters to Damascus, Jesus had appeared to him, and his whole life was changed. Then, after the language that speaks of a profound humiliation, "I persecuted the Church of God," he breaks out into exultant and triumphant words, "But by the grace of God I am what I am." That does not merely mean he owed everything to grace. It does mean that; but it means also he had paid his debt, he had yielded to grace.

Then he goes on. I did not receive the grace of God in vain. I yielded to Him, and it mastered me. What was he? A Jew first, but a Greek by upbringing, and a Roman citizen—"But by the grace of God I am what I am." What I am is the supreme proof of the value and power of the Gospel that I heard, and that came to me through the appearance at the beginning. However this began, whether it be

I or they, whether it be either prophet, teacher, or evangelist, so we preach, and so ye believed.

The resurrection is the great central fact to Christian faith and experience. It is that fact of the resurrection that becomes the rock, the anchorage of faith in the meaning of the death; and it is that fact of the resurrection which produces an effect upon experience, so that we are saved, so that we stand.

It has been justly said that this fifteenth chapter is one of the deepest, and in some senses, the most mysterious in the Bible, using that word "mysterious" in the New Testament sense of the word, which does not mean something incomprehensible, but revelation. We have seen the reason for this whole section, which is found in the opening verse of this paragraph (verses 12–34), "Now if Christ is preached that He hath been raised from the dead, how say some among you that there is no resurrection of the dead?" There were evidently those in the Corinthian church who had taken up that attitude, and were denying the fact of resurrection generally. Here we must remember the Corinthian atmosphere in which this church existed, and in which she had been called upon by God in His great grace, to be in fellowship with His Son in His business in Corinth.

In this Corinthian atmosphere these Christian people found certain lines of supposedly philosophic teaching and outlook upon life. We but refer to them without discussing them. There were three views held by the Corinthian teachers and philosophers: Epicureanism, Stoicism, and Platonism. These were three distinct schools of philosophy, and they all held certain views on this subject of resurrection. The position of the Epicurean was that of blank materialism. He denied any existence at all beyond death. The position of the Stoic was that at death the soul was merged in Deity, and so the loss of personality. Third, there was Platonism, which insisted upon the immortality of the soul, but absolutely denied the idea of bodily resurrection.

This Corinthian church existed in a city permeated with this teaching, and had imbibed it in some measure or degree. We may be safe in saying that the view taken by some members of the Corinthian church was the last, rather than the first or second, that is, a belief in the immortality of the soul which denied a bodily resurrection, a continuity of personality, but no resurrection. That undoubtedly was the peculiar view to which Paul referred here, "How say some among you that there is no resurrection of the dead?"

In the first eleven verses of the chapter he had dealt with the subject, the resurrection of Christ. In the presence of this view he brought the Corinthian Christians back face to face with the resurrection of

Christ, by giving them three lines of proof. The first was the Gospel in itself, and the effects it produced in them. That is the final proof that Jesus rose from the dead, the effects produced by the Gospel in the lives of men and women constituting the Church. Then he passed on to show the proof of the Scriptures, the Old Testament, notably certain great passages that stand out, Isaiah liii, Psalm xxii, or the opening part of Hosea vi. The whole outlook of the Old Testament Scriptures reveals a hope of a victory, that there should come somehow to humanity through travail a great triumph. In other words, they were looking for death, but they were looking also for resurrection in some form. Whereas it may be one cannot find in the Old Testament any very definite tabulated reference to resurrection, one goes back to the language of Job, and we are justified in so doing. But the great fact is that He rose, according to the Scriptures. Then the final proof was that he massed the witnesses, those who actually saw Jesus after His resurrection—Cephas, and the twelve, and five hundred brethren at once, and James, and last of all Paul also.

Now, still further, in this paragraph he emphasizes the importance of Christ's resurrection. In our next paragraph he went beyond the fact of Christ's resurrection. However, here he brought these Corinthian people back to the fact of Christ's resurrection, showing the importance of that fact, and the importance of the truth of that fact, in three movements: first of all, the importance of Christ's resurrection in regard to our salvation (12–19); then the importance of Christ's resurrection in regard to the programme of God (20–28); and finally the importance of Christ's resurrection in regard to our present conduct (29–34).

Take that first section. What is Paul declaring there? That to deny the resurrection of Christ is to deny the fact of resurrection at all, and then it is to invalidate the whole Christian message and experience. He is telling them if Christ be not risen, then our preaching is vain, void. That is the meaning of the word *vain* there, void, empty, there is no value in it, no meaning in it, no truth in it.

Moreover, he says, when we preached that Gospel, we were false witnesses, we were lying about God. We have declared God raised Him from the dead, and if He was not raised, then what we have said is untrue.

And, finally, "your faith also is vain," the faith you professed. That is to say, if Christ be not raised, that invalidates the whole Christian message, and the whole Christian experience. You were fastening your faith upon unreality. We see how basic this fact of the resurrection is to the Christian faith and message, and that is what the apostle is teaching.

He then summed up. If our faith is vain, what then? Sin remains. "Ye are yet in your sins." What does that mean? That Christ's death was a failure. Hope is deferred or destroyed. What does that mean? That Christ's promises were all false, and the whole superstructure of the Christian faith and experience goes to pieces; it is false entirely if Christ did not rise. That is his first line in this application, showing the importance and value of the resurrection. Those who have fallen asleep in Christ also are perished, and if in this life only we have hoped in Him, we are of all men most miserable, pitiable is the better translation; because our hope was so great, so bright, so full of glory; if it is all put out, we are in darkness, we are to be pitied. Our faith is destroyed and our hope also, which means that if Christ did not rise, then whatever His intentions may have been, they were not fulfilled. He failed to deal with sin, and if Christ be not raised, all the promises in Him of life for evermore break down, and we are of all men most pitiable.

At the twentieth verse he says, "But." All these things are suppositions, and fair suppositions, logical suppositions. "But" they are all groundless, says Paul. There is no ground for any such view. There is no ground for thinking for a single moment that preaching is vain, and faith is vain, and hope is destroyed. "But." What? "But now hath Christ been raised from the dead," just a plain, glorious, definite affirmation. All those suppositions were not true. There was no reason for them. Christ had been raised from the dead. A great cry that, the confident assurance of faith, in answer to all these speculations of unbelief, those we have referred to, and those imbibed by the Corinthian Christians who were denying the fact of resurrection. This is the answer of faith, and it is based upon the fact that the Corinthian Christians and all Christians are living, not in the conditions in which they would have been living if Christ had not been raised. They are not yet in their sins. Hope has not perished. They have known what it is to be loosed from their sins, and that is experience again. We are back again on the value of experience, and the ultimate proof of the affirmation that Christ is raised. No, our faith was not a mirage, a humbug, a phantasy. He had been raised, and the first line of proof is there; the conditions in which the Corinthian and all Christian people find themselves demonstrate it. We are not yet in our sins. Hope has not perished. Hope abides.

Then going on, Paul dealt with this great fact, by showing its relationship to the programme of God. He surveys this in a few sentences. We miss a great deal if we miss the sweep of his outlook. He surveys the whole sweep of human history. He did this more than once in remarkable applications. "In Adam." He has gone back to the very beginning of human history. What is the history? "In Adam all die." What a sentence it is! How true it is! How they are led to look back at the programme of God and see that fact, " In the day that thou eatest thereof thou shalt surely die," and in the day that man ate of the forbidden fruit taken from the sacramental tree that marked the limitation of his liberty, under the government of God, he died. Oh, what is the stupid remark? He did not die? The devil said that. He died then spiritually. He was severed from his fellowship with God. Death is the fiat of Divine judgment on sin. Men were dead, living there while he was teaching and preaching. " In Adam all die."

But here, said he, is a new beginning. Here is the " last Adam," the second Man. The word Adam there is used in the sense of headship of a race, the one from whom the race springs. But God's second Man was the *last* Adam. If we say second Adam, we presuppose the possibility of a third Adam, another from whom a race shall spring. There will be none such. It is " first Adam " and " last Adam."

What does relationship with Him mean? In the programme of God all are to be made alive in Christ. We have no right to take that and make it apply apart from the relating phrase, " in Christ." If we are not " in Christ " we are still " in Adam," and death is the ultimate. If we are in Christ, we are in the place of life.

Then Paul traced the process. Everything will happen in order, " Christ the firstfruits." That is the first resurrection, the great resurrection. Afterwards, " they that are Christ's, at His coming," at His parousia, at His presence, " at His coming." Two great resurrections are in view, the individual resurrection of our Lord Himself, the last Adam emerging from the tomb victorious over sin and sorrow and death. He the Firstfruits.

Then he sweeps the centuries again. We have not arrived yet. I am not trying to find out when, but at last it is coming, the resurrection of all His own in the programme of God. It is all linked to the resurrection of Christ. Christ the firstfruits, and in Him as the firstfruits the evidence, the proof, the assurance that all in Him shall not only live in the spiritual sense, but shall come with Him into the place of the mystery and wonder and glory of the resurrection, at His coming.

Then it always seems to me as though Paul could not stop. He looked on again. He has gone back to the beginning of human history. He has swept the dying centuries. He has swept on to the ultimate resurrection, and he could not stop, but has gone on and says, " Then," after that great resurrection, at His coming, " Then cometh the end." Here in this little paragraph that needs thoughtful consideration we have a glance furthest ahead of any glance in the Bible. This is beyond the second coming, and we have this marvellous declaration, "Then cometh the end, when He shall deliver up the Kingdom of God, even the Father; when He shall have abolished all rule and all authority and power. For He must reign, till He hath put all His enemies under His feet." He must reign *till!* Do not merely think of the fact that He is going to reign by and by. That of course is true in a certain sense. We sing,

> "Jesus shall reign, where'er the sun
> Doth his successive journeys run."

We have a perspective outlook, and a very blessed one. But it is not only true that He shall reign. He is reigning now. He must reign till He put all enemies under His feet. While the enemies are there, while these forces of evil are rampant, He is reigning. The fact remains that God has given to Him a name that is above every name, and has highly exalted Him. Before He left this earthly scene He said, "All authority hath been given unto Me in heaven and on earth," all authority; and the Man at God's right hand, the risen and ascended Lord, is King. He is King today. But there will come a time when He will deliver up the Kingdom. In what sense will He do so? Only in one. He will deliver up what we may accurately describe as the mediatorial Kingdom, when His work of mediation is completed, and it is not completed yet, for "He ever liveth to make intercession for us." He is still our Mediator between God and man; but the time will come when all involved in mediatorial Kingship will be accomplished. "Then cometh the end," and then He will "deliver up the Kingdom of God, even the Father . . . that God may be all in all." But till then He must reign, and all the truth of that depends entirely upon the resurrection. If He did not rise He did not ascend. If He did not ascend He is not reigning. If indeed He died as other men die, and did not emerge from death victorious and supernaturally, then until this very moment His ashes are mixed somewhere in Syrian soil still, and the whole Church of God is false and a humbug. Oh, may I be forgiven for suggesting such a thing; but Paul is doing so here. There is the great fact, and the whole programme of God for humanity circles around, and centres in, as to its ultimate accomplishment, the fact of the resurrection.

So we turn to the last paragraph. "Else," if all this is not so, "Else what shall they do which are baptized for the dead?" If the things Paul has been saying are not so, he asks several questions. What will it profit them if they are baptized for the dead? Here we are in the presence of a difficulty which lacks any final, positive, and dogmatic interpretation. Many attempts have been made to explain what Paul meant. It has been suggested that someone died, and another filled the gap in the ranks, and were baptized for them, and carried on their work. Personally, I cannot see there is any point in that view. Certainly the apostle was referring to some custom current at the time, and Paul uses it as an argument, but he does not justify that particular custom, whatever it was. There were those who were baptized for the dead. Possibly there had entered into their thinking, that if a man had believed, and yet had not been baptized, that it was necessary for someone to take his place and submit to the rite of baptism. One cannot be dogmatic, but quite evidently a rite was being practiced. Paul takes it. He does not say whether it is right or wrong. He does not justify it, but he names it, and asks what is the use of being baptized for the dead, if they are not raised. He takes this illustration, the uselessness of the rite if there be no resurrection.

Then he comes to that which is more evident. Why should we endure suffering? It is emphatic. Why should we stand in jeopardy every hour? As they did literally. He was in danger daily, "I die daily." He had fought with beasts at Ephesus. What is the use of it all if the dead are not raised? Then he summarizes in the language of the Epicureans, "Let us eat and drink, for tomorrow we die." That is exactly what the Epicureans were saying. Let us enter into life with all its experiences. Let us eat and drink, and give full rein to license, to every desire of the flesh; it is all right. We shall die tomorrow. If we are right, and there is no resurrection, let yourselves go, and give up this standing in jeopardy, give up these rites, whether correct or not, that express our belief in resurrection, and let us settle down to materialism. "Let us eat and drink, for tomorrow we die."

Then, finally, Paul says, "Be not deceived," and uses that remarkable declaration, "Bad company doth corrupt good manners," good dispositions, good thinking. They had been in the wrong company, listening to the wrong teaching. That makes for the corruption of your thinking and your manners. He calls them from the state of mental intoxication and drugging into which they had passed. He says, "Awake" from your drunkenness. It is a sharp rebuke. He says, "I speak this to move you to shame." Here emerges the great teaching that materialization of thinking is due to wrong fellowship. They had been in the wrong company, had been listening to the wrong teachers. That goes on today.

As we study this section we see how the spiritual in life is maintained by the outlook created by the abiding sense of the resurrection and our relationship thereto; because that view maintains the true interpretation of personality as being more than material, as being continuous, and as passing through the mystery and marvel of death into resurrection, and to a larger and fuller life that lies beyond.

iii. Intellectual Difficulties	xv. 35–57
a. The Two Questions	35
b. The Two Answers	36–50
iv. The Assurance and Challenge	51–57
a. The Assurance	51–54
b. The Challenge	55–57

I CORINTHIANS xv. 35–57

THIS is our second study in this great resurrection chapter. As in our previous consideration, we remind ourselves that the reason of this section is discovered in the twelfth verse of this chapter, in which Paul said, "How say some among you that there is no resurrection of the dead?" It was that fact known to the apostle that drew forth the whole of this wonderful section on the subject of the resurrection. It is quite evident that there were those in the Corinthian church who were influenced by the materialistic philosophy of Corinthian philosophers and teachers, the Epicureans, the Stoics, and the Platonists.

Now, the purpose of the apostle throughout this section was to correct these false views and teaching by constructive exposition. In the first two movements we have seen that he laid emphasis on the fact of the resurrection of our Lord, gathering the proofs, and showing the importance of it. Now he briefly turned aside to discuss the possibility of resurrection on the grounds of reason. In the beginning of the letter, when declaring the foolishness of the wisdom of this age, he had said, "Howbeit we speak wisdom, yet not of this age." That is to say, the philosophers were teaching what was supposed to be wisdom. But we have a philosophy, he said. We teach wisdom, but it is not of this age. It is not bounded by this age. It is something larger than any teaching that is of this age.

In this paragraph we shall see that Paul turned aside to show, in one sense, the wisdom that is not of this age, but which is possessed by the preachers of the Gospel, the teachers of the way of Christ. This paragraph divides itself quite naturally into two parts. The first is only a verse, asking two questions (35), and the rest (36–50) consists of the answers to these questions. The answers are not *seriatim,* because in his answer he keeps the two questions in mind all the way through.

What were the two questions? They are very revealing. Paul says, "But some one will say, How are the dead raised?" Secondly, "With what manner of body do they come?" As a matter of fact, the second question reveals the unbelief in the fact of the resurrection, and accounts for the first question, "How are the dead raised?" We notice that these questions are concerned with the manner, rather than with the fact, of resurrection. The fact is denied, because the manner is not understood. It is the manner, "How?" "With what body?" While the two questions in themselves are concerned with the manner of resurrection, they reveal the reason in the mind of the thinker who asks them, for denying the fact of the resurrection. To summarize that, inability to comprehend the manner or the method of the resurrection has resulted in a denial of its possibility. No, we cannot understand how, and therefore we do not believe the thing can take place. That is to put the matter bluntly, but that is what the questions mean.

Let us look at the questions. The first, "How?" It is quite simple. There is no need of exposition. It means, How? In what way are the dead raised up? In what way? Death is seen as the disintegration of the body. That is what these people were saying. Someone died, and immediately the process of disintegration set in; and soon that whole body will be dust, or resolved into the elements, and scattered. The disintegration of the body is seen. How can that body, disintegrated as it so evidently is, however can it be so reconstructed? How? It is quite a simple question, a natural question. *Natural* is the right word. I have heard people ask it today. They ask this very question in the presence of the great teaching of the New Testament about resurrection, whether it be the resurrection of Christ or of His people, or resurrection at all, it does not matter. They ask this question, How can it be? Go through the length and breadth of the land, and look at the graveyards, and think of the bodies there, they are gone. How can there be reconstruction?

Then the second question, emphasizing the difficulties of the first, "With what body?" What sort of body? It is a sort of exclamation, to imagine the dead rising. What will they be like? With what manner of body do they come? This is the emphasis, explaining the How. How is it done? We have seen their bodies disintegrate, scattered. How are they going to be gathered together, and what will they be like when they are gathered together? We see the deduction in the mind of those who asked such questions was that the resurrection is a question. There can be no resurrection. There can be no gathering together of those disintegrated bodies. One cannot imagine bodies resulting from that, and therefore there are those who say there is no resurrection.

Paul now set himself to answer the questions. Notice his first words, "Thou foolish one." The revisers have softened that, and made it a little more polite. The old Version had it, "Thou fool." I am not quarrelling with the change. If you are a fool, you are foolish! But Paul is looking with contempt upon those people who were raising some difficulty and making deductions, and were expressing themselves in these questions. "Thou foolish one," he shows his contempt for their thinking. Then he keeps the two questions together, and begins with that most remarkable illustration from Nature (36–38). Notice he says, "A bare grain," a naked grain, a simple grain of wheat, or of some other kind. Take that simple grain in your hand and look at it, says Paul. There it is. You put it in the ground and it dies; but it comes again, but not the body you put into the ground, but a new body. And yet, in some infinite wonder and mystery, that new body that you see coming up has come out of the old body. The old body, the bare grain—keep that in mind—is put into the ground, and it comes again, and the quickening into life is the result of the dying. There would be no coming again of that grain except through death, and yet through death there is the mystery resulting from the putting of that grain into the earth.

I have heard people say that it is not quite fair to take the spring season of the year, when first the blade and then the ear and then the full corn in the ear appear, and make it typical of the resurrection; but that is exactly what Paul has done here. He asks us to look at Nature, and says, in effect, There is no greater mystery in the resurrection of the human body than in the coming again of the new manifestation of life of a bare grain. He said, You foolish one, if you are going to stand and say, There are mysteries here I cannot fathom, therefore I do not believe in resurrection, then you may say you do not believe in the harvest, which is the result of the sowing of bare grains, because you do not understand the process. I declare it here and now, on the authority of the Holy Word of God, there is no greater mystery than when you put into the ground a seed that presently comes back in new life; and there is no greater mystery in the resurrection of the body than there is in that of the coming again of the bare grain that dies, with the new body.

You say, That does not solve it. Of course it does not, but it faces the fact of the mystery. It sees that in this realm over which God reigns supremely for evermore there is a unity. What we can see any day if we take a bare grain and watch results coming from it is the working of God.

He now says, "God giveth it a body even as it pleased Him, and to each seed a body of its own." Now the mystery is solved, but the mystery remains, but the fact is self-evident. Keep your eye on the grain. Look at the grain put into the earth now, and presently look at the harvest. Look how that one grain has come back and taken on a new life, a new body in some infinite mystery, out of the old. Well, what shall we do with the mystery? Put God at the back of it. "God giveth it a body." There is the little seed that we put into the ground, or take that dry, curious looking bulb that some put into the ground, look at it, withered, dead. Dead? Wait, and presently see the springing leaves, and presently see the flowers, and the new life. How is that done? "God giveth it a body," and so all the vast expanses of the harvest fields of earth are an eternal witness to the activity of God, taking hold of death, and transmuting it into life, giving to the bare grain a new body, something different. That is the solution of the mystery. "How are the dead raised?" "God giveth it a body." What that means who shall tell except in the results that are seen, and will be seen in the resurrection, manifest in those who are raised from the dead?

We have not seen that yet. Oh, yes, we have, in One, "the Firstfruits," Christ Himself. And at once there opens up that whole subject. Go through the New Testament, and ponder carefully and not hurriedly the stories of Jesus after the resurrection, and notice the new body. Oh, it is the old one in a sense; but it is not, it is entirely new, not subject to the laws that bound that body before, which God had prepared for His Son for the accomplishment of His purposes in the world. There we see it. Now Paul took that simple, natural thing, and said, in effect, There is no more difficulty in believing in the resurrection of the human body than the resurrection of the bare grain put into the earth. Behind the coming back of the grain and the human form, in new forms, is God. "God giveth it a body."

That led Paul aside as he drew attention to the infinite variety of the work of God. Keep in mind the previous statement, "God giveth it a body." Paul looked out at the differing forms there are of bodies. On the earthly level there is one flesh of man, one of beasts, one of birds, and one of fishes. It is the creation of a body. It is not resurrection. "God giveth it a body." Look round and see the infinite variety in the work of God.

Then he made the broad distinction. There are bodies celestial, bodies fitted for the skies; and terrestrial bodies. Whether he is referring to bodies of man, beast, bird, or fish, the bodies now, or bodies he is about to refer to, I think both are true.

He then climbs into the stellar spaces, and without giving any detailed description, he says there is the sun, moon, and stars, all having their own peculiar glory, all the work of God. He gives the body of man, of beast and bird and fish; the sun, moon and stars. The body is always the medium of the revelation of something superior to it, and dwelling within it, and showing through it, whether it be man or beast or bird or fish; whether sun, moon or stars. The great thing however is this, God has done it. Do not limit God. We ask, What sort of body? Look out upon the variety that is found in this world, and in the universe, all the work of God, and though we cannot imagine that resurrection body, if we remember it is God's work, we shall be able to believe in the fact of it.

Paul then takes these things, and applies them. " So " is the resurrection body, and we have that wonderful little passage, " It is sown in corruption; it is raised in incorruption; it is sown in dishonour, it is raised in glory; it is sown in weakness; it is raised in power." Take those first words all through, and we have seen all that as we have stood by the grave of our loved ones. What have we seen as we have gone back and visited that grave? Corruption? That is true of every human body. Death brings corruption, dishonour; however ornate we may make the funeral, we have to hurry the body away. It is a case of dishonour. Weakness? Of course, absolute weakness. Corruption means decay and withering away. Dishonour means just what it says. Weakness means feebleness. Paul said, That is the body put into the ground, but the body that will come with resurrection contradicts all those things. First of all, incorruption, that is, undecaying, an immortal body. Dishonour as we bury, but in the resurrection, glory, something to be honoured. Weakness, absolute weakness, the uttermost in weakness, feebleness in power; but in the resurrection power, force, dynamic.

Then Paul says this, There is " a natural body," " a spiritual body." Take two other words, and what did he really say? He said there is a psychic body and there is a pneumatic body. The word pneumatic is today used in other realms, which is unfortunate, but pneumatic is really the Anglecizing of the Greek word here, and behind that word is the word *pneuma,* spirit. The psychic body is the natural body, that is, the body soul-governed, mastered by the life element. But the spiritual body is the body spirit-governed, no longer a body under the mastery of the mere animal life that is ours in this world. But the body that shall be under the complete control and mastery of the spiritual essence, that will be the resurrection body. Paul puts his emphasis here, " If there is a natural body, there is also a spiritual body."

As already referred to, take the post-resurrection stories, that going into the garden, that walk to Emmaus, the appearance in the upper room, that meeting of the disciples in Galilee; go through them and watch Jesus, reverently I use the human name; because it is the same Personality, but entirely different, on a different plane of human life. It is well to remember that up to that time there had never been a resurrection at all. We search the Old Testament in vain. We find resuscitation. Lazarus was not a resurrection. It was a resuscitation. There was brought back the spirit life to the actual same body, but the body was still under the laws of the earthly. "First that which is earthly." Lazarus was brought back to that. Our Lord had passed beyond that. He had come into the possession of the heavenly body; hence doors need not be opened; hence, if He so desired, He was not known; hence He was able to make Himself known. All those mystic and wonderful stories are revelations of the body celestial, the spirit-governed body, no longer mastered by that which is merely the animal life, the soul-governed body; no longer the psychic, but the pneumatic; no longer the soul-governed, but the spirit-governed, that is, resurrection.

Paul then showed, with that great sweep over history again, how it all came about. The first man Adam was made a living soul. Yes, we are told, "The Lord God . . . breathed into his breathing places the breath of lives; and man became a living soul." This last Adam is different, and He is different in the way of resurrection. He is not only in Himself a living One, He is "a life-giving spirit." Paul is showing the relationship we bear is first to the natural, that is, to human life, as it has descended from Adam. Then if we are Christian the earthly will be followed by the heavenly, and into the full glorious, completely orbed realization of that we shall come at the resurrection, and not until that resurrection.

So he concluded everything with stating the new conditions. " Flesh and blood [a phrase that describes the soul-governing body] cannot inherit the Kingdom of God" in its ultimate; but only the spiritual body, and that God will prepare in the resurrection.

This whole section is intended to show and does show the reasonableness of the resurrection. Keep that bare grain in mind. The resurrection is reasonable when the universe is seen as God-centred and human life is seen as related to God. Then the difficulty passes away. Still there are things that are beyond our ken. We may still say, How? and With what body? but the answer that is full and final and satisfactory, if we believe in God, is this, "God giveth it a body, even as it pleased Him."

Here in verses 51–57 we have the culmination of the great section dealing with resurrection.

In the course of this argument Paul spoke of Christ as "the Firstfruits," and "they that are Christ's at His coming." That phrase is separated in its application by at least 1944 years. How many more I do not know, and am not asking to know. The resurrection of Christ—the resurrection of the saints. The years 1944 have passed away, looking on these things from the standpoint of human almanacs and calendars. The whole fact of resurrection is in the phrase, "Christ the Firstfruits, then they that are Christ's at His coming." Christ's coming, and Christ's resurrection. Christ's coming, and the saints' resurrection. Those are the boundaries of our Christian faith, and Christian experience, and Christian hope, and Christian life. As Paul put it when he was writing one of those short epistles which we call pastoral, "The grace of God hath appeared." That was the beginning, the epiphany; and he says, the glory shall appear. The Christian age, and the Christian experience and campaign are bounded by these things, the first and the second coming. The consummation of the first coming was when Christ rose from the dead; and the consummation at the second coming will be that the saints shall be raised. That has been seen in the earlier part of the chapter. All through he had insisted upon and emphasized that first fact—Christ's resurrection.

Now, in what is comparatively a brief and yet marvellous paragraph, Paul looks on to the consummation, the resurrection of the saints at His second coming, at His presence. Our attention is directed to that great consummation. Having stressed the resurrection of Christ as the Firstfruits, he closes with the resurrection of the saints as harvest. The Firstfruits, the risen Christ. The harvest, the resurrection of the saints. This paragraph may be divided into three sections. It really ends with verse 57, so far as resurrection is concerned. First, the assurance (51–54); then the consequent challenge, the great ringing challenge to death (55–57). Then we have one other verse (58) which is the ultimate appeal of the whole letter, based not merely upon the great doctrine of resurrection, though closely allied to that, but also going much farther back in the letter.

Take first the assurance. Notice how Paul introduced this in an arresting way. "Behold." It is a challenging word that means, Now think, now look, now ponder. "Behold," here is something I have to say to you that demands your close attention, and Paul certainly meant to arrest our wandering attention. "Behold, I tell you a mystery." A mystery in the New Testament, and in Christian faith and doctrine, never means something that cannot be understood. It always means something that man by intellectual effort cannot find out; but it means something that is revealed, and that man can apprehend, because it is revealed. Now, says Paul, "Behold, I tell you a mystery," I tell you something you will never find out by the process of reasoning, that you will never discover by the searching of the intellect. It is a mystery, but I tell it to you. There is the emphasis—I declare it, I tell it.

What is the mystery? It is this, "We shall all be changed." That is the mystery in itself. That is the sum totality of it. We shall be changed. We have been looking at the resurrection in the previous part of the chapter. In the case of the analogy we saw how the seed is changed; so the body will be changed. "We shall all be changed." That is the great wonder, the mystery; but it is declared to you, says Paul. I tell it to you, I announce it to you, that life is not always to continue as we are living it now. We shall be changed. Something will happen, and the something will be within our own personality. We shall continue. Our personalities will continue, but very differently. "We shall be changed." That assumes the whole fact of the resurrection. Notice that Paul says we shall not all sleep when we shall all be changed. That to which he looks forward is an event which will take place in time. There are people who will be living, but many will have passed on to the life beyond. The change will come in the midst of ordinary things. There are those who will be alive. One can see how this opens up much food for thought. There are those here in London, in the villages, on the highways, and on the sea, here and there going about their ordinary avocations, just living life on the human level. "We shall all be changed."

But this event will take place in the ordinary processes of life, on the human level. We shall not all sleep. There are those who will be alive when this great complete change takes place.

Then this wonderful description of the method: "In a moment, in the twinkling of an eye, at the last trump; for the trumpet shall sound, and the dead shall be raised." Notice that Paul does not tell us when. The New Testament never tells us when this will happen. We are always to live on the border line of this event. It may take place before this day is over. May the Lord lead us into the patient waiting for Christ, not impatient. Yet have we not felt it day after day, what a thing it would be if this took place now, if He came. The resurrection will take place at the exact and right moment in the economy and purpose and programme of God. No date is named, but the fact; and it will be sudden.

One cannot refrain from going over to another of Paul's letters, written, as I believe, earlier than that to the Corinthians, and I think he had that in mind when he wrote this paragraph. In the letter to the Thessalonians (1. iv. 13–18) he wrote this:

"But we would not have you ignorant, brethren, concerning them that fall asleep; that ye sorrow not, even as the rest, which have no hope. For if we believe that Jesus died and rose again, even so them also that are fallen asleep in Jesus will God bring with Him. For this we say unto you by the word of the Lord, that we that are alive, that are left at the coming of the Lord, shall in no wise precede them that are fallen asleep. For the Lord Himself shall descend from heaven, with a shout, with the voice of the archangel, and with the trump of God; and the dead in Christ shall rise first; then we that are alive, that are left, shall together with them be caught up in the clouds, to meet the Lord in the air; and so shall we ever be with the Lord. Wherefore comfort one another with these words."

We see how closely related that is to this briefer statement:

"We shall not all sleep, but we shall all be changed, in a moment, in the twinkling of an eye, at the last trump; for the trumpet shall sound, and the dead shall be raised incorruptible, and we shall be changed. For this corruptible must put on incorruption, and this mortal must put on immortality."

There is the victory. There is the change, the change from corruption. That is the story of our lives. The word has no pleasant sound. It has no pleasant meaning, but we all know the process of corruption, even now. We are dying while we live. Oh, do not let that sound dolorous. It is a fact. Some of you can hardly believe it, and I do not blame you. You do not feel like dying. I do! I am quite sure of it. The pins are being loosened. The tent is being taken down. The virility has almost ceased, and is no more. Dying, corruption; there is no cure for it. But then this corruptible will put on incorruption. No more failure, no more dying. Death will be swallowed up in victory in that great and wondrous hour. That will be the hour when death ends. Death ended for our blessed Lord when He rose. Again I quote Paul, because it is so apropos to this thought. He says in his letter to the Romans, " Knowing that Christ being raised from the dead dieth no more, death no more hath dominion over Him. For the death that He died, He died unto sin once; but the life that He liveth, He liveth unto God." That is the resurrection of Christ, and that is the story of our resurrection. We shall die no more. We shall be changed into that new order of life; our personalities continuing in those bodies that God will prepare for us, which are superearthly, supernatural. That is what Paul was looking forward to here, the end of death for Him, and if it be so, for us also.

He then broke out, " When this corruptible shall have put on incorruption, and this mortal shall have put on immortality, then [and not till then] shall have come to pass the saying that is written, Death is swallowed up in victory." That will be the complete triumph over death. Then death is ended in that final hour of resurrection.

Then he broke out, " O death, where is thy victory? O death, where is thy sting? " I think I am familiar with the reason why the revisers have changed that. The Old Version read, " O death, where is thy sting? O grave, where is thy victory? " The revisers have put the word " death " in twice, evidently the result of an opinion based

THE CORINTHIAN LETTERS OF PAUL 203

upon the comparison of certain differing Greek texts. Taking Westcott & Hort's and Nestlé's Greek text, we find that the word "death" occurs twice. But if we go back, as the Authorized translators did, to the *Textus Receptus,* we find they used the words "death" and "grave," or Hades. Who am I that I should express an opinion against the view of Westcott & Hort or Nestlé. I do, however, express the opinion, and I think they were wrong. I think the old *Textus Receptus* was right. How does it read there in the actual Greek sentence? "Where of thee, O Death, the sting? Where of thee, O Hades, the victory?" There is a double challenge. Hades, of course, may mean death, but it refers to the whole region of death, the place of the dead, the place of departed spirits, the land of shadows, they called it. I think here the apostle was using those words. He was challenging death itself, and the region and the shadow of death, Hades. Whether Hades or death, perhaps it really does not matter. We have the double challenge, death itself and the grave, the place of the shadows, the place to which the dead pass.

Paul inquires first, Where is the sting of death, where is the victory of the grave? The question abides, Where?

He proceeds to tell us that the sting of death is sin. It always is. There would be no such thing as the fear of death if there were no sin. The sting, the thing that fills the heart with fear and foreboding, is that of sin. Then that remarkable declaration, the strength or power of sin is the law; and because of that we are all our lifetime subject to bondage. Paul is not dwelling upon that. He is challenging it, laughing at it. "O death, where is thy sting? O grave, where is thy victory?" No, the victory is not with you, Death; the victory is not with the grave. "Thanks be to God, which giveth us the victory through our Lord Jesus Christ." What a glorious and daring challenge that is!

We are tempted to dwell there upon the whole outlook on death. The outlook on death is created always by the long view that sees the resurrection. If that is seen, and seen as the ultimate, not death the ultimate but the resurrection, then what a light and a glory it sheds on the way. I never read that without thinking of Bishop Taylor's little poem. I love the challenge of it, in which he seems to have caught up the apostolic challenge:

> "Death, the old serpent's son,
> Thou hadst a sting once, like thy sire,
> That carried hell and ever burning fire;
> But those black days are done;
> Thy foolish spite buried thy sting
> In the profound and wide

> Wound of our Saviour's side;
> And now thou art become a tame and harmless thing;
> A thing we dare not fear,
> Since we hear
> That our triumphant God, to punish thee
> For the affront thou didst Him on the tree,
> Hath snatched the keys of hell out of thy hand,
> And made thee stand
> A porter at the gate of life, thy mortal enemy."

That is the true view of death to the Christian, and the culmination is in order to that resurrection that lies beyond.

FINAL APPEAL		xv. 58
ILLUSTRATIVE CONCLUSION		xvi
	I. Concerning the Collection	1–4
	II. Paul the Worker	5–9
	III. Timothy the Worker	10, 11
	IV. Apollos the Worker	12
	V. Injunction to Workers	13, 14
	VI. Interrelation of Workers	15–18
	VII. Salutations	19–24
	i. Of Others	
	ii. Of Paul	

I CORINTHIANS xv. 58–xvi

THE final verse of the fifteenth chapter is arresting in its opening word, "Wherefore." This word implies an antecedent. It is evident that the apostle was now going to write something resulting from what he had already written. Having brought to conclusion the particular subject of the resurrection, he now wrote, "Wherefore."

It is interesting to note the different views that have been held concerning the "Wherefore." Upon what does it lean back, what is the antecedent? It has been the general interpretation that it leans back upon the truth concerning the resurrection. I have no doubt that is true, but I have equally no doubt it is not all the truth. Unquestionably, the resurrection was in his mind. Having challenged death and the grave as to their sting and victory, and having declared in triumphant language that God giveth us the victory, he immediately says, "Wherefore, my beloved brethren, be ye steadfast, unmovable, always abounding in the work of the Lord, forasmuch as ye know that your labour is not vain in the Lord." Your labour is not vain. The harvest will yet be gathered. The resurrection will be the hour in which you will find your reward for all your labour and all your toil. Undoubtedly there is that close connection.

But I do not think that is all the truth. To find the antecedent to the "Wherefore," that upon which the "Wherefore" leans, in order to gain the emphasis of that which is now to be said, we have to work our way back through all the letter to the first chapter and the ninth verse. We have made constant reference through the whole course of the study of the letter to that verse, because that is the fundamental affirmation upon which everything is built in the letter. Paul was writing to the church in Corinth, and the Church universal, "all who call upon the name of our Lord Jesus Christ in every place, their Lord and ours." He says to that Corinthian church what he would say to any church, that "God is faithful, through Whom ye were called into the fellowship of His Son Jesus Christ our Lord." That is of vast importance as it reveals the calling and function of the Church. She is called into the fellowship, the *koinonia*, the business enterprise, the fellowship of love, the fellowship of Jesus Christ; and the principle is that she is called into fellowship with Him in His enterprises, and God has so called her. After writing the whole letter, the corrective part, because of their failure; and the constructive, showing the secrets of success and power, now he says at the last, "Wherefore," which takes in everything he has said about the failure of the church through its carnalities, and everything he has said about the secrets of power through the spiritualities.

Putting the two statements together, we see how intimate the connection, and how amazing and arresting it is. "God is faithful, through Whom we were called into the fellowship of His Son Jesus Christ our Lord." "Wherefore, my beloved brethren, be *ye* steadfast, unmovable, always abounding in the work of the Lord." We are called by God into the fellowship of His Son, the fellowship of His mission and enterprise; and Paul starts by reminding them that whoever breaks down, God will not, God is faithful. Now, at the close of all the arguments and the teaching, he says, Wherefore, because God will be faithful, and because God calls us into this fellowship, be ye faithful. He does not use that word, but it is the same thought, "Be ye steadfast, unmovable, always abounding in the work of the Lord."

We have taken time to see the connection which is there when this letter is taken as a whole. The letter was read by that church, and has been read by the Church universal. Paul has had two great things to say, with a good deal of corrective and constructive instruction in between. The first is, God has called the Church into fellowship with Jesus Christ, Who will be faithful. Secondly, on the basis of that, interpreted by the whole of the teaching, the Church has one duty. What is it? "Be ye steadfast, unmovable, always abounding in the work of the Lord."

That is the principal thing here. What did Paul tell us to do? He makes an immediate appeal, " Be ye." Leave out the qualifying words for the moment, though they are important. What is the statement? " Be ye . . . in the work of the Lord." God has called us into the fellowship of His Son, therefore " be ye . . . in the work of the Lord." We are in fellowship with Him. Be in the work of the Lord. Be about His business. Fulfil your vocation. Do that which God intended you to do when by His grace and through His redeeming power He put you into fellowship with Jesus Christ. " Be ye . . . in the work of the Lord."

Of course, there a great theme opens out. What is it we are to do? Did Paul say, You people who belong to the Church must do all you can to help God; or you must find out things to do for Him? Oh, no, that is one of the fearful mistakes the Church is making. She is always trying to find out things to do for God. No, get into His own work; get into fellowship with your Master; live in the power of the fellowship into which God has put you.

What is the work of the Lord? That is not possible to say in any lengthy way. All we must do is to go back to the New Testament, and watch Him in that earlier career. Listen to Him. Take out from the things He said some of the outstanding sentences, and we shall find out what the work of the Lord is. " The Son of man came to seek and to save that which was lost." " Be ye in the work of the Lord." He " came not to call the righteous, but sinners to repentance." " Be ye in the work of the Lord." Oh, said His critics, look at Him; He is making Himself one in common with those sinning, polluted crowds. There is no hope for Him, He eateth with publicans and sinners. Jesus answered them in the threefold parable of Luke xv. That is the work of the Lord. First, the shepherd seeking the sheep; second, the woman sweeping, till the coin is found; third, the father singing and rejoicing when the boy comes home. That is the work of the Lord.

We may take that simple and hurried analysis and ask ourselves how far are we in the work of the Lord. Do we know what it is to take the journey over the mountains to seek the lost? " Steadfast, unmovable, always abounding." No, that is not tautology. That is not a repetition of the same thing thrice over. Every word has its meaning.

" Steadfast," that refers to personal faithfulness, sticking to it. That is not an elegant phrase, but it is a great one after all. Sticking to it steadfastly, personal fidelity. Does not the next word mean the same thing? Not at all. " Unmovable " means faithfulness against opposition. Some people cannot stick. They are not always there.

We really cannot depend upon them, even if they take a class in the Sunday school. That is a passing illustration. "Steadfast" means always there. That is the great idea, and we cannot be in the work of the Lord without confronting opposition. There are many adversaries. So says Paul in the next chapter. Yes, we shall have adversaries. Not only be faithful within yourselves, but do not be moved from your loyalty. Stay there in spite of all adversaries. Then he puts in that little phrase, "always abounding." Abounding? Yes, that is running over, more than is demanded. That means getting rid of a foot-rule and balances, and measuring up a certain quantity. The same Greek word occurs in the account of the feeding of the multitudes, when they gathered up the fragments that remained. That is the word, the overplusage. That is the idea. Faithful personally, and faithful against opposition, and going on, and always on, and for evermore, always abounding.

Then the last word, "Forasmuch as ye know that your labour is not vain in the Lord." Not your work merely but your labour, that kind of toil that has in it the red blood of sacrifice, that kind of toil that wears and weakens by the way. That is not vain in the Lord. So that final verse.

Briefly take this sixteenth chapter. This last section of the letter has peculiar interest and value. It is different in many ways from the rest of the letter. The great system of correction and instruction is completed, and the great appeal has been made in that last verse of chapter fifteen. Paul now turned to this chapter, which has been variously described by expositors. One writer says it is wholly concerned with personal matters. Another says it contains sundry practical directions. Both are right, and yet there is more than that in the chapter. Its value is more than personal. As we consider it, the Church comes into view, the church in Jerusalem, local; the church in Corinth, local; the churches in Galatia and Macedonia, but all of them constituting the one Church with mutual responsibility. The whole Church is in view.

Once more in this chapter we see the principles wonderfully illustrated that have run all through the letter. I take only the fundamental affirmation and the final appeal. Fellowship, that is the fundamental affirmation, fellowship with the Lord, and fellowship with each other; and that finds fundamental and final and practical application in this chapter. These members of the Church are seen, whether of Jerusalem or Corinth, or wherever they may be; we see them united in fellowship, first with the Lord, and therefore with one another; so that if one suffers, all suffer, if one rejoices, all rejoice. The thrill of a common life pulsates through the whole body of Christ, and that is illustrated here.

When we turn to the final appeal, to the call to work, here we have a group of persons, who are all seen in relation to that work, in fellowship with the whole Church. It is a remarkable list here, Paul, Timothy, Apollos, Stephanas, Fortunatus, Achaicus, Aquila, and Priscilla, or Prisca. They are all named, individuals, but they are all members of the Church, and they are all seen in relation to the work of the Church. That is the glory and beauty of this whole chapter.

In the first movement the whole Church is in view. We must remember, first of all, the background of conditions obtaining at that time, and then note Paul's instructions as to the practice of fellowship under those conditions.

What were the conditions? The reference here is to the church in Jerusalem, and it is remarkable. It is a reference to the fact that the church in Jerusalem had practically evidently no wealthy people by this time. They were poor. When Paul wrote his Roman letter he referred to the same fact, "the poor among the saints that are at Jerusalem." And the word "poor" is the strongest, it describes absolute penury. There is no doubt that in that church at the time they were a poor crowd as to this world's goods. The church in Jerusalem is seen, difficulties arising from material conditions. There would seem to have been none wealthy. I think if there had been such Paul would have had a strong word to say to them. No, he speaks of the poor, and I think the necessary deduction is that there were no wealthy people in that church.

The whole history of the church in Jerusalem is an interesting one. It is appalling. This church utterly broke down and failed. The Lord had charged them to go forth, beginning at Jerusalem, and to be His witnesses in Jerusalem, and in Judæa and Samaria, and unto the uttermost part of the earth. That commission was given at the beginning of the Acts. They never did this until they were driven out by persecution. They hugged the church, and hugged their privileges, and lost their real spiritual power, until persecution arose; and then they were driven forth, and under the stress of persecution and suffering they went forth through Judæa and through Samaria, and towards the uttermost part of the earth. The Book of the Acts of the Apostles is the story of how they went. But by this time they had been largely driven forth, and those remaining were a poor folk. The church was in difficulty. There would have seemed to be no wealthy people, and there were those in definite and extreme need in Jerusalem.

What had that to do with Corinth? What had that to do with the churches in Galatia? What had that to do with any of the other churches scattered here and there, Corinth founded through the ministry of Paul, and others? It is quite evident that it had something to do with them, and those other churches were responsible to go in and practice a fellowship of life and giving in the case of those suffering saints in Jerusalem. We see the beauty of the ideal, of the community of the Christian Church, and the commonwealth of the Christian Church breaks upon us. Paul here gave instructions as to that giving.

Let it at once be said that the instructions were unquestionably to meet those local conditions in that church, but they contain principles of giving which at least we may do well to ponder. They were to give. They were to send money to help these people. They were to feel the poignant suffering of their brethren and sisters in Jerusalem, and they were to help them. These are the instructions as to how they were to do it. It is a collection *ad hoc,* to that particular necessity. At any rate, it is interesting to note the instructions, whether they have universal application I am not going to argue at any length. What did Paul tell these people to do in the matter of giving?

First of all, their giving was to be regular and systematic on the first day of the week, that is, the first day after the Sabbath, that is, on our first day of the week. They were to give on that day, and they were to give according to their prosperity. Every man and woman, every member of the church was to go alone on the first day of the week. That is the second thing. The gifts were to be personal. They were to be alone. "Let each one of you lay by him in store," a lonely act; in store, that is, treasured up and stored regularly.

Then Paul is careful to show that their giving was to be subservient to the spiritual. It was to be a solemn dedication, according to prosperity that had come to them. On the first day of the week part of their wealth was to be at the disposal of the church, and it was to be done in order not to interfere with the apostle's coming visit to them. Let us get hold of that. Every one of you lay by him in store on the first day of the week regularly, and in loneliness, with definiteness. Test all your giving by your own prosperity, dedicated, consecrated, and do that regularly, in order that when I come there may be no collections. That is very remarkable. What was Paul coming to them for? To minister to them in spiritual things, and he wanted all the material things out of the way. He did not want them going around trying to whip up a collection. "That no collections be made when I come."

He did not want their giving to be the result of extortion, because of his own presence. I know how constantly that has been done, and some evangelist, some prophet, some preacher, some pastor, and the real purpose is to extort money from those assembled. It is an iniquitous idea. When writing his second letter to the Corinthians, Paul said this, "I thought it necessary therefore to entreat the brethren, that they would go before unto you, and make up beforehand your afore promised bounty, that the same might be ready, as a matter of bounty, and not of extortion" (II Cor. ix. 5). Wonderful instructions these!

Then he was careful to show that these gifts were to be distributed by the church, and by those appointed by the church. He says if it is meet for him to go also, then they can go with him. But everything is to be done in a business-like way by the properly appointed officers of the church.

That is a little paragraph on giving. These instructions were undoubtedly for local conditions, but the underlying principles of fellowship, and fellowship is giving, abide. There are cases where these actual words of Paul are necessary today concerning the Church in Norway, and the Church in Finland, and in the Netherlands. They need that the whole Church of God should feel with them in their pain, and far more, minister to their necessities. Whereas these are local conditions, wherever such conditions recur the same principles abide.

The application of these principles to much obtaining today in the matter of the Church's finances is by no means to our advantage. How constantly the Church arranges for the visit of some follower of Paul, some evangelist, some prophet, some preacher, some pastor, and the whole purpose of that visit is a good collection. I have not been wandering up and down in this country and America for all these years without having seen it, and felt it acutely. I have felt again and again the real value was not the spiritual but the material. Oh, Paul, I thank you for that word. I fain would use it when my next invitation comes—I will come, providing you get the collection over before I come!

This sixteenth chapter is largely a page of illustration. While it has correctly been described as containing the final words of Paul, and salutations of a personal nature, to read it only in that way is to miss a good deal. As a matter of fact, everything insisted upon in the course of the apostolic writing is here seen in operation. It is a page of illustration, but it is a page that illustrates the fellowship of the Church in the work of the Lord.

That at once takes us back to the beginning of the letter, where Paul laid down the great fundamental truth that God is faithful, Who has called us into the fellowship of His Son, the Lord Jesus Christ. That has been the theme all through the letter, the Church in fellowship with the Son of God. Consequently, the members of the Church are in fellowship with each other, in order to the doing and carrying out of the work of the Lord.

We have seen in the first four verses of the chapter this fellowship of the Church acting mutually. The church at Jerusalem was passing through difficult times that had reduced its members to absolute penury, and the churches scattered through that whole region where Paul had been travelling were making contributions financially to aid the church at Jerusalem. Paul writes to the Corinthian church as to their duty, and how they were to carry it out. This is technical, but we see what a revelation we have of the oneness of the Church, how it is linked together, that if one member suffer, all the members suffer, and if one rejoice, all rejoice. The whole Church lives one common life, the life of fellowship with the Lord, and consequently the life of fellowship with each other, so that when the church in Jerusalem is in distress, the other churches come to its help by contribution.

We come now to verses 5–12, to a group of individuals. Notice how this thought of work, the fellowship of the Church in work, is present all through. Paul says of Timothy in verse 10, "He worketh the work of the Lord." In verse 16, when speaking of the house of Stephanas, he refers to them as "every one that helpeth in the work." The work, the service of the Church, is in view. It was also in view when he was dealing with the collection for the saints in need. He is illustrating the operation of that work in the Church of God. In the cases quoted here to the end of the chapter, the word work does not occur, but the fact is present. Paul, Apollos, Fortunatus, Achaicus, Prisca, Aquila, they are all seen at work, and Paul's reference to them is always in relation to their work and their service in the Lord. In these verses 5–12 we have Paul, Timothy, and Apollos. They are presented to us.

We have a very arresting little picture of Paul incidentally drawn in verses 5 to 9. To turn aside for a general statement, it is wonderful how, self-effacing as he was, Paul has nevertheless yielded himself up to his readers, so that there is no one of these early servants of the Lord with whom we are better acquainted than we are with him. In the Philippian letter he contributed the great autobiographical passage, and there are other references in other letters of his service and suffering. Here, however, the reference is quite incidental, but none the less interesting. He is a worker, one among the multitude, a member of that whole ecclesia, that Church of God, which has been called into the fellowship of God's Son in His work. Paul is seen as a worker.

We are first arrested by his unsettled outlook. We find a good deal of comfort in that:

"But I will come unto you, when I shall have passed through Macedonia; for I do pass through Macedonia; but with you it may be that I shall abide, or even winter, that ye may set me forward on my journey whithersoever I go. For I do not wish to see you now by the way; for I hope to tarry a while with you."

That is gloriously unsettled. We do so love a programme, don't we? I know the slavery of it, and it took me a good many years to break through that slavery. I found I could not keep the elaborate programme I had made, that it was the Holy Spirit breaking down the little arrangements for a larger purpose. Paul here was quite uncertain, though he was certain about some things. He was going through Macedonia, and he intended to come to Corinth. If he came, he would stay with them for a little, even winter with them, but he did not say he would. It was all open. If he wintered with them, he would have them set him forward on his journey whithersoever he went. The uncertainty is very manifest, the glorious uncertainty of the worker.

Yet there is no uncertainty in words not yet referred to. The uncertainty is qualified by the words, "If the Lord permit." That qualifies everything. It may be Macedonia. It may be Corinth. It may be a little while in Corinth. It may be all the winter there; and then he will be going on. He could not stay. Where was he going? He did not know, "Whithersoever I go." But the one qualifying, authoritative, steadying fact is that he was under the command of his Master, "If the Lord permit." It is a wonderful picture of the apostle moving constantly, and going on, having no definite programme.

There is another illustration of the same thing when Paul wrote to Timothy. He said, "These things write I unto thee, hoping to come unto thee shortly; but if I tarry long." He was not sure. He hoped to get down to see Timothy, who was probably then in Ephesus; but he did not know, and he did not want Timothy to wait for the instruction, because he was uncertain about his own movements.

I know the fascination of having a programme, and having everything in order, and knowing where we are going; but let us leave room, at any rate, for the interference of God. "If the Lord permit." That is a very remarkable word, *epitrepho*. It is, if the Lord turn over, in that indication; if the Lord indicate, if the Lord transfer me, turn me over. It is the picture of Paul as the worker under his Master's authority. There were all kinds of possibilities; Macedonia, Corinth, "whithersoever," the regions beyond—that was his watchword, not knowing whether he would stay there or here; but knowing one thing, that all his life was under the authority of his Master. It is the picture of Paul at work. "Wherefore, my beloved brethren, be ye steadfast, unmovable, always abounding in the work of the Lord." Paul here was carrying out his own instructions to the Corinthians. This first little section shows him "always abounding," Macedonia, Corinth, whithersoever I go, if the Lord permit, always abounding, that is the abiding principle.

But he was quite sure he could not move at present, that he was a fixture for the time being. That is what he told them in the eighth verse. "But I will tarry at Ephesus until Pentecost." Then he gave two reasons for staying where he was at the moment. First, "A great door and effectual is opened unto me," and the second, "There are many adversaries." These two reasons made him perfectly sure that he could not at the moment come to Macedonia and Corinth, that he could not continue his journeyings, that he had to stay there for a period. As a matter of fact, he stayed there in Ephesus for three years, which was a long time for Paul. It was a short pastorate.

What were the things that made him sure that he must stay there? First of all, the open door, "a great door and effectual." Go back from Paul's own description to Luke's account of the things that happened at Ephesus, and see what a remarkable door was open to him. It was one of the greatest cities of the world, having a temple to Diana or Artemis, one of the wonders of the world; and all the life of that great pagan city was centred around that temple. It was the banking house of the merchants. It was where the confederacy of the Ionian states met in legislative capacity. All the life of Ephesus circled around that temple, and there was the church of God, contradicting everything that was central to the life of the city. Paul saw the greatness of it, "a great door and effectual." He could not go on yet. He must stop there, that was his first reason. To go back once more to his final appeal, he is not only "always abounding," he is "steadfast," faithful, standing by the open door; he must abide, he cannot go on; he is in the "work of the Lord."

Then the second reason. "There are many adversaries." So we get his word "unmovable." "Steadfast," I must stay here, the door is open. "Unmovable," no adversaries can deflect me. I have to stay there. What a wonderful pen portrait it is of that great apostle, in a few incidental sentences! The door was wide open, and the opportunities were great; and, moreover, the forces of evil were massed against his Master and His Gospel. "There are many adversaries." Do not forget that is one great reason for staying where you are. If you have no adversaries, you had better move out and find the places where you get them. There is not much in Christian service if we do not know the power of opposition beating against us.

In two verses Paul referred to Timothy (10, 11). "Now if Timothy come, see that he be with you without fear." Does that mean, So receive him that he will not be afraid? Or does he mean, Do not be frightened? I do not know which he meant, and cannot be quite sure. I am inclined to think it means that he shall have no consciousness of fear, for mark it, "he worketh the work of the Lord, as I also do; let no man therefore despise him. But set him forward on his journey in peace, that he may come unto me; for I expect him with the brethren." Again an almost incidental reference to Timothy, and yet how remarkable! Paul had already referred to him in this letter. He said, "For this cause have I sent unto you Timothy, who is my beloved and faithful child in the Lord" (iv. 17). There is no doubt about it, Timothy was very near and dear to the heart of Paul. That is proven most conclusively by the two letters Paul sent to him. Timothy then was unquestionably at Ephesus, and they were the letters of an old man to a young man. There are many suppositions. Many think that Timothy was a weakling and Paul had his work to encourage him. I do not believe it for a moment, and think there is no proof of it. Timothy was a most remarkable personality. He had been brought up in the knowledge of the Holy Letters, which are able to make wise unto salvation, and had been taught by his mother and his grandmother. When Paul, as I believe, went on that journey around those churches, and was left for dead at Lystra, I think it was then that Timothy heard him, heard his message, and saw how it fulfilled all the aspirations and hopes of the teachings of his mother and grandmother, and he became a Christian. Be that as it may, Paul here speaks of Timothy as his beloved and faithful child. How is he to be received? So as not to cause fear to himself. These Corinthians were a strange crowd, forming all sects and parties around Paul, Cephas, and Apollos; and Paul knew they might look askance at this young man, so he charged them they were not to browbeat him, or make him timid. Moreover, they were not to despise him, and they were to set him forward on his journey. So he commended Timothy to them.

Again, to refer to Paul's letters to Timothy, he said to the Corinthians they were not to despise him; but to Timothy he said in his first letter, "Let no man despise thy youth; but be thou an ensample to them that believe, in word, in manner of life, in love, in faith, in purity." To the Corinthians, Do not despise him. To Timothy, Do not be despicable. See to it that you are living so that they cannot despise you. See to it that your life and work are such that you become an ensample in word, what you say, and in manner of life, in your love and faith and purity. Live in the power of these great things, so that they cannot despise you. "Let no man despise thy youth." That seems to have been the difficulty.

At any rate, Paul was writing to these Corinthians that they were not to despise him, this young man who was coming down. These were learned people in Corinth. They were so learned that they proved their stupidity by giving themselves up to philosophic vagaries. They were very clever people. This young man was coming down to them.

Why were they not to despise him? Because "he worketh the work of the Lord, as I do." There at once is a picture of the true attitude of the Church towards God's own workers and messengers. That is fellowship. Paul says he is in this fellowship; he is also a worker. "He worketh the work of the Lord, as I do." Paul was not commending this young man to the church at Corinth by reason of his wealth. We do not know that he had any. He was not commending him to them because of any position Timothy occupied in a worldly sense. There is but one commendation. He is in the business, he is doing the work, he is working the work of the Lord; and that creates the right to a true attitude towards him on the part of those to whom he is sent.

In one verse, we turn to Apollos. "But as touching Apollos, the brother, I besought him much to come unto you with the brethren; and it was not at all his will to come now; but he will come when he shall have opportunity." I am bound to say I love that verse because there is so much in it. First of all, Paul's reference to Apollos here is very brief, but it is arresting. Apollos was one around whom certain of the divine elements in Corinth were gathering themselves, who said they were "of Apollos." Now, Paul wanted this man to go down to Corinth. Notice his description of him, "Apollos the brother," showing that there was perfect fellowship between them in spite of the difficulties created by the Corinthians, and the difficulties that might have still been there, accentuated by the attitude of certain of the Corinthian people toward Apollos and himself. Oh, no, we understand each other. He is my brother, "Apollos the brother."

Then is not this very arresting? Here is a difference of conviction between them. Paul wanted Apollos to go to Corinth; indeed, he says he besought him much to go. It may be speculative, but why was Paul anxious for Apollos to go down to Corinth? Most likely because of the faction, and Paul perhaps felt if Apollos went it would be easy for Apollos to show that there was no real division between himself and Paul. But it was not at all Apollos' idea to go, and Paul said it with equal definiteness. "It was not at all his will to come now." Why did he refuse? Perhaps for the very reason Paul wanted him to go, from the other side. I admit that is speculation. Perhaps Apollos felt that the division would be accentuated by his presence and that he had better keep away, and he did not go.

Here is a remarkable side-light on Paul. We have been told that Paul was dogmatic, and especially when he talked about women. It depends. Yes, he was, but that is not all the truth. He was dogmatic in certain respects and in certain matters; but here he is seen giving way to Apollos, and writing the letter and telling them that he was not coming; and Paul does not insist upon his own will, or if he cannot have his own way, decide that he will have no more to do with Apollos! Oh, this is so human. Apollos the brother, I want him to come to you, and he will not, but he will come some day, said Paul, when he has the opportunity. We see the mastery of the law of love in the case of these two outstanding messengers and teachers in the Church, both workers together with the Lord, workers together with each other, and therefore able to differ in opinion without separating, in love. It is a beautiful picture.

These cases are illustrations of the principle of the Church in fellowship in the work of the Lord. This is a most delightful chapter, a revelation of the Church in its entirety, in its individual membership, in its mutual responsibility and its fellowship in service and work. That very eminent cleric of the olden days, that bright wit, Sydney Smith, was once asked how he accounted for the success of the Methodist people springing up everywhere. His reply was very characteristic. " They are all at it and always at it." That was the success of Methodism, all at it, and always at it, " always abounding." It was the success of the early Church. They were all at it and always at it, and even though differences arose, we see the law of love in the case of these workers. When the work of the Lord is supreme at the passion of the Church, there is room neither for indolence nor for strife.

This concluding paragraph (13–24) breathes the spirit of the whole letter, and proceeds upon the assumption of its teaching. The Church is still viewed in its fellowship with the Lord, and in its intercommunion in the fellowship of that one church of the one Lord with each other.

This little section falls into three parts naturally. First there is a group of remarkable closing injunctions (13, 14); then some personal references, and a charge growing out of them to these people in Corinth (15–18); finally, the salutations (19–24).

The injunctions: " Watch ye, stand fast in the faith, quit you like men, be strong. Let all that ye do be done in love." That cannot be read carefully without seeing that there was in the mind of the apostle the consciousness of the perils surrounding the church. He had written the letter to correct them, and to give them the secrets of power in the church. Now he has finished all the system of his correction and instruction, and he gathers up in these brief, short, epigrammatic forceful words certain definite charges. " Watch ye," and he felt there was a necessity for saying that. " Stand fast in the faith." Go back in the letter, and see where they failed. " Quit you like men." He had to say at the beginning he could not write unto them as men, but as unto babes. " Be strong," or, more accurately, " Be strengthened."

Then the final word of those charges, "Let all that ye do be done in love." There flashes back upon the mind the memory of conditions Paul had corrected, as revealed in the earlier part of the letter, and there necessarily comes to the mind with new force the great description of the unfailing law of the Church, which is the law of love. Here, gathered up in epigrammatic form, are things needing to be said, and things already said.

Notice there are four personal words and one relative. The four personal words are addressed to individuals; there is an individual note about them. "Watch ye, stand fast in the faith, quit you like men, be strong." Then there is a relative word that covers all the fact of their interrelationship with each other, "Let all that ye do be done in love."

Notice in those first four there are really two couplets. First, "Watch ye, stand fast in the faith." That is a complete couplet in itself. Then, "Quit you like men, be strengthened." That is the second. Notice how these epigrammatic sentences laying these charges upon these people at Corinth, and upon us all, carry out the instruction, the commandment, the charge of the final appeal of the letter, "Wherefore, my beloved brethren, be ye steadfast, unmovable, always abounding in the work of the Lord." There are two words that stand out. He charged them to be steadfast, unmovable. The first of these couplets qualifies, explains, and enforces the first word, to be "steadfast." "Watch ye, stand fast in the faith." The second couplet emphasizes, illustrates, and enforces the second word, "unmovable," "Quit you like men, be strengthened."

These sentences need very little exposition, yet how powerful they are. Be steadfast. How shall we be steadfast? Be watchful, literally, keep awake, do not go to sleep, do not imagine you can take a vacation from your vocation. I am not speaking against a vacation. Vacations are very trying to me, but are very necessary. But we can never have a vacation from our holy vocation in the Christian Church. Watch ye, keep awake, do not go to sleep. There is tremendous force in that.

Then mark this: Stand fast, be steadfast, but stand fast in the faith. That is to say, there are limits to our liberty, and the only way to be steadfast is to remain in the faith. Keep awake, stay in the faith; do not be deflected from it for a single moment. There is a tremendous significance in these little, brief, forceful sentences of the apostle.

Then, "unmovable," "Quit you like men." That word "quit" literally means, Grow up, do not be children, do not be babes, be able to stand up. Be unmovable, stay in your Christian maturity, grow up, "Quit you like men," so that you cannot be moved, so that forces that are against you cannot deflect you by a hair's breadth from the line of your duty and loyalty. And "be strengthened." That means progressively going on, not being content with the point at which you have arrived, growing up—let Peter tell you—"Grow in the grace and knowledge of our Lord and Saviour Jesus Christ." So in these little words we see these charges of a personal nature laid upon this Corinthian church, and for all Christians, which are to affect the whole of their outlook on life.

Paul then gathers everything up in the relative word, "Let all that ye do be done in love." That is simple, and is a relative word, and yet it has an application to the personal. There are involved in those personal couplets the alert life of watchfulness and the active life of conflict. Whatever it is, whether watching or fighting, let love be the reason for it. "Let all that ye do be done in love." It is the unfailing law revealed so perfectly in the thirteenth chapter, and it is the condition of fellowship which answers all else, and conditions all else. There is a company of individuals. Paul says to every individual the same thing, "Watch ye, stand fast in the faith, quit you like men, be strengthened," progress in your growing; but whether watching or fighting, be love-mastered. If that is true in every case, the interrelationships within the Church will be what they ought to be.

The personal references and charge are very interesting. Paul had had some visitors. He names them, Stephanas, Fortunatus, and Achaicus. Who were these people? We know very little about them. One thing we do know about Stephanas and his household. Paul had baptized them. In i. 16, he says, "I baptized also the household of Stephanas; besides, I know not whether I baptized any other." He was not very particular about that subject. This household of Stephanas was definitely one that owed everything to Paul in their spiritual life. He had been to see Paul, accompanied by Fortunatus and Achaicus. We know nothing about Fortunatus except this, that Clement, the great writer whom Paul mentions in his Philippian letter (iv. 3), says that Fortunatus carried this letter to Corinth on behalf of Paul. There is no inspired authority for that, although I think it is interesting and true. Then the other man, Achaicus, this is the only reference to him, and that is all we know of him. He was one of these three who had been to see Paul, and what we gather is this, the helpfulness of their visit, and the consequent charge he laid upon these Christian people concerning these three men, and all others of like ilk. Paul says, "Be in subjection to such." They have refreshed me, and they will refresh you. The reason why they are to be subject to them is that of the service they have rendered to Paul and to others. We are in the same realm of the whole letter. Here the members of the church, the individuals, emerge. We see them in a wonderful action, men who are serving their fellow members in love, visiting Paul, and now evidently going to Corinth.

We come to the salutations (19-24), and at once we are brought into the atmosphere of the catholic Church, the universal Church, the whole Church. It is incidental, apparently at the very end, the whole Church is seen in relationship to one church. Numbers of people in churches scattered here and there, all parts of the one Church, and all interested in this one church at Corinth. That is what Paul meant when he said, "The churches of Asia salute you." We are not to suppose Paul had any special message from all the churches in Asia; but he knew them, and knew their attitude. Some of them had proved their attitude in their gifts of love, which Corinth was called upon to give for the church at Jerusalem. Here is this unity, the fact that these were linked up with others. He was finishing this letter to correct this church in the interest of all churches. He says, "All the churches of Asia," and there is a breath of glorious catholicism, of unity, of oneness in that simple phrase, "All the churches of Asia salute you."

Having said that which is inclusive, Paul went on, and took two illustrations, a man and a woman, Aquila and Prisca, or Priscilla, as the Old Version had it. Just two people, but they "salute you much in the Lord, with the church that is in their house." Again we get a glorious glimpse of these two people. It is an interesting story. We find from Acts xviii. 2 that they were exiles in Corinth, driven out of Rome because of their religion. In that same chapter we find that when Paul went to Ephesus, they went with him, they accompanied him. They were there for some time in Ephesus. It is very interesting that Apollos learned from Aquila and Priscilla all the fulness of the Christian Gospel. He was undoubtedly a great man, one whom Paul had just called "the brother," a man Paul loved, who had done a great work in Corinth. We know that when he came to Ephesus, Aquila and Priscilla found that he did not know all the fulness of the Christian Gospel. He knew Christianity only so far as it had been revealed in the teaching of John the forerunner. That is the meaning of that story in the Acts when Paul came down there, to find a group of people who were believers, but lacking something. Paul said, "Did you receive the Holy Ghost when you believed?" and they said, "Nay, we did not so much as hear whether the Holy Ghost was given." And Paul said, "Into what then were ye baptized?" and they said, "Into John's baptism." That is what Paul had seen. Then there came a day when this man and woman, that tent-making couple, took Apollos in hand, and opened his eyes to see the glory of the fulness of the Gospel. We find from the Roman letter (xvi. 3) they eventually returned to Rome, from which place they had been exiled. Paul now named them, and they saluted these Corinthians much in the Lord, and the church in their house.

So we have a glimpse of the whole Church, and the churches of Asia, of two individuals, and of a local church, a comparatively small one, in their house; but there is the same principle of love.

We come to the last paragraph, which evidently is one in which Paul, usually dictating to an emanuensis, now took the stylus from the hand of his stenographer and did some writing for himself. We remember that in writing to the Galatians he said, "See with how large letters I have written unto you with mine own hand." There was a touch of sanctified humor there. If the view be correct that he suffered from his eyes, one can see him bending down, and writing, "The salutation of me Paul with mine own hand." He is going to write something himself, something that is going to finish the whole of his message, and gather it up. What is it? "If any man loveth not the Lord, let him be anathema. Maran atha. The grace of the Lord Jesus Christ be with you. My love be with you in Christ Jesus. Amen." A wonderful paragraph.

What does he say? "If any man loveth not the Lord, let him be anathema. Maran atha." It is unfortunate that the Authorized Version has no period after the word "anathema," for it misses a good deal of the tremendous force of these words Paul wrote with his own hand. As a matter of fact, Paul wrote three words here, not two. "Anathema," that is one word. "Maran," that is a separate word. "Atha," that is a separate word. These three words are not linked together save in a secondary, yet important, way.

"Anathema" is a Greek word, as all the letter is Greek. After Paul had written, "If any man loveth not the Lord, let him be anathema," he broke off into Aramaic; and the next two words are not Greek, but Aramaic, "Maran Atha." They stand in lonely isolation. Yes, linked with what has gone before. It is the great exultant cry of the apostle's heart, in which he dropped into the language probably with which he was most familiar in his young manhood, Aramaic.

"Anathema" is a Greek word, not found very often in the New Testament, and it is not always translated in that way. It is found six times in the New Testament altogether. The first occurrence apparently has no relation to this subject, and is in Acts xxiii. 14, when the enemies of Paul bound themselves with a great curse to take his life. They were bound by an anathema, that is, they were accursed unless they ended the life of Paul. Then it is found in the Roman letter (ix. 3), in that passage of pregnant power and passion, when Paul said, "I could wish that I myself were anathema from Christ for my brethren's sake." That is the supremest word ever coming from a human writer, expressing the fulness of his fellowship with his Lord. Then it is found in the earlier part of this epistle (xii. 3), in which he says, " No man speaking in the Spirit of God saith, Jesus is anathema," no man speaking in the Holy Ghost can call Jesus accursed. That is not really a malediction. It is the statement of an inevitable fact. If a man does not love Him, there is no hope for that man except that he should wither, perish, be accursed. Paul has gathered up into one tremendous sentence the conviction of his heart and purpose. The word for love there is the word of human affection. If any man does not love Him, does not go out emotionally to Him, there is nothing for that man. He is lost, he will perish. It is that very sense of the supreme and final glory and beauty of the Lord that led to these two Aramaic expressions.

"Maran," that word simply means the Lord. "Atha" is a verb, part of the verb to come. Scholars have spent a good deal of time over this word, and I am not going to attempt to decide between them, but use all of the readings. Some say "atha" means, "is coming." There are those who say that it is present, "cometh." Others say it is a past tense, "has come." One of the most eminent scholars I know accepts that first view. Experts differ, but whether it be "has come," or "cometh," or "is coming," the great thing is "the Lord," the fact of His Lordship. That is why I like to employ all three suggestions. It may mean, The Lord has appeared, has come. Or it may be, The Lord cometh all the time. Or it may mean, The Lord is coming. It is the advent into human life of the supreme Lord. It is the great exclamation out of Paul's very heart, revealing his conviction that it is no fiction that He has come, that He comes, that He is coming, that He is the great reality.

Then the last words, " The grace of the Lord Jesus Christ be with you," the Lord, Jesus, Christ be with you all, in Christ Jesus. That is everything. And yet there is a personal touch, and he ends with it, " My love be with you all in Christ Jesus." Did ever any letter have a more glorious close than that?

II CORINTHIANS

INTRODUCTION i. 1-11	A. THE MINISTRY i. 12-vii	B. COLLECTION FOR THE SAINTS viii, ix	A SEQUEL C. PAUL'S COMING TO CORINTH x-xii. 10	
I. Salutation 1, 2	I. Personal Vindication i. 12-ii. 11	I. The Example of the Macedonians viii. 1-5	I. His Authority	x
i. The Authoritative note 1a	i. A Defense of Principle i. 12-22	i. The Manner	i. His Appeal	1-6
ii. The Inclusive Note 1b	ii. An Explanation of Action i. 23-ii. 4	ii. The Method	a. Its Grounds	1
iii. The Salutation 2	iii. Parenthesis ii. 5-11	II. The Deputation viii. 6-ix. 5	b. Its Plea	2
II. Thanksgiving 3-11	II. Concerning the Ministry ii. 12-v	i. The Privilege of the Church after the pattern of Christ viii. 6-12	c. A Description of Spiritual Authority	3-6
i. The Values of an Experience of Suffering 3-7	Introductory ii. 12, 13	ii. The Method of Christian Equality 13-15	ii. His Answer	7-11
ii. The Experience from which the values came 8-11	A Parenthetical Reference	iii. The Business Side of Things 16-24	a. Their Mistake	7-10
	i. Its Power ii. 14-iv. 6	iv. The Appeal and Confidence of Love ix. 1-5	b. His Warning	11
	a. Declaration of Power ii. 14-17	III. The Results to follow ix. 6-15	iii. His Claim	12-18
	b. Testimonials of Power iii. 1-3	i. The Enrichment of Liberality 6-11	II. His Apostleship	xi, 1-xii. 13
	c. Nature of Power 4-18	ii. The Church at Jerusalem 12-14	i. His Apology for Boasting	xi. 1-4
	d. Exercise of Power iv. 1-6	iii. Thanksgiving for the One Gift 15	a. "Foolishness"	1
	ii. Its Tribulation iv. 7-12		b. Its Reason	2-4
	iii. Its Hope iv. 13-v, 10		ii. His Boasting	xi, 5-xii. 10
	a. The Principle 13		a. Of His Apostleship	5-15
	b. The Confidence 14-18		b. The Comparison Emphasized	16-33
	c. The Contemplation v. 1-10		c. Of the Supreme Matter	xii. 1-10
	iv. Its Impulse v. 11-19		iii. His Only Apology	11-13
	v. Its Aim v. 20, 21		III. His Programme	xii. 14-xiii. 10
	vi. For Consistency vi. 1-10		i. The Subject Approached	xii. 14-18
	III. The Consequent Appeals vi, vii		ii. The Purpose of His Writing	19-21
	i. The Appeal 1a		iii. The Procedure at His Coming	xiii. 1-4
	ii. The Arguments 1b-10		iv. The Last Appeal	5-10
	a. "Working" 1			
	b. "Giving" 3			
	c. "Commending" 4-10			
	ii. For Consecration vi. 11-vii. 1		CONCLUSION xiii. 11-i. 4.	
	a. Appeals			
	b. Arguments		I. Exhortations	11
	iii. For Continued Fellowship vii, 2-16		II. Salutations	12, 13
	a. The Appeal 2-4		III. Benediction	14
	b. The Arguments 5-16			

II CORINTHIANS

INTRODUCTION	i. 1–11
I. *Salutation*	1, 2
i. The Authoritative Note	1a
ii. The Inclusive Note	1b
iii. The Salutation	2
II. *Thanksgiving*	3–11
i. The Values of an Experience of Suffering	3–7
ii. The Experience from Which the Values Came	8–11
a. The Experience. Darkness of Death	8
b. The Anchorage. God of Resurrection	9
c. The Deliverance	10
d. The Fellowship of the Saints	11

II CORINTHIANS i. 1–11

THE second letter to the Corinthians was evidently the outcome of the first. Titus, and perhaps Timothy also, had communicated to the apostle certain facts concerning the reception of his first letter to the Corinthian church. What they told him disturbed him, and called forth this letter.

If the first epistle was that of the church prepared for work by corrective and constructive statements, this may be said to be a picture of the apostle himself as a worker in suffering, in love, and in the consciousness of authority conferred on him by God. It has been said with truth the apostle here really reveals himself as to his personality. It is largely personal from beginning to end, and it is a defence of his ministry. As in the first letter we saw the Church, in this we have a remarkable picture of the ministry within the Church, as depicted and exemplified in Paul himself.

It is a difficult letter to analyze. There is a sense in which there is very little system in it. We have an introduction contained in the first eleven verses of the first chapter. Then Paul dealt with the ministry (i. 12–vii). It is a defence and an interpretation of the work of himself as an apostle, and consequently of the Christian ministry generally. Then in two chapters (viii. ix) we have a section, very local, yet containing principles of perpetual application concerning the collection for the saints. That leads up to the second line of argument concerning the ministry, and concerns Paul's coming to Corinth (x–xiii. 10). There we have a remarkable picture of the man himself, and a valuable one. Finally we have a conclusion (xiii. 11–14).

It should be remembered in studying these first eleven verses of the introduction that there were those opposed to Paul. This fact makes the more remarkable the beautiful tenderness of his greeting as he approached them. He had gained the knowledge from Titus, and perhaps from Timothy also, that there were those in the church who were denying his apostolic authority, questioning whether he was a minister of Christ at all. He saw that this must undermine the truth as it had been revealed to them through him, and consequently it must be borne in mind, that background of criticism of himself, that existed in Corinth amongst some in the church.

He greeted them with affection, and then spoke to them, as to those likely to be interested, of a period of suffering through which he had passed. In dealing with this he was careful to show that he recognized what large values accrued from such experiences of suffering. All this in order finally that he might recognize especially how they had helped him by their supplications and gifts.

First of all, he struck the authoritative note in the first part of the opening verse, "Paul, an apostle of Christ Jesus, through the will of God," the note that claims authority. Some of them were denying his apostleship. He claimed to be an apostle, and by the will or purpose of God. No man can have any higher authority than that, and he started there. He struck the keynote of all that he was going to do afterwards "by the will and purpose of God."

But there is an inclusive note. He was writing not only to the church at Corinth, but to all in Achaia. That is a general geographical term. Probably there were not many people in that district who were believers, but he included them. There is a touch of fine art in that. Not only the Corinthians, but all in Achaia.

Then the salutation, "Grace to you and peace from God our Father and the Lord Jesus Christ." Grace and peace! He is going to complain. He is going to scold them a little presently, but he is not doing it yet. He is greeting them, and his greeting is with the great words, grace and peace, and telling the origin, "From God our Father, and the Lord Jesus Christ," the origin and the source, God the Father; and the channel of communication, the Lord Jesus Christ; grace and peace be with you.

Then he dropped into thanksgiving. We have a remarkable passage beginning at the third verse, and running through the seventh. The theme is comfort, comfort granted in terrible trouble. Notice that he first spoke of the values of the experience, and then of the experience. He was going to tell them of the experience only after he had described the effects of that experience. That is part of his method. If they would grasp the values, then they would turn to the experiences and would be surprised. That is apparent in a natural reading of the passage.

The values, what are they? First of all, " Praise be to the God and

Father of our Lord Jesus Christ," or, " Blessed be the God and Father of our Lord Jesus Christ." " Praise be " is the meaning of " Blessed." It is the eucharistic expression of worship and adoration. " Praise be to the God and Father of our Lord Jesus Christ, the Father of mercies, and the God of all comfort." The Father of mercies, and the God of comfort, the One from Whom all mercies flow.

"Praise God from Whom all blessings flow," or mercies flow; so we might sing it, and that is what it means. If there is a mercy, God is the Father of that mercy, whatever it may be; and He is the God of all comfort. That word "comfort" is the key word. In some form or another it occurs no less than ten times in five verses, "comfort," "the God of all comfort."

What is comfort? We are often weak and sentimental in our thinking about comfort. The word literally means strengthened, sustained. It is a cognate word with the name given to the Holy Spirit. That name is Paraclete in our translation, which is a transliteration of the Greek word. Here this word "comfort" is *paraklesis* all through this paragraph. We may interpret comfort by the work of the Holy Spirit and say that the Spirit is the Comforter. Said Jesus, I will send you Another, and He will disannul your orphanage. He is the Comforter. In that connection a comforter means far more than a consoler. Once some of our translators introduced the word consolation. This is more than consolation, it is underpinning. It is coming to the side of someone and disannulling all his loneliness and his difficulty—comfort, "the God of all comfort." The apostle says that God comforted him.

God also gave him through the comfort He ministered to him ability through the experience to minister comfort to others. That is the thought and the teaching.

It also means fellowship with Christ in His suffering and in His comfort. It means the fellowship of the saints. I remember my dear old friend Chadwick saying once publicly in my hearing that the best word for Paraclete is Comforter, not Advocate. I told him that I did not agree with him, and then he said his lawyer was his advocate, but he did not call him his comforter! I told him, I did. In the matter of law, about which I am an ignoramus, I put the matter into the hands of my lawyer, and left it. He was my advocate, and in that way he was my comforter. It is not consolation, it is the great thought of underpinned, strengthened comradeship called to the side of, and being by the side of, upholding. That is the great word, the upholding power that comes from God.

The apostle then told them of the circumstances that drew forth this action and this experience of comfort. What was it? The darkness of death. There is a difference of opinion over what Paul was referring to here. He was not explicit. Some think it was something that happened at Ephesus, when he said he had fought with wild beasts there. It may have been so. Possibly it was a serious sickness that he had been through. Personally, I think that is what it was; but, at any rate, it was so serious that he "had the sentence of death" in himself, and the anchorage that he found when the sentence of death was there, when he could not indulge in hope at all, was the comfort ministered by God. "We have had the answer of death within ourselves," so that our hope might not be in ourselves. Death was accepted, but his hope was in God, Who is able to give life to the dead, and comfort of God. In such an hour as that, death does not end all. The comfort is that beyond death there is life. God is the God of resurrection, and that was whispered to Paul in the midst of this experience of suffering, this terrible experience, and that it was so there is no question.

He will refer later on in the letter to another matter, the thorn in the flesh. We do not know whether that was his meaning here. Undoubtedly he names the locality in Asia, where he had been sick unto death. There was no strength in him. He looked out upon the future and saw nothing. The sentence of death was in him, and then God comforted him with the assurance that He could bring the dead to life, and that through Him death was not consummation. He might die, but he said the experience through which he had passed had taught him that God was the God of resurrection, able to give salvation, deliverance.

Yes, he was comforted because God was the God of resurrection. He was able to give life to the dead; but Paul was comforted also in that the sentence of death was not carried out. He was looking back now, but in the hour of darkness the assurance that came to him was that of the everlasting arms underneath him, and the fact that God was by his side, and all that in order that he might help and comfort others.

We see the great Christian principle in that. When God comforts us, it is that we may be able in our turn to comfort others. That is the very genius of Christianity. Everything received is received on trust. Everything that you and I have from God we have on behalf of others—the comfort of God, the strengthening of God, the upholding of God, the revelation that God is able to make alive from the dead, and then presently salvation from that death which he had feared, on which he had looked with so much trembling. We have put our hopes in Him.

Now, the chief interest in this particular introduction is its relation to the personal note running through the letter. Paul was writing to these Corinthians, and he turned aside to describe to them an experience through which he had been passing, and he told them the values of it in his own soul, and the values of it for them. Comfort is the great word, comfort from God, comfort for others. So he prepared for whatever he had to say presently of rebuke, by a revelation of great tenderness. He called them to sympathize with him, and he assured them that God had sympathized with him, and that He would sympathize with them as they are asked to sympathize with him. It is the sympathy of sharing the activity of God, Who is the God of all comfort.

A. THE MINISTRY	i. 12–vii
I. *Personal Vindication*	i. 12–ii. 11
i. A Defense of Principle	i. 12–22
a. The Testimony of Conscience	12–14
b. " I Purpose According "	15–22
ii. An Explanation of Action	i. 23–ii. 4
a. The Declaration	i. 23, 24
b. The Method	ii. 1–4
iii. Parenthesis	ii. 5–11
a. The Discipline Exercised	5, 6
b. The New Responsibility	7–11
1. Restoration	7–10
2. Reason	11

II CORINTHIANS i. 12–ii. 11

PAUL now proceeded to the subject of his ministry, the authority of which was threatened by the attitude of some in that Corinthian church. In dealing with the ministry he has first a personal vindication (i. 12–ii. 11); then he dealt with the subject of the ministry itself in a wonderful passage (ii. 12–v); and he ended with a consequent appeal (vi, vii). In this study we deal with the personal vindication.

Here we find that a defence of principle (i. 12–22); an explanation of his action that had caused the difficulty (i. 23–ii. 4); followed by a parenthesis concerning the action of the church in the past (ii. 5–11).

We will first compare two paragraphs. In the sixteenth chapter and verse 5 of the first epistle, Paul wrote: " But I will come unto you when I shall have passed through Macedonia; for I do pass through Macedonia." Now, he had not done what he said he was going to do in the first letter, and he was charged with fickleness, of being a " yea " man and a " nay " man, of saying he was going to do something and then not doing it. Is that a serious charge anyhow? It depends. Paul evidently thought it was a serious charge, because it hinted his unpreparedness to stand by his authority as declared, and this questioned his ministry. That of course is what some of these people were doing. They were even saying he was not an apostle. They were saying he had no right to any authority whatever, and the charge under consideration at this point is that of his fickleness, as they said.

Now he defended himself. It was a defence first of all of the principle. Notice carefully that he took trouble to defend himself. Apparent inconsistency or fickleness may be consistency on the highest level. That is what he was trying to show them. First he claimed he had the testimony of his own conscience. That is a remarkable passage:

> "For our glorying is this, the testimony of our conscience, that in holiness and sincerity of God, not in fleshly wisdom but in the grace of God, we behaved ourselves in the world, and more abundantly to you-ward. For we write none other things unto you, than what ye read or even acknowledge, and I hope ye will acknowledge unto the end."

Notice the tender appeal, and the personal claim of a clear conscience, that he had acted in holiness and sincerity. It is a great claim when a man can make it.

Then he went on, and he asked them to look at the apparent fickleness. He asked them a question, and then gave them the abiding principle as an answer:

> "God is faithful, our word toward you is not yea and nay. For the Son of God, Christ Jesus, Who was preached among you by us, even by me and Silvanus and Timothy, was not yea and nay, but in Him is yea. For how many soever be the promises of God, in Him is the yea; wherefore also through Him is the Amen, unto the glory of God through us. Now He that establisheth us with you in Christ, and anointed us, is God; Who also sealed us, and gave us the earnest of the Spirit in our hearts."

Notice three things there, the faithful God, the certain Lord, and the indwelling Spirit. Paul claims that the will of God had been made known to him, realized through the Lordship, interpreted by the Spirit. Those were the lines on which he had acted, when he did not come, but went another way. His action was because of these things. He claimed the guidance of the Spirit, interpreting the Lordship of Jesus, and the faithfulness of God. Jesus is the Yea and the Amen. That is to say, He is the One Who says, Yes, it shall be so, and Who ratifies it by the Amen, the unvarying and invariable Christ. They had told him he was fickle. He said, No, there is a meaning in what happened. I said I was coming. I did not come, but I did not come because of that twofold fact, the faithfulness of God, and the certainty of the

Lordship of Christ as interpreted by the Spirit to me. There is the personal note all through this paragraph.

Then he went on to explain his action. He said he had a solemn witness, God Himself, that he did not come for certain reasons. He did not come that their faith might have freedom to act. Mark that carefully. If he had gone then, instead of writing that first letter, he would have apparently gone to insist upon his own authority. Now he flung himself back upon that which is authoritative, claiming that he himself had been obedient to it. He told them they stood in faith, not under his government, but under the government of the One in Whom they were believing. This is very high ground, and this is the true ground of the true minister of Jesus Christ. As Peter said, "Neither as lording it over the charge allotted to you," or "God's heritage." The word "heritage" is the word clergy, and the only place in the New Testament where it occurs. There it does not refer to the ministry, but to the laity. Those we speak of today as the clergy are not to lord it over the real clergy of God. That was why Paul did not come after he wrote that first letter.

It is well to remember what he said to them about that first letter. It is the key to this. I sometimes think we ought never to read the first letter without studying this paragraph in the second letter (ii. 1–4):

"But I determined this for myself, that I would not come again to you with sorrow. For if I make you sorry, who then is he that maketh me glad, but he that is made sorry by me? And I wrote this very thing, lest, when I came, I should have sorrow from them of whom I ought to rejoice; having confidence in you all, that my joy is the joy of you all. For out of much affliction and anguish of heart I wrote unto you with many tears."

That is the account of the reason, and inspiration, and method of the first letter. "Not that ye should be made sorry, but that ye might know the love which I have more abundantly unto you."

We recall the fact that the first letter was divided into two parts of correction and construction, growing out of that preliminary declaration that God is faithful Who has called us into the fellowship of Jesus Christ His Son, and reaching its great climactic in the 58th verse of the fifteenth chapter, "Wherefore, my beloved brethren, be ye steadfast, unmovable, always abounding in the work of the Lord." All through the letter he was first of all correcting the weakness of the church, and then constructing, showing the things of the church's strength. Here we find out how he did it. He wrote it with tears and much anguish, not desiring to make them sorry, but desiring that they might know the love he had towards them. The letter was love-inspired. Similarly, now he had not come to them because his coming might have had the effect of inducing them to think that he claimed authority over them. No, he said, it is by faith you must live, and by faith you must act. He said, I left you without a visit in order that your faith might be strengthened, that you might stand. That is the personal vindication.

Then he dropped into a concluding passage in this section (5–11), "But if any hath caused sorrow, he hath caused sorrow, not to me, but in part (that I press not too heavily) to you all. Sufficient to such a case is this punishment." A student of these letters will know that this is a reference to the incestuous person that he quoted as an example of the failure of the church in Corinth, and told them that they were to exercise discipline. Evidently they had done so, and had denied to that man, guilty of a gross immorality that was not common even in Corinth, which they had countenanced and sheltered under the ægis of the church, the privileges of the fellowship. Paul had said he must be put outside, and that they must use discipline so as to maintain the church's purity. She had no right to tolerate any in her membership who were not pure and true to their Lord.

Now, in this letter he again referred to this man. It had come to his knowledge they had exercised discipline, and refused the man the sanctions of church membership; but now he saw there was a new probability. That man might be overwhelmed with sorrow, and that very sorrow might become his undoing. Their business now was to forgive him and to receive him again. This does breathe the very tone and spirit of our Lord. We recall what our Lord said about the sinning brother. They were to go and see him alone. If he would not hear, then take two or three others. If he would not hear these, tell it to the Church. Mark carefully the rest of the statement, if he will not hear the Church, "let him be unto thee as the Gentile and the publican." How do we recite that? What is the tone of voice? If it is hard, that is Romanism at its worst. That is a papal bull of excommunication. Who is the Gentile and the publican? He is the man for whom Christ died. Treat him that way. Go after him, seeking him as the Son of man, Who came to seek and to save that which is lost. So go after that man. Restore such a one in "the spirit of meekness," as Paul says elsewhere. So he charged them that they now had new responsibility, that of the restoration of the man.

He then closed the section with the reason, "that no advantage may be gained over us by Satan, for we are not ignorant of his devices." What are the devices of the devil? Let us confine ourselves to this case. First of all, he lured this man by temptation into lust. Now he told this man that there was no forgiveness. He was being submerged in sorrow. He was being overwhelmed in sorrow. Paul said, Restore him, forgive him, love him, take him back, lest he be overwhelmed with grief; and take him back that Satan may gain no victory. He had gained a victory by overcoming this man through his lust. Do not allow him to gain a second victory by overcoming this man through sorrow that is overwhelming. Restore such a one, again to quote from the first letter in another connection, in "the spirit of meekness," "comfort him, lest by any means such a one should be swallowed up with his overmuch sorrow."

We are not ignorant of his devices, temptation and destruction by lust; the temptation to feel that there is no hope, despair settling upon the soul. "We are not ignorant of his devices."

Then the devices of the devil within the Church, what are they? First the tolerance of evil. The first letter told them that they must not tolerate evil. Now, the second device of the devil is undue severity, the hounding of the failing man until he is overwhelmed and in despair. It is a wonderful little illustration of the apostolic mind, and of the Spirit as it works still in all those who share the apostolic function, in the case of the sinning man in the Church. Deny him the privilege of membership in the Church. Excommunciate him, if you like the word, and it is a correct word. Then, if he repent, you have gained your brother; take him back again.

So we come to the end of this section, Paul's vindication of his own authority, and absence of fickleness; and the explanation of that action is in the closing parenthesis, it is in the ministry, "that the ministry be not blamed," as in another of Paul's words. He is not anxious about his personal authority, but the authority of the truth, and the authority of the life of God, the authority of the faithful God, the certain Lord, and interpreting Spirit.

II. *Concerning the Ministry*	ii. 12–v
Introductory	ii. 12, 13
A Parenthetical Reference	
i. Its Power	ii. 14–iv. 6
a. Declaration of Power	ii. 14–17
b. Testimonials of Power	iii. 1–3
1. The Author. Christ	
2. The Pen. Paul	
3. The Ink. The Spirit	
c. Nature of Power	iii. 4–18
1. Covenant	4–6
2. Ministration	7–11
3. Courage	12–18
d. Exercise of Power	iv. 1–6
1. The Courage	1
2. The Method	2
3. The Issues	4–6

II CORINTHIANS ii. 12–iv. 6

WE now come to the discussion of the subject of the ministry generally, which occupies the whole section of the letter from ii. 12–v. Perhaps nowhere in the New Testament is the subject of the ministry set forth in its sublimity as it is here. We now take the introduction (ii. 12, 13) and the subject of the power of the ministry (ii. 14–iv. 6). In our next study we will take what remains of the section concerning the ministry, and consider what the apostle teaches about the tribulation, hope, impulse, and aim of the Christian ministry (iv. 7–v).

Take first of all the two verses constituting the parenthetical introduction. Paul made reference to some of his movements, seeing he had not immediately got to Corinth. The charge against him was that of fickleness, that he had said he was coming, and had not come. " Now when I came to Troas for the Gospel of Christ, and when a door was opened unto me in the Lord, I had no relief for my spirit, because I found not Titus my brother; but taking my leave of them, I went forth into Macedonia." The statement of these two verses simply means this, that he came to Troas, saw the open door to Corinth, but did not enter it. He turned aside and went into Macedonia. He was troubled at not finding Titus, and so he changed his plan, and went aside into Macedonia. They had charged him with fickleness, and he showed them that fickleness may be of the very essence of loyalty to the Divine guidance, and he referred to it again now.

Our next section is concerned with the power of the Christian ministry (ii. 14–iv. 6). Here we see the declaration of power (ii. 14–17), the testimonials of power (iii. 1–3), the nature of power (iii. 4–18), and the exercise of power (iv. 1–6).

In verse 14 we see the secret of the power. There is no question that the figure Paul employed in this verse is that of a Roman triumph. Some difficulty has been experienced with the text here. In such a Roman triumph the conspicuous figures were those of the victor and the vanquished. The victor rode in triumph, and the vanquished was often chained to his chariot wheels; and the whole procession was accompanied by the burning of incense. Without dogmatizing, I believe that Paul here was viewing those engaged in the ministry as the victors, and he was describing their work as that of a triumphant march, and the vanquished, those that they had mastered, and again are accompanying on the march. That to me is the meaning of the figure.

Notice then the verses that speak of the manifestation of power (15, 16). It is a tremendous picture, and again we must keep in mind the Roman triumph, the burning of incense all the way, and the victor and the vanquished. Now, the burning of incense was a savour to those who were beaten, to those who were about to be imprisoned or to die. To them it was a savour of death unto death. It was a savour of life unto life to those who were set free and were victorious. The incense spoke of the victory of the one, and of the good things that were to come.

But notice carefully that Paul asked that question, "Who is sufficient for these things?" It is a separate question. He breaks in with the consciousness of the tremendous thing he is saying, and the tremendous work of the Christian apostle and minister. He drops in this letter from the plural to the singular, and from the singular back to the plural again and again. He referred to Timothy and to Titus, thinking of the whole work of the Christian ministry, and he says, "We are a sweet savour of Christ unto God." Then he cries out, "Who is sufficient for these things?" He did not answer his question now, but he will answer it presently. He left the question, marking the magnificence of the ideal of the Christian ministry as he saw it, a triumphant procession. "He leadeth us in triumph everywhere," as one rendering has it.

He goes on. Incense is ascending, and it is a savour of life unto life, and of death unto death, for he says, "We are not as the many, corrupting the Word of God; but as of sincerity, but as of God, in the sight of God, speak we in Christ." That is the answer to his question, "Who is sufficient for these things?" Those are sufficient who are not making merchandise of the Word of God, not corrupting it, not distorting it in making merchandise of it; but in sincerity as to God, in the sight of God, speaking in Christ.

This is the whole scheme of the Christian ministry, not corrupting the Word of God, not making merchandise of it, but in sincerity speaking the things of God in Christ.

The next paragraph touches upon the testimonials of power, that is, the power of the ministry (iii. 1–3). This is a commendation. "Need we, as some do, epistles of commendation to you?" You are our epistles, says the apostle, you Christian people in Corinth. He carries out the idea in the most remarkable way. The author of the epistle is Christ, the pen is Paul, and the ink is the Spirit. That is to say, Christians are the true credentials of the power of the ministry. "Ye are our epistle," written not in tables of stone, not with ink, but by the Spirit in the heart, "known and read of all men." That is to say, the evidences of the power of the Christian ministry, the testimonials of the power are found in Christians.

He then goes on, and in a long section he spoke of the nature of that power (iii. 4–18). Notice first there is a three-fold contrast here, between the old and the new, a contrast of covenant (4–6), a contrast of ministration (7–11), and a contrast of courage (12–18).

The contrast of the covenant is this. "The letter killeth," that is to say, the letter reveals, and so condemns. The Spirit realizes, that is, communicates life equal to the accomplishment of the revelation of an ideal.

Then the ministration of death and of the Spirit. Here we reach this remarkably interesting paragraph about Moses' veiling of his face. Why did Moses veil his face? Not because of the excellent glory of it. We recall the fact that he came down from the mountain, and veiled his face—we are told in the history—seeing that his face was shining, but he did not veil it to hide the shining. He veiled it because the shining was passing away; it was fading, and he veiled his face that they might not see its passing. That is the contrast. Christ needs no such veiling, for His glory never passes. That is the whole meaning of the paragraph.

The same contrast is seen in the rest of this chapter. Why Moses veiled his face we are told. Why Christ does not need to veil His face is revealed to us; and we are told that "the Lord is the Spirit; and where the Spirit of the Lord is, there is liberty. But we all, with unveiled face, reflecting." The word here in the Revised Version is "reflecting." I prefer the word found here in the Authorized, "beholding as in a mirror the glory of the Lord." The idea is not that of reflection in order to transform, but rather that of beholding until transformed, in order to reflect. "We, beholding as in a mirror the glory of the Lord, are transformed into the same image from glory to glory, even as from the Lord the Spirit." So we are revealing the very glory of our Master, and that is the result of the Christian ministry.

Going on to the first six verses of the fourth chapter, Paul speaks of the power of the ministry. "Therefore seeing we have this ministry, even as we obtained mercy, we faint not." Courage, strength. Why do we not faint? "For we have renounced the hidden things of shame, not walking in craftiness, nor handling the Word of God deceitfully." That is why. We are not handling the Word of God deceitfully. We are not walking in craftiness, "but by the manifestation of the truth commending ourselves to every man's conscience, in the sight of God."

"But if our Gospel is veiled, it is veiled in them that are perishing." Here is the exercise of power. We faint not. We have renounced the hidden things of darkness, of shame, and we preach Christ as Lord. That is the central clause. The negative result only is referred to by the apostle. The Gospel is veiled to those who are perishing. But why is it veiled? The reason of the veiling is that the god of this world, or the god of this *age* more accurately, has blinded their minds. But why has the god of this age blinded their minds? Because of their unbelief. That harmonizes very largely with the teaching of our Lord about His parabolic method, and why He adopted it. It is said that our Lord adopted the parabolic method in order to hide the truth. He did nothing of the kind. He adopted it because of their blindness, and as a lure. He told them stories and gave them illustrations, by means of which to awaken their interest, if possible. But they were blinded, as men are blinded still.

Why are they blinded? Because the god of this age has blinded them. Why has he had power to blind them? Because of unbelief. The whole teaching of the letter to the Hebrews has dealt with that. The one sin that will bring men ultimately to perdition is the sin of unbelief, unbelief as refusal of Christ, refusal of the Gospel, refusal to accept what God is offering to them. To put it quite bluntly, if anyone goes down to perdition, why will they go? Because of their sins? No, but because of their sin, the sin of rejection of Jesus Christ. "If our Gospel is veiled, it is veiled in them that are perishing." Who are they? Those who refuse that Gospel, blinded by the god of this age, blinded because of unbelief. Refusal to believe is the secret and reason of the blindness that happens to men. Oh, it does not matter, people are told, what we believe. Believe me, it *does* matter. It matters very much what we believe, and whether we believe at all. That is the whole picture here.

We have looked very roughly at this paragraph in this study, but it is a marvellous picture, which is not yet finished. Paul has yet to deal with the tribulation and hope of the ministry. He has also to deal with the impulse and aim of the ministry, to which we shall come in our next study. But the Christian ministry is here viewed as a triumphant procession where men who are in the ministry are led everywhere in triumph; and the credentials of their authority are found in those who are won by their message, the unveiling of the glory in Jesus Christ shining in the faces and the lives of Christians. These are the letters of commendation in which Paul rejoices in the Corinthian church. He reminds them he has to point out many things of failure, but that is the basic idea, the ministry consisting of a triumphant procession, in which those proclaiming the glory of Christ and the Word of God in sincerity and truth are led everywhere in triumph; and their triumph consists in souls won and transformed, reflecting by beholding, knowing the transforming power, reflecting the glory of the Lord.

ii. Its Tribulation		iv. 7–12
a. The Principle		7
b. The Strain and the Strength		8, 9
c. The Issues		10–12
iii. Its Hope		iv. 13–v. 10
a. The Principle		13
b. The Confidence		14–18
c. The Contemplation		v. 1–10
iv. Its Impulse		v. 11–19
a. The Double Motive		11–15
b. The New Viewpoint		16
c. The Ministry of Reconciliation		17–19
v. Its Aim		v. 20, 21
a. The Office		20a
b. The Aim		20b
c. The Basis		21

II CORINTHIANS iv. 7–v

WE have considered the power of the ministry (ii. 14–iv. 6), and now come to its tribulation and hope, its impulse and aim, which are all dealt with in this paragraph (iv. 7–v).

Its tribulation (iv. 7–12). There is an undercurrent all through this section, revealing Paul's sense of his own physical weakness. He had opened the letter by speaking of great trial coming to him, that he had despaired almost of life. I think there is no doubt the sense of physical weakness was upon him. He was talking all the time about weakness in the bodily realm, and contrasting it with the power in the spiritual realm. That covers the whole ground of this section.

He has dealt with the power and authority of the ministry, which is so full of triumph in Christ Jesus. Yet the exercise of it is through tribulation. The pressure is in the earthen vessels, and these are subject to affliction. There is a revelation of a great principle of all successful work. It is through the breaking of the earthen vessels that light flashes out upon the pathway of others. We are reminded of the story of Gideon, and the breaking of the pitchers, so that the light shone forth. Yet the other truth is recognized, that the power is such that all the pressure upon the earthen vessels is not sufficient to destroy them. Tribulation is the principle, the weak vessel for the mighty power, and that power sustaining the weakness of the vessel and making it unconquerable. That is the whole story. Those two phases show the strain and the strength, and are remarkable. "Pressed on every side, yet not straitened." We see the pressure from without, but it cannot hurt the vessel. It does not make the vessel straitened. "Perplexed, yet not unto despair; pursued, yet not forsaken; smitten down, yet not destroyed; always bearing about in the body the dying of Jesus, that the life also of Jesus may be manifested in our body." It is physical weakness that he is thinking of all through this paragraph, not mental; and it is a singularly appropriate passage for us just now. While not wanting to discourage any, it may be some are serving in fulness of health and vigour. Thank God for it, but do not trust too much in that health and vigour. Do not put any confidence in that. We shall find that when we are weakened in the way, then we are strengthened. "When I am weak," said the apostle in another connection, "then am I strong." We shall see it again in another application lower down. "We which live are always delivered unto death for Jesus' sake, that the life also of Jesus may be manifested in our mortal flesh. So then death worketh in us, but life in you." Through the weakness and the paralysis in powerlessness life is communicated to others.

Suffer me to use a personal illustration. A young fellow entered the ministry, and had remarkable success, and great blessing has attended his life and work. At the time he was a young man fresh from college, a brilliant preacher even then. He preached in my church in Birmingham, and I went home after the sermon and said to Mrs. Morgan, "Was that not wonderful?" She quietly remarked, "Yes, but it will be more wonderful when he has suffered." Well, he suffered, and it *was* more wonderful. Through weakness, great weakness, strength is made perfect.

Turn now to the next paragraph (iv. 13-v. 10), the hope of the ministry. Verse 13 contains the principle, faith creating testimony. We believe, therefore we speak. That is one secret of power and success in the Christian ministry. If you do not believe, shut your mouth. That is a word for young ministers. If you do not believe do not talk.

In verses 14–18 he is looking on to the gathering of the harvest and the reward at the resurrection. He does not consent for a single moment that the Christian ministry is bounded by time. It runs on and on. He is lifting his eyes, looking on to that day when the outward man which is decaying day by day shall be renewed, and shall be superseded by the spiritual and the new resurrection body. He is looking on to the resurrection, for as "He raised up the Lord Jesus, He shall raise up us also with Jesus, and shall present us with you." It is a glance ahead to the day of which we all think sometimes, not often enough perhaps, when this mortal shall put on immortality, when there "shall come to pass the saying that is written, Death is swallowed up in victory," and we are in the presence of the Lord.

"Wherefore we faint not, but though our outward man is decaying, yet our inward man is renewed day by day. For our light affliction"—we go back to the beginning of the letter again and read what he said about almost despairing of life; now he has called it a light affliction—"a light affliction, which is for the moment, worketh for us more and more exceedingly an eternal weight of glory." The light affliction is for the moment, passing, not abiding. But mark carefully, how is that? When is that so? "While we look." It depends upon where our eyes are looking. "While we look not at the things which are seen, but at the things which are not seen; for the things which are seen are temporal," passing, transient. "But the things which are not seen are eternal," abiding. That is his outlook. "While we look." That is an arresting phrase. If you are looking at the things seen, you have no such confidence as this. You have no such hope as this. But when you look at the things unseen, what are they? The spiritual forces that are resident within us, making us superior to all the pressure, and enabling us still to continue. "While we look."

Then he goes on and declares, "For we know that if the earthly house of our tabernacle be dissolved, we have a building from God, a house not made with hands, eternal, in the heavens." For that word "tabernacle" I should prefer reading "tent." The tent is for pilgrimage; the house is for settlement. Lift your eyes to the heavens, and measure the present by that outlook and that eternity. "For verily in this [that is, in this tent] we groan, longing to be clothed upon with our habitation which is from heaven." It is possible to enter into the heavenly condition with no results accruing from the earthly testimony. We may be found naked.

"For indeed we that are in this tent do groan, being burdened; not for that we would be unclothed, but that we would be clothed upon, that what is mortal may be swallowed up of life. Now He that wrought us for this very thing is God, Who gave unto us the earnest of the Spirit. Being therefore always of good courage, and knowing that, whilst we are at home in the body, we are absent from the Lord (for we walk by faith, not by sight); we are of good courage, I say, and are willing rather to be absent from the body, and to be at home with the Lord. Wherefore also we make it our aim, whether at home or absent, to be well-pleasing unto Him. For we must all be made manifest before the judgment-seat of Christ; that each one may receive the things done in the body, according to what he hath done, whether it be good or bad."

Please draw a distinction between the judgment seat of Christ and the great white throne. This is not the great white throne, but the *bema*, the judgment seat of Christ. Those who appear there will be His own children, His own followers.

Once again notice, he is looking on to the things unseen, the things that are eternal. And is there anywhere a finer or more beautiful description of the life on the other side than that—" at home with the Lord " ? In the body we are absent from the Lord, that is, as to bodily presence, not as to spiritual sight. But at last, when we cross over, we shall be " at home with the Lord." Make that a homely phrase. We all know what it is when we feel at home. Everyone has a spot on earth where he feels at home, with no restraint, no keeping up of appearances, at home; just in perfect quiet and ease. As Mrs. Craik wrote about friendship:

"Oh, the comfort, the inexpressible comfort of feeling safe with a person, having neither to weigh thoughts nor measure words, but pour them all right out just as they are, chaff and grain together, knowing that a faithful hand will take and sift them, keep what is worth keeping, and then with the breath of kindness blow the rest away!"

That is being at home, " at home with the Lord." I believe that is what the Lord meant when He said, " I go to prepare a place for you, that where I am, there ye may be also." I do not think there is any necessity for His furnishing the mansion. Nothing like that. No, I am going before, that when you come, you will not feel strange, for you will know Me. At home with the Lord! Those are the things to look at. Those are the things which bear one up. It is while we look at those things that we are filled with courage.

A comparison of the tent with the house is very beautiful. As I have said, the tent is for pilgrimage. We can strike our tent and move away. Happy is the man down here who lives in a tent. I do not mean literally, but spiritually. If we are living in a tent we know what it means to be ready to move, and be disturbed, and therefore never to be disturbed. The one secret of not being disturbed is readiness to be disturbed by the Master. That is what we mean when we sing:

> "And nightly pitch our moving tent,
> A day's march nearer home."

By and by it will not be a tent. It will be "an abiding place." That is what our Lord meant, "In My Father's house are many abiding places." I go to get ready for you, to prepare a place for you, that where I am, you may be also, at home with the Lord. It is a beautiful description of the life that lies beyond. I do not want to know anything beyond it than that. It is enough that I shall be with Him, at home with Him, at my ease with Him. No more confession of sin, no more sinning, at home with the Lord. Oh, one could linger and ponder over that. The beauty of it is great. That is the tribulation and hope of the ministry, and that hope is centred in the life that lies beyond. That is where the glory shines, and will for ever shine; and it is for us to live and serve and bear tribulation in the light and inspiration of that coming glory.

The impulse of the ministry (v. 11–19). "Knowing therefore the fear of the Lord, we persuade men." I am glad the revisers have substituted the word "fear" for the Authorized word "terror." That word did not convey the idea of the apostle at all. It is "the fear of the Lord." What does that mean? What is the fear of the Lord? The old way of defining the fear of the Lord is that I used to be afraid that God would hurt me. Now the fear is, or should be, that I should hurt Him, that I should grieve Him, that I should cause sorrow to the Holy Spirit. "Knowing the fear of the Lord, we persuade men." The outstanding message of the first paragraph (11–15) is that two motives are there, fear and love. "The love of Christ constraineth us." Do not make any mistake, it is not because of love for Christ that we serve. It is the love of Christ working in us, mastering us, driving us, constraining us, "the love of Christ shed abroad in our hearts," constraining us. The fear is linked with that love. It is fear lest we should hurt love, and the only way in which we can fulfil that obligation is that of service.

"We are made manifest unto God; and I hope that we are made manifest also in your consciences." He is not very careful about that, but he hopes that it is so. The supreme thing is the sight of God. "We are not again commending ourselves unto you, but speak as giving you occasion of glorying on our behalf, that ye may have herewith to answer them that glory in appearance, and not in heart." Fear and love.

Then the new viewpoint. "Wherefore we henceforth know no man after the flesh; even though we have known Christ after the flesh, yet now we know Him so no more." That is an amazing statement. It is when we do look at men after the flesh that we see their wealth, their poverty.

> "Only like souls I see the folk thereunder,
> Bound who should conquer, slaves who should be kings—
> Hearing their one hope with an empty wonder,
> Sadly contented with a show of things:—
>
> "Then with a rush the intolerable craving
> Shivers throughout me like a trumpet-call—
> Oh, to save these! to perish for their saving,
> Die for their life, be offered for them all!"

So F. W. H. Myers interpreted Paul. I do not know any lines that are more full of suggestiveness than those.

But he says, We do not know Christ after the flesh any more. What does he mean? Go back in his life history. When he knew Christ after the flesh he considered Him as the leader of a new sect, the leader of a new party, a menace to holy religion. He says we do not see Him like that any more. We know Him now in the Spirit, by the Spirit. We know neither man whom Christ died to save, nor Christ Who saved him, by worldly, fleshly standards. We look upon men and the Saviour from the higher standard, and the standpoint is that of the purpose of God. "God was in Christ reconciling the world unto Himself." He was not being reconciled to the world. I do not know whether that is a distinction without a difference. I do not think it is, but I never could comfortably sing the hymn:

> "My God is reconciled,
> His pardoning voice I hear."

Oh, I do sing it! It is a great hymn, but it is not God Who is reconciled, but it is the world is reconciled to God. God never turned His back upon this world. Man turned his back upon God. It is not God Who turned round and changed. He cannot do it. He is the same.

> "But He the same, abiding,
> His praise shall tune my voice."

But man has to change, and God was in Christ, in order to produce that change on the part of man, reconciling him to God, restoring him to the Divine kingship and favour and love. I do not mean that God ever ceased to love man, but man ceased to enter into all the benefits of love, and still is doing so. But "God was in Christ, reconciling the world unto Himself, not reckoning unto them their trespasses, and having committed unto us the world of reconciliation."

Now mark this. "We are ambassadors therefore on behalf of Christ, as though God were entreating by us." What an amazing statement! "We are ambassadors." What are ambassadors? Those who represent the King, those who stand in the courts of human conscience, authoritatively representing the authority of the King. Ambassadors serve. "We are ambassadors therefore on behalf of Christ, as though God were entreating by us," as though God was beseeching by us, entreating and beseeching. "We beseech you on behalf of Christ, be ye reconciled to God. Him Who knew no sin He made to be sin on our behalf; that we might become the righteousness of God in Him." That is the aim. That is the purpose.

We should not stop there. It goes right on. "And working together with Him, we entreat also." But that is our next study. We have glanced at the tribulation, the hope, the purpose and the aim of the Christian ministry. Notice throughout that the apostle is looking at it from a very human standpoint, and yet from a Divine height. He is conscious of weakness, but he is also conscious of the mighty power sustaining him, and sustaining all those who are in that ministry, for he uses the plural number "we." So the power of the ministry works through tribulation, in hope, having as its purpose and its aim the delivery of the Divine message, and promulgation of the Divine purpose, that the world shall be brought back; and in spite of sin there shall be the triumph of righteousness.

```
III. The Consequent Appeals                          vi. vii
    i. For Consistency                               vi. 1-10
        a. The Appeal                                    1a
        b. The Arguments                                 1b-10
            "Working"                                    1
            "Giving"                                     3
            "Commending"                                 4-10
    ii. For Consecration                             vi. 11-vii. 1
        a. Appeals
        b. Arguments. Series of Questions
                      Series of Promises
    iii. For Continued Fellowship                    vii. 2-16
        a. The Appeal                                    2-4
        b. The Arguments                                 5-16
            1. His Suspense in Macedonia                 5
            2. His Comfort in Titus' News                6-12
            3. His Comfort in Titus' Reception           13-15
            4. His Hope                                  16
```

II CORINTHIANS vi, vii

IN these two chapters (vi, vii) we come to the consequent appeals.

The true aim of the ministry is incidentally and clearly set forth. It is that of leading men to Christ, so that they may live the Christ life. The way into right relationship with Christ is the way of being reconciled to God through Christ. That is the whole subject, the theme of the Christian ministry. It always has been. It always is if we understand our work as ministers of Jesus Christ, and the whole Church is in direct co-operation with us in those aims.

The apostle now therefore appealed to the Corinthians to vindicate himself, and those associated with him in the ministry, by giving no occasion of stumbling. The vindication of the value of all the toil and suffering, and the tribulation, will be in the consistent life of the saints. That lies at the back of all we have studied. We have seen this before. Now in order to do this, they are urged to complete separation from all the forces that are contrary to Christ, and that is the burden of this appeal.

It is a threefold appeal; first for consistency (vi. 1–10), secondly, for consecration (vi. 11–vii. 1), and then for continued fellowship (vii. 2–16).

The appeal for consistency. The appeal itself is found in the first verse. Then the arguments for that appeal are in the remaining verses (2–10). The first phrase, "and working together," is linked closely with the last verse of our previous study. That is the meaning of "and." It is a sequel. "We are ambassadors . . . working together with God." Verse 2, in which Paul quotes from Isaiah, is in parenthesis. Notice therefore the statement, "working together with Him . . . giving no occasion of stumbling in anything, that our ministration be not blamed; but in everything commending ourselves as ministers of God."

The appeal is in the first verse. "Working together with Him, we [the ambassadors on behalf of Christ] entreat also that ye receive not the grace of God in vain." This appeal is in harmony with Paul's letter. Again and again we remember how he says this. In effect, he says, You are reconciled, be reconciled. In another connection he said, You have put off the old man. He constantly drew attention to the fact of their standing, and urged them to live up to it, to let their conduct square with their position. That is what he meant here. "We entreat also that ye receive not the grace of God in vain." You have received the grace of God. He so saluted them at the beginning, and all through he has emphasized it. But now he said, Do not let that be in vain. Do not let it be an empty thing. Let it be a full and forceful fact. "Do not receive the grace of God in vain." Notice the linking up of those two participles, "working together," "giving no occasion of stumbling." That does not link to the charge to the people not to receive the gift of God. That links with the apostolic work of the ministry. "Working together with God we entreat" you; and in order that we may emphasize our entreating, we must give no occasion of stumbling, that our ministry shall not be blamed, but in everything commending ourselves as ministers of God. Working together with God, giving no occasion of stumbling, in commending ourselves as ministers of God. That describes the work of the Christian minister. He is working with God, but he is entreating men to be reconciled to God, as though he would entreat them by Him. He is appealing to those so reconciled not to receive the grace in vain; and he goes on to show how the Christian minister exercises the gift, working, and giving no offence, "commending ourselves in the midst of you, as ministers of God."

Then comes that remarkable passage in which Paul seems almost to exhaust himself in describing how the minister is to commend himself in the sight of God as a minister of God to those to whom he is called upon to minister. There have been many attempts to analyze that description. This is by no means dogmatic, but I am inclined to analyze it thus in a threefold division. He speaks first of the physical, then of the mental, and lastly of the spiritual, in the exercise of the ministry. "In much patience, in afflictions, in necessities, in distresses, in stripes, in imprisonments, in tumults, in labours, in watchings, in fastings"—all those touch the physical. "In fastings," how far is that literal? I think it means what it always does in the New Testament, abstention under certain circumstances from everything, not merely food, but everything that hinders our work. Some fast at special seasons, at special times. Many fast all through Lent. While respecting them, I do not think Lent is marked off as a necessary period for fasting. It may be perfectly proper. I do not give up sugar in my tea in Lent. "Fastings"—every minister knows what that means if he is worthy, and has entered into the real spirit of his ministry.

In the next verses, taking the Authorized rendering, "By pureness, by knowledge, by longsuffering, by kindness," all those mark the mental.

Now, "by the Holy Ghost, by love unfeigned, by the word of truth, by the power of God, through the armour of righteousness on the right hand and on the left"—there the preposition is "through,"

"through the armour of righteousness on the right hand and on the left, by glory and dishonour, by evil report and good report, as deceivers, and yet true; as unknown, and yet well known; as dying, and behold, we live; as chastened, and not killed; as sorrowful, yet always rejoicing, as poor, yet making many rich; as having nothing, and yet possessing all things."

Those are the spiritual elements of strength that lie behind the work of the ministry. Let us ponder these when we are alone and on our knees. They harmonize very largely with all Paul had said before of the work of the ministry, despised, "pressed, yet not straitened; perplexed, yet not unto despair." There we have the arguments for the appeal he makes. Help us that we may fulfil our ministry as we ought to fulfil it. Help us, that the ministry be not blamed, that there be no blame attached to us. Help us that we may give no occasion of stumbling in anything, and that we may commend ourselves in all these ways. That is the first appeal for consistency.

Then we come to the appeal for consecration (vi. 11–vii. 1). Notice the introductory outburst of tenderness. "Our mouth is open unto you, O Corinthians, our heart is enlarged. Ye are not straitened in us, but ye are straitened in your own affections." Your love to us is not equal to ours for you. "Now for a recompense in like kind (I speak as unto my children), be ye also enlarged." Let your love abound. You are restricted in your love. The secret of very much of your criticism is to be found right there, that your love is not what it ought to be. So the tender outburst is of the nature of an appeal.

What is the appeal? Three little sentences mark it. "Be not unequally yoked together with unbelievers." That is the first element. The next is, "Come ye out from among them, and be ye separate." The next is, "Let us cleanse ourselves." Then we have the arguments in favour of that attitude so described, the attitude of complete separation. Be not unequally yoked with unbelievers, come out and be separate, and let us cleanse ourselves from all defilement of flesh and spirit. There is a defilement of the spirit which is independent of the defilement of the flesh. The spirit can be defiled in many ways. I sometimes think that the sins of the spirit are more deadly than sins of the flesh. So the apostle says, "Let us cleanse ourselves from all defilement of flesh and spirit," and his arguments consist of two things, a series of questions and a series of promises.

The questions, "What fellowships have righteousness and iniquity? What fellowship has straightness with crookedness?" That is what the words mean. "What communion hath light with darkness? What concord hath Christ with Belial? What portion hath a believer with an unbeliever? What agreement hath a temple of God with idols? for we are a temple of the living God." Those questions are unanswerable. There can be no coalescing between the things, straightness and crookedness, light and darkness, between Christ and Belial They cannot do it, and so surely as any attempt is made, that which will suffer will be the high and true and noble, not the low, the untrue and the base.

What is the ground of Paul's appeal? What is he leading up to? To those great and gracious promises. "I will dwell in them, and

walk in them; and I will be their God, and they shall be My people."
And once again,

> "I will receive you,
> And will be to you a Father,
> And ye shall be to Me sons and daughters,
> Saith the Lord Almighty."

These are the great promises of God, that transcend the possibility of our understanding in all the full glory of them. Wherefore, come out from among all those opposed, into a complete separation. Those are the arguments.

Finally, then, he appealed for continued fellowship (vii. 2–16), "Make room for us," as the margin has it. "We have wronged no man, we corrupted no man, we took advantage of no man." That is a great claim, and perfectly true. So he says to them, Open your hearts to us, make room for us. He had just told them they were straitened in their own affections. Enlarge your heart, open your hearts, make room for us. "Great is my boldness of speech toward you, great is my glorying on your behalf. I am filled with comfort, I overflow with joy in all our affliction." Why? Because he thinks of them. He has been correcting them all through the letter. He is correcting certain attitudes taken up by certain of their number; but for the church as a whole he has every confidence in them as a whole, and he believes they will indeed do exactly what he says. That is why he is glorying on their behalf.

These appeals, on the basis of principle, merge into one, which is directly personal in those opening sentences, and which thrills with urgency and tenderness, "Make room for us."

Paul goes on in a very local way to tell of his experiences, and why he gloried in them. "For even when we were come unto Macedonia, our flesh had no relief, but we were afflicted on every side; without were fightings, within were fears." What did Paul mean by that? Surely he was thinking of them, and of the failure manifest in that church. When he came into Macedonia, he had said he was going to Corinth, but turned aside, and went on into Macedonia, and he was afflicted in the realm of thought and haunting fear for the sake of those his children to whom he had written in Corinth.

"Nevertheless, He that comforteth the lowly, even God, comforted us by the coming of Titus." This epistle opened with the declaration that God was the God of all comfort. Paul has now gone back to that thought. "God comforted us by the coming of Titus." What a human touch that is! When he got into Macedonia he did not find Titus there, but Titus arrived with tidings, resulting from Paul's first letter. That is what he is writing about now, and the effect it had produced. It is very human all this paragraph (verses 7–9). In it we see into the mind of the apostle. He had suffered, because of that first letter he had written. He had had no rest to his spirit, no rest to his flesh, because of his mental argument with himself, an agony as it seems, "fightings without, fears within." But Titus had come, and he had brought news of the effect produced by his first letter; and Paul now says, If I did regret it, I do not regret it any more. He thought his first letter was a mistake, but now, because of the result brought about, he says he is glad he wrote it. Why was he glad? Because of the effect produced on the church in Corinth. It had produced sorrow, expressing itself in repentance, not in regret merely, but in that sorrow which "worketh repentance," a change of mind, and a change of conduct consequent upon a change of mind. It is quite evident that they had done all he told them, and he describes the whole attitude of these people. What searchings of heart, with fightings, what fears! But he is very glad he wrote, and he is glad because his letter had produced the desired effect, the repentance of the church, growing out of sorrow. Repentance is not sorrow only. It may be unaccompanied by sorrow. It often is, and mostly is, perhaps, unaccompanied by it. There is the chief difference between the Roman and Protestant theologians, the difference between *recipicencia* and *pœnetentia*. The Roman theologians insisted upon the element of sorrow. The Protestants said, No, it is not sorrow, but a change of mind rather. That may not be accompanied by sorrow at the time, but sorrow will always follow, sorrow for the past; but the change of mind is the great thing. If sorrow has produced this change of mind, then, Paul says, I am thankful that I wrote that letter.

Then, again, he is comforted not only because Titus had told him of the effect of his letter. He is comforted by the church's reception of Titus (13–15). They had fulfilled his expectations, so he was comforted because of that also.

So he ended on a high exultant note of hope (16) "I rejoice that in everything I am of good courage concerning you." That is the end of his appeals, and the end of his dealing with these Corinthian Christians about the subject of the ministry. He is not downcast. He is rejoicing, and he is glorying. He is of good courage concerning them, full of hope. Such is the closing note of the appeal.

B. The Collection for the Saints   viii. ix
   I. *The Example of the Macedonians*   viii. 1–5
     i. The Manner
        a. Source. Grace of God
        b. Spirit. { Joy / Liberty
     ii. The Method
        a. Self First
        b. Substance Therefore
  II. *The Deputation*   viii. 6–ix. 5
     i. The Privilege of the Church, After the Pattern of Christ   viii. 6–12
     ii. The Method of Christian Equality   13–15
     iii. The Business Side of Things   16–24
     iv. The Appeal and Confidence of Love   ix. 1–5
  III. *The Results to Follow*   ix. 6–15
     i. The Enrichment of Liberality   6–11
     ii. The Church at Jerusalem   12–14
     iii. Thanksgiving for the One Gift   15

II CORINTHIANS viii, ix

These two chapters form the second movement in this letter, that concerning the collection for the saints. The section has a local background which it is necessary to see, for even though the local colour has faded, the main revelation of principles abides. At that we will now look.

The church at Jerusalem was at this time poor and suffering, and the whole subject is that of the gathering of a fund to help them. In his first letter Paul had given explicit instructions concerning that collection (I Cor. xvi. 1–4). That is different from things today. Now the churches send for us in order to have a collection! I like the apostolic method better myself. I have always objected to be the instrument of extortion of money out of anyone.

Now, the value of this whole section is the revelation of abiding principles, and the whole activity is described by the repeated use of the word "grace." It occurs seven times in the eighth chapter, and three times in chapter nine. "The grace of God" (viii. 1). "This grace and the fellowship" (4). The Authorized Version translates this, "That we would receive the gift," but the Revisers have quite properly translated the word in the same way, "grace." "This grace also" (6). "This grace also" (7). "The grace of our Lord Jesus Christ" (9). "Thanks be to God" (16). That word "thanks" in Paul's letter was the same word, "grace," "Grace be to God." The translators undoubtedly felt there was something difficult about that, so they put in "thanks," which is not inaccurate, which expresses the thought there, but it is "Grace be to God." Then "this grace" (19), seven times in all in that chapter. "All grace abound" (ix. 8); "the exceeding grace of God in you" (14); and "Thanks be to God" (15). The word is again "grace be to God."

Thus the whole subject of the fellowship of the saints with each other is lifted into the high atmosphere of looking upon it as an activity of grace. Let us look at this word, the Greek word for grace, *charis*. It underwent a change of meaning, or of different application in the Greek language and literature. Then it gathered a new meaning when the Christian writers took hold of it. It first meant everything in the realm of beauty, as against ugliness, of strength as against weakness, of health as against sickness, of love as against hate. The whole æsthetic realm, the realm of beauty and glory and health and strength, all that is high, as opposed to all that is low—grace, *charis*.

Then in later writings it took on a new meaning, and it was the desire to impart these things to other people. I am referring still to Greek literature. Then these New Testament writers took hold of it, and lifted it into a higher realm, and it became a word standing for the activity that fulfils the desire to impart the things of health and beauty and glory, instead of shame, to other people.

Now, the grace of God is first of all, all that in God which is of health and beauty and glory and strength. It is the desire of God to impart it to others, until, finally, grace had its glorious manifestation in His Son and in His Cross, the activity that provides for others these things of glory and of beauty. So much for the study on the word "grace" and its high meaning.

The abiding principle of this is self-evident. The Church is one, and the grace of God is upon it. At the commencement of his first letter, and at the beginning of this, Paul said, "Grace to you and peace from God our Father," the grace of God: God's activity answering the desire of His heart, put at the disposal of those who lacked all the things of health and strength, beauty and glory, the grace of God.

Now, the whole of this subject of giving, of the collection for the saints, is looked upon throughout this paragraph as an activity of grace. The Church is one, and it has mutual responsibilities and privileges. The great word of course is the word fellowship, *koinonia*. That comes from another word which means to have all things in common. That is the same word in Acts, where it is said that the early Church had all things in common. So that the Church is one, looked upon in that way. Paul had already stated that in his first letter when dwelling upon the Church as the body of Christ. He had said, "Whether one member suffereth, all the members suffer with it; or one member is honoured, all the members rejoice with it." There is the high ideal. A pain suffered by a member of the Church runs through its membership, and is shared by all. A joy entered into by a member of the Church ripples and runs through all the Church itself. The Church is viewed as one, and consequently this whole subject of giving, giving for the relief of the saints, is looked upon as an activity of grace.

Passing over the ground we may observe the application of this principle. Paul first quoted the example of the Macedonians (viii. 1–5). Then he dealt with the subject of the deputation that was being sent to Jerusalem, in the interest of this activity of grace (viii. 6–ix. 5). Then he showed the results that would follow that activity of grace (ix. 6–15).

The example of the Macedonians, what was it? First of all, the source of their activity was the grace of God, and the spirit of it was joy and liberality. That is in the first four verses.

Then the method of grace, the method of the activity of this grace is in verse 5. Here we have the principle, " First they gave their own selves to the Lord." That is often misquoted, or misunderstood. It is often quoted, They first gave themselves to the Lord, and then they gave of their substance. No, they gave themselves first to the Lord, and then " to us by the will of God." Their method was that they were first devoted to the Lord, and, secondly and consequently, they were devoted to the apostles and the work of the ministry and the work of the Christian Church. The whole fellowship is included. That includes of course the giving of their substance, and interprets the reason of their giving. First to the Lord, there is the principle. Give yourselves first to the Lord. Be careful about that. If you do not, you will give of necessity, you will give grudgingly. We shall see later on that is what they did not do in this matter of giving. First devotion to the Lord means the abandonment of self to Him, and then self at the disposal of all the rest of the ministers and leaders in Jesus Christ. Such were the manner and method.

This whole paragraph concerning the deputation begins by a statement of the apostle as to the privilege of the Church, giving after the manner of Christ (6–12); self-emptying, for the filling of others, and that " according as a man hath, not according as he hath not." Which means to say, we cannot be mechanical about giving. As Paul had instructed them in his first letter, they were to give as they had prospered. That cuts across this gospel of tithing. Tithing may be all right, but it is a minimum. The tithing of a man earning a pound a week is two shillings, and is generosity. The tithing of a man whose income is £10,000 a year would be £1,000. That is poor. It cannot be computed mechanically. It is " according as a man hath, not as he hath not." So the apostle lays down a principle, and the instructions given in his first letter is " as he may prosper," " upon the first day of the week, let each one lay by him in store." A most healthy exercise. Think it out. That instruction is qualified in this letter, "As a man hath, not according as he hath not." If we have not got it, we are not responsible. That may mean in many cases a reconsideration constantly, every week perhaps. On the first day of the week, what of the income? Did you do better last week than you have done for a long time? What effect has that on your giving to the cause of God? Oh, we are not doing so well. All right, then in the presence of your Lord act accordingly. That is a very important principle, which I am sure we do well to ponder and observe.

What is the method of Christian equality? "Your abundance . . . for their want." "Their abundance . . . for your want." What abundance had the Jerusalem church? The abundance of spiritual influence and power. All these churches that Paul was founding owed it to Jerusalem that they had come into existence. They owed their Gospel to Jerusalem. The spiritual abundance had emanated from Jerusalem. I think it might be shown that Jerusalem broke down, and did not fulfil its obligations. Our Lord had told them to go to the uttermost part of the earth, and they hugged Jerusalem for years, and did not go out until persecution drove them. But they went everywhere, and when scattered through persecution, they preached the Word, and there is the abundance that came from Jerusalem.

In the paragraph (16–24) two principles are revealed. Two things are to be observed in the matter of giving and of collections. First it must be "to the glory of the Lord"; secondly, "in the sight of men." That is why Paul sent Titus and that other brother, whose praise was in all the churches. I have never decided who he was. They were sent ahead in order that there might be a completion of the gathering in Corinth for the saints in Jerusalem, before he arrived. He was coming, but he sent them ahead, and if need be, he would go with them. What for? "To the glory of the Lord"? Certainly, but also that the Church might be in no matter of suspicion as to the gathering of money, "in the sight of men." Here he emphasizes the importance of the business side of things in the finances of the Church. We may apply that, and carry it out. I remember that when the Salvation Army started its work William Booth was charged with dishonesty. People said that all the property was in his name, and he might at any time have realized on that property, and so forth. That was criticism of the work. He was very careful from the first to publish his accounts, and in the process of the years that criticism ceased entirely. It is never heard now that the Salvation Army officers are making money out of the work. "In the sight of men" all things upright, all things honourable. That is the principle of the Church.

Then, at the beginning of the ninth chapter comes his appeal, not for their giving. He knew they would give. But he appealed for their state of heart, for their readiness, for their preparedness, that their service might not be as the result of extortion, but of bounty. That word "bounty" is blessing. He says, As you were prepared, as your will was right, so now complete the doing. The great point however is that the will should be there. There must be a willing. "God loveth a cheerful giver." The Greek word there might be transliterated "hilarious," "God loveth a hilarious giver." Does that startle us? It is a fact, and it means exactly that, laughter, and song, and cheer. The Lord loves a cheerful giver. In some churches they have a habit of singing a hymn during the taking of the collection. It is rather good, providing the hymn does not interfere with the finding of the money! It must be hilarious giving, giving out of the heart, because you love to give, not because you are bound to give; not of necessity, nor grudgingly, that is, wanting to hold on to it all the time, of necessity, under compulsion. That is not the way to give. "The Lord loveth a cheerful giver," and our giving should be of that nature.

He ends this section by that very remarkable challenge and charge, "Thanks be to God for His unspeakable Gift." That is to say, when we give, remember God's gift to you, and that Gift as interpreted in the Cross, the grace in that when He was rich, yet for our sakes He became poor. That is the only occasion where that Greek word for *poor* occurs in the New Testament. It means pauperism. He became a pauper on this earth, that we might become rich, that we might be made rich in Him and in His grace. Remember that. If you do, your love, your giving will be of the nature of His. Love will be the inspiration of it. Sacrifice will be the measure of it, and rich blessing to others will be the result of it, giving your money, not grudgingly, not of necessity, but freely, cheerfully.

Those seem to me to be the principles underlying this very local section. That collection was being made for the poor saints, and all the churches in Macedonia were making a contribution to the suffering and needy saints of Jerusalem. This is very applicable today. How many churches today are suffering, are homeless? All the churches should help them in every way they can. There ought to be equality of contribution to the need, just as those churches are contributing to our need in things spiritual, by their courage, and their very carrying on, in spite of all the turmoil and strife and desolation. How wonderful they are! How heroic they are! How splendid they are! They are making a great contribution of their abundance, the abundance of their faith, the abundance of their courage and their love.

This is a small matter comparatively, and yet Paul says two things run together, that we should make our contribution, if we have it, to their necessities in things material, for there must be, and so there will be, equality.

```
C. PAUL'S COMING TO CORINTH                                x-xiii. 10
   I. His Authority                                              x
      i. His Appeal                                            1–6
         a. Its Grounds                                          1
         b. Its Plea                                             2
         c. A Description of Spiritual Authority               3–6
     ii. His Answer                                           7–11
         a. Their Mistake                                    7–10
            1. Declared                                    7 and 10
            2. Corrected                                    8 and 9
         b. His Warning                                         11
    iii. His Claim                                          12–18
         a. His Opponents' Self-Glorying                       12
         b. His Limits of Glorying                          13–16
            1. The Divinely Appointed Work                     13
            2. The Work Done, and to be Done              14–16
         c. The Final Test                                 17, 18
```

II CORINTHIANS x

IN this final division of the letter Paul vindicated his authority in an argument that centred around his proposed visit to Corinth and the criticisms of him. In this chapter he deals with his authority. In the second division (xi–xii. 18) he dealt with his apostleship; finally, with his programme (xii. 19–xiii. 10).

He first pleaded with them that there might be no necessity for him to change his methods that had characterized his actions when amongst them. In answer to the criticism of those who had declared themselves to be Christ's, he in turn also declared that he was Christ's, and announced his ability to use his authority if necessary, finally claiming that he had such authority directly from the Lord.

When dealing with the subject of the authority of the ministry in the earlier part of his letter, Paul was addressing himself principally to the loyal majority. Now he evidently has in mind the minority in definite opposition to him. This opposition may have been that of one man, with a weak following. Paul's words are so personal at one point that they make me feel that is so. "If any man trusteth in himself that he is Christ's . . . even as he is Christ's, so also are we." The nature of the opposition can be gathered from his reply. The background of that opposition is clearly revealed. They were denying his authority, and were speaking disrespectfully of him. They were saying when he was there he was weak. His letters were strong, but he was not able to exercise authority when present. They were little criticisms, but Paul felt it worth while to deal with them, and that he did in this particular section. His joyful ending of the earlier section on authority ended with the words, "I rejoice that in everything I am of good courage concerning you," and opened the way for the financial business. The grateful ending dealing with the financial business was, "Thanks be to God for His unspeakable Gift." That afforded, and was the platform of approach to the unpleasant matter of the opposition of a certain minority.

In the first six verses he appeals to them. "Now I Paul myself entreat you by the meekness and gentleness of Christ, I who in your presence am lowly among you." That is what they were saying, that in his absence he wrote letters that were strong, but when he was there he was not strong at all. "In your presence I am lowly, but being absent am of good courage toward you." The fourth verse is in parenthesis, so read in close connection verses 3 and 5. "For though we walk in the flesh, we do not war according to the flesh; casting down imaginations, and every high thing that is exalted against the knowledge of God, and bringing every thought into captivity to the obedience of Christ." That is a remarkable passage. It reveals the ground of his authority: first, the personal note, "I Paul myself"; but that personality interpreted by "the meekness and gentleness of Christ." "Lowly among you," yea, verily. So they said. So I was, but I am of good courage. That is also true.

What, then, is his plea? "I beseech you, that I may not when present shew courage with the confidence wherewith I count to be bold against some, which count of us as if we walked according to the flesh." That is his appeal, that he should not be made to change his attitude. He is quite capable of doing so. He can be courageous when with them. He can be severe when with them, but he much prefers to proceed as he had before, by the meekness and gentleness of Christ. "I am meek and lowly," said Jesus. So Paul appealed to them.

In the next verses we have a description of his spiritual authority, a definition of things wherein that authority consists. It was not "according to the flesh." That means not according to human personality, or human cleverness; not according to human activity at all. What then? There is a negative and a positive note, and these two in harmony create spiritual authority. The negative, "casting down imaginations," or, to take the marginal reading, "casting down reasonings, and every high thing that is exalted against the knowledge of God." That is the negative note, "casting down." His presence and his teaching had moved in that direction, "casting down every imagination," or reasoning, which was contrary to the knowledge of God. "This is life eternal," said our Lord, "that they should know Thee, the only true God." Any reasoning that is contrary to the knowledge of God, that is revealed in Christ, is to be denied, it is to be cast down. That is the negative side of spiritual authority.

But the positive side is this, "bringing every thought into captivity to the obedience of Christ." That is one of the most remarkable phrases in the New Testament, "bringing every thought into captivity to the obedience of Christ." Let us ponder that, and examine ourselves and our thinking. Especially is that true of those in the ministry. Is our every thought brought into captivity to the obedience of Christ? Are we submissive to Christ? Do we submit all things to Him, for that is the first qualification? Do we submit all things to Him for His jurisdiction and government? Do we ask, Is this the will of our Lord, before we go anywhere, or do anything, or before we plan or think? We must do that. Yes, but do we submit the plan and thinking to Christ? That is the secret of spiritual authority, and there is no man in authority unless he knows what it is on the negative side to cast down imaginations, or reasonings, which exalt themselves against the knowledge of God, and that in order that every thought may be brought into captivity to the obedience of Christ. That is a great phrase. If our gathering together has any value at all it is practical. Here was a man whose authority was being questioned in the realm of the flesh. Yes, he said, that is not the realm in which we are living or serving, thinking or planning. We think and plan and work in spiritual power, and the objective is that of the casting down of all imaginations, all reasonings, all cleverness, that exalts itself against the knowledge of God, and the knowledge of God has only come to us through Christ. But we are also bringing every thought into captivity to the obedience of Christ.

He now made his answer, first showing them their mistake (7-10), and then warning them (11). In verses 7 and 10 we have their wrong thinking that Paul was correcting. "Ye look at the things that are before your face." You are seeing that which is near, and that which is near alone. You are judging by appearance, a most evil thing to do at any time, and under any circumstances. "If any man trusteth in himself that he is Christ's, let him consider this again, that even as he is Christ's, so also are we." Notice he did not say that man was not Christ's; but he was objecting to his claim. He objected to being excluded from that privilege. He says, We are Christ's, as that man is Christ's. That man who claimed to be Christ's really excluded the apostle, denied his authority as from Christ, and his relationship to Christ. Paul said, Let him remember we also are Christ's.

Then verse 10. "For his letters, they say, are weighty and strong, but his bodily presence is weak, and his speech of no account." Let him remember there is no inconsistency in our attitude. That was the mistake they were making. They were looking upon the face only. They were judging by appearances. There creeps in the thought of bodily appearance. In presence he is mean and contemptible. That is what they said, and they were judging by that. He is weak in words. That comes of his gentleness manifest when with them, and that expressed itself in his previous letter. Now that is corrected by verses 8 and 9. There is the correcting element to their false thinking. Their false outlook was that they were judging by appearances, and holding him in contempt for what he appeared to be, and turning their back upon the central verity of his authority, that which he had already done, the authority that sought to bring every thought into captivity to the obedience of Christ; and casting down every imagination and reasoning that exalted itself against the knowledge of God. That is his authority. They were looking at the man, and judging by those human expressions.

He now made his claim (12–18). This is a remarkable passage, in which we see Paul's view of his limitations. Those limitations are created by the will of God. That word "province," which occurs three times, means there the sphere appointed by God. His opponents are glorying in themselves. He will do nothing of the kind; but he will glory in the Divinely appointed task and work, and the work done, and so to be done. That is the theme of his glorying and of his authority. Everything here is leaning back upon the apostle's conception that he stated at the beginning of the letter, that he is an apostle "by the will of God," and that God has made His plans for him, and that he is working within them. He said he was not trespassing on any man's sphere or province, but was working within the bounds laid down by God. That is what he was doing. The solemn teaching of the whole passage is this that the right test for work is not the opinion of others. Other people may say everything is all right, and that one is doing splendidly. That is of no value. It is not the opinion of oneself in comparison with others. That is a very tempting line of thought. I may look at others, and may be well satisfied with myself. That is no good. The test is not a man's opinion of himself within his own personality. There is only one test, and that is the commendation of the Lord. Does the Lord commend me? Does the Lord approve of my service? That is the only test. Here Paul shows his magnificent and absolute independence of the thinking of others, or of his thinking about himself. Everything is relegated to the arbitrament of his Master, the Lord Himself, the only thing worth thinking about.

The secret of spiritual power, or the work of spiritual power, is that of casting down reasonings exalting themselves against the knowledge of God, and bringing every thought into captivity to the obedience of Christ. Here this is what Paul was doing as to himself. He is bringing everything to submit to the Lordship of his Lord. The sphere in which he is working is an appointed sphere. He does not go across into the sphere of another man. The city of Corinth was marked for him, and he went there, and he is hoping to go beyond that. His sphere stretches out beyond that, but the whole thing is he is testing his work by the opinion and thought and judgment of his Lord.

That need not be stressed. It is important.

> "Men love thee, praise thee not,
> The Master praises, what are men."

So run the lines of a hymn, and there is a tremendous truth in them. To go to rest every night, submitting the life to Him, and to hear His word of commendation, that is the highest reward. I would rather submit my life to Him for judgment than to any of you. He is more patient. He is more understanding. I know perfectly well that He knows my desire as well as my activity, and that He judges me by my aspiration as well as by my achievement.

In this chapter Paul has argued for his authority, an authority derived from the authority of his Master, an authority that acts for the pulling down of all imaginations that are contrary to the knowledge of God that we have had in Jesus Christ. Anything that contradicts that is to be cast down, is to be destroyed, and all thought is to be brought into captivity to the obedience of Christ.

260 THE CORINTHIAN LETTERS OF PAUL

II. *His Apostleship*	xi–xii. 13
i. His Apology for Boasting	xi. 1–4
a. " Foolishness "	1
b. Its Reason. " I Am Jealous "	2–4
" I Fear "	
ii. His Boasting	xi. 5–xii. 10
a. Of His Apostleship	5–15
1. As to Official Authority	5
2. In its Exercise	6–15
b. The Comparison Emphasized	16–33
1. The False Teachers	16–20
2. The Apostle	21–23
On the Level of the Flesh	21, 22
On the Level of Spiritual Authority	23–30
The Witness	31–33
c. Of the Supreme Matter	xii. 1–10
1. The Vision and the Voice	1–6
2. The Thorn and the Grace	7–10
3. The Effect	7 and 10
4. The Great Word	10
iii. His Only Apology	xii. 11–13

II CORINTHIANS xi–xii. 13

PAUL now dealt with his apostleship (xi–xii. 13). In this whole section we hear the apostle boasting: first making an apology for so doing (xi. 1–4), and then indulging in the boasting (xi. 5–xii. 10); lastly, making his only apology (xii. 11–13).

He begins this apology for boasting, and then gives the reason for it. He first records the foolishness of boasting, and then he tells the Corinthians why he has done it. He starts this by saying, " Would that ye could bear with me in a little foolishness." Chapter ten had closed with the words, " For not he that commendeth himself is approved, but whom the Lord commendeth." There he had stated his independence of the opinion of other people, and warned those to whom he wrote that the commendation of others was of no value at all, that the commendation of a man's own soul of himself was not of any value. The only commendation that is of any value is that of the Lord. " Would that ye could bear with me in a little foolishness." It is interesting how this idea runs through the whole of this section. Paul reverts to it again and again. What is " foolishness " ? The Greek word means mindlessness. That is not an adequate interpretation. Let us try another word, " stupidity," or by implication, " ignorance," " egotism." Paul says, Bear with me in a little egotism, a little mindlessness. He is undervaluing what he is going to do, and yet he does it, and was warranted in doing it. Of that there is no question. He thinks very little, he sets very little value, from his own soul's standpoint, upon what he is compelled to do. It is remarkable how the thought of foolishness runs all through this section, in different forms, the word, or cognate words, through this chapter, and again in chapter twelve.

Why was he doing this? For two reasons, "I am jealous," "I fear." Those two phrases record the movement of his mind; and declare his reason for indulging in this little foolishness, that is of so small a value in itself, and yet he is constrained to do it. "I am jealous over you with a godly jealousy; for I espoused you to one husband, that I might present you as a pure virgin to Christ." Is there anything more beautiful than that as a description of the Christian life and position? Espoused to one husband, and the word of course meant far more than it does now. In espousals today one is not sure of anything. Two people are espoused, and that does not mean much. It ought to. It does in some cases. It rather depends upon one's outlook on life. Espousal, to the mind of the Hebrew, to the mind of the Jew, to the mind of Paul, was equivalent to marriage. "I have espoused you to one husband." That is the meaning, one husband, not to one fiancé—excuse me! I have espoused you to one husband, a pure virgin to Christ. We see all the light shining through that, with its suggestion of relationship to Him.

And "I fear, lest by any means, as the serpent beguiled Eve in his craftiness, your minds should be corrupted from the simplicity and the purity that is toward Christ." One could stay there, but go back to the story of the beguilement of Eve. How did the serpent beguile Eve? He slandered God. He told her God did not mean what He said. He was "a liar from the beginning," as our Lord Himself did say; and on the basis of a lie that was partly the truth. We remember Tennyson's lines:

> "A lie that is all of a lie can be met with and fought outright;
> But a lie that is partly the truth is a harder matter to fight."

"Yea, hath God said, Ye shall not eat of any tree of the garden?" No, He had not. He had limited their liberty by one tree only. Follow that out. "I fear, lest by any means, as the serpent beguiled Eve in his craftiness, your minds should be corrupted from the simplicity and the purity that is toward Christ." I presented you to Christ, to one husband, but I fear that your minds should be corrupted. It is leaven that corrupts. Well did our Lord warn against the leaven of hypocrisy, the leaven of making believe, the leaven of wearing a mask, the leaven of a lie. "I fear."

Why was he fearing? "For if he that cometh preacheth another

Jesus, Whom we did not preach, or if he receive a different spirit, which ye did not receive, or a different Gospel, which ye did not accept, ye do well to bear with him." There are those who look upon that as irony. I do not think it is. I think the apostle meant if a teacher should come with an entirely different message he might be borne with, he might be tolerated. But those in the apostle's mind who were coming with the message were questioning Paul's authority, and therefore challenging the authority of the message.

He now turned to his boasting. " For I reckon that I am not a whit behind the very chiefest apostles." He has begun his " foolishness," his boasting. Do not be misled by any definition of the term which I have suggested. Do not get away with the first meaning of that Greek word, " stupidity," but take the accepted meaning, egotism, boasting. The apostle said he was going to indulge in that, and he does so first of all by a tremendous statement as to authority. " For I reckon that I am not a whit behind the very chiefest apostles." Some tell us that he was comparing himself now with the false teachers. I do not think so. I believe he was thinking of the actual apostles, and was claiming an equality with them, because of the Lord's appointment. He was referring to the fact there that he also had been called of God, and appointed to this apostleship.

Then, in the next paragraph (5–15) he shows his authority, arguing for that authority as to its manner, its method, and its motive.

As to its manner, verse 6: " But though I be rude in speech, yet am I not in knowledge; nay, in everything we have made it manifest among all men to you-ward." " Rude in speech " ! Surely there he is quoting his critics. Well, he said, I may be; but the thing I say, I am not rude in that; the thing I have taught you bears the hall-mark of Divine authority. So much for his manner; if rude in speech, not in knowledge.

Then his method, and there is a local touch here. Was it a sin that he was not chargeable to them? His need had been supplied by the brethren from Macedonia. He took nothing from these Corinthians, and he now boasted in that. When he wrought with his own hands for his own support, or when he was in want, that want was supplied by others, not by them. He makes a very strong statement there. He says he robbed other churches to serve them. That is very local.

Then he goes on and shows his motive (11–15). What was it? " Wherefore?" Why did he do all this? That is the meaning of the " Wherefore?" Why did I determine not to be chargeable to you? Wherefore? because I love you not?" Was that it? It was a question. " God knoweth," and He knows, and he is commended by his Master; and when a man knows that, it delivers him from all care of the opinion of others. You Corinthians say I do not love you; well,

God knows. "But what I do, that I will do, that I may cut off occasion; that wherein they glory, they may be found even as we." What does he mean? Surely he means that these people who are troubling him, he wishes they also had to work for their living, that "they may be found even as we," not dependent on you for their support.

"For such men are false apostles, deceitful workers, fashioning themselves into apostles of Christ. And no marvel; for even Satan fashioneth himself into an angel of light. It is no great thing therefore if his ministers also fashion themselves as ministers of righteousness; whose end shall be according to their works."

Notice the appeal of that passage. He was putting himself into comparison, definitely with these false teachers now, and he described them drastically as false apostles, deceitful workers, and said that they fashioned themselves into apostles of Christ. They are not appointed. They are not ordained. They are not apostles within the will or purpose of God. They "fashion themselves." It is a very cutting criticism of them. He says, What wonder. The devil himself fashions himself as an angel of light. What wonder if his ministers do the same, false apostles, deceitful workers, fashioning themselves as apostles of Christ, being ministers of the devil, of Satan, after the manner of Satan.

Again go back to the Garden of Eden, where Satan appeared as a bright and brilliant being. That is the story. The idea of the devil appearing as a snake is of course ridiculous. That is not the word at all. It is a shining one. Eve was beguiled by a brilliant appearance, and a lie, a slander on God. The apostle claims that these false teachers have been received, and they have been exercising authority which has been characterized by great severity and harshness such as Paul never used.

The apostle then compared himself with them, first of all on the level of the flesh. "Are they Hebrew? so am I. Are they Israelites? so am I. Are they the seed of Abraham? so am I." Then he rises to the highest height and portrays himself in comparison with them as the ministers of Christ. "Are they ministers of Christ? (I speak as one beside himself) I more." And that marvellous paragraph follows, showing him, not on the level of the flesh, but on the level of spiritual authority. The only thing to do with the paragraph is to read it and attempt to draw the picture for oneself. "In labours . . . in prisons . . . in stripes . . . in deaths." In personal suffering, "beaten . . . stoned . . . suffered shipwreck, a night and a day . . . in the deep; in journeyings often." Watch him and read his story as he there describes it. "In perils of rivers . . . of robbers . . . my countrymen . . . Gentiles . . . in the city . . . in the wilderness . . .

in the sea . . . among false brethren; in labour and travail, in watchings often, in hunger and thirst, in fasting often, in cold and nakedness." These are all pictures. He was giving them his apostolic credentials, the credentials of his authority, the proof, in comparison with others, of the authority of his teaching, the authority of the truth, the authority of that simplicity and purity to which they were called, when he betrothed them to Christ, espoused them to Christ, to one husband. All these are his credentials.

He then finished by saying, "Beside those things that are without, there is that which passeth upon me daily, anxiety for all the churches." That is the point where the value of episcopacy comes in, "all the churches." The *episcopus* is an overseer. Paul said, "All the churches," those he had planted, and the churches planted by others. He was anxious about them day by day, perhaps the same anxiety that he had concerning these Corinthians, fear lest they should be corrupted from the simplicity and purity that is in Christ.

Well, if this is foolishness, it is not stupidity; it is great boasting. It is the boasting of a man conscious of the witness of God. He says, "The God and Father of the Lord Jesus, He Who is blessed for evermore, knoweth that I lie not." He knows the comfort of it, the strength of it. It is a comfort and a strength to any man called to the ministry, "God knoweth." He knows what? Knows all the suffering, knows all the trial, knows all the facts, which he has already referred to, that he is led everywhere in triumph in Christ. Through travail he has come to triumph all the way. "God knoweth." That is the secret of his deepest boasting.

The last two verses of the chapter introduce the next section, in which he becomes even more personal. We end this paragraph with this thought, that this man is indulging in boasting, about which there is no doubt. He is boasting on a high level of the privilege that has come to him of bearing witness and proclaiming the truth, and that through all circumstances, suffering, and deprivation, desolation, and peril; but all the time "God knoweth."

> "He knows, He loves, He cares,
> Nothing this truth can dim.
> He gives His very best to those
> Who leave the choice to Him."

Here (xii. 1-13) Paul dealt with his apostleship. As we saw in the previous chapter (xi) he had adopted a new method, that of boasting. Reading the last verses of that chapter we have the sequence. The 30th verse tells the purpose of his boasting, "If I must needs glory, I will glory of the things that concern my weakness." The next verse is one of solemnity and of great value, in which he called God to witness that he was not lying.

Then immediately proceeding, he tells of his escape from Damascus. That is closely connected with all that follows in the process of his argument. It is important that we should notice it. Can any picture be more one of weakness than that, of his being let down in a basket over the wall of Damascus? Could we think of anything more likely to rob a man of any sense of dignity than that? "In Damascus the governor under Aretas the king guarded the city of the Damascenes, in order to take me; and through a window was I let down in a basket by the wall, and escaped his hands." Yet that led on to all that followed, in his life and ministry. That hour of weakness was the hour in which he found entry upon the ministry of power which followed.

Let us look at that incident in its setting. Luke in his historic narrative, the Acts of the Apostles, does not notice it. Indeed, there is a great gap historically at Acts ix. 19. That reads, "He took food and was strengthened." That was when he came to Damascus. Then Luke's narrative goes on, "And he was certain days with the disciples which were at Damascus. And straightway in the synagogues he proclaimed Jesus." Reading that, in spite of the fact that the revisers have made a break in the middle of the verse, one might imagine that was an immediate sequence. That was nothing of the kind. Two, or probably three years are passed over, during which time Paul was in Arabia. Turn over to the Galatian letter, and there (i. 15) we read, "But when it was the good pleasure of God . . . to reveal His Son in me, that I might preach Him among the Gentiles; immediately I conferred not with flesh and blood; neither went I up to Jerusalem to them which were apostles before me; but I went away into Arabia; and again I returned unto Damascus." It was this return to Damascus of which Luke wrote in what remains of that nineteenth verse of the ninth chapter of Acts and following verses. Paul had been away from Damascus for two or three years. That is a subject worth thinking about. Paul, apprehended by Christ on the Damascus road, was sent to Damascus. A disciple there was told by the Lord that he was coming; received him, welcomed him, gave him food, strengthened him. Then Paul went away from Damascus to Arabia. Speculation may be perfectly proper about that period in Arabia. He went under the shadow of Mount Sinai, and he had to reconstruct all his thinking in the light of the experience on the Damascene road; and there was no more fitting place than to do it at that place where the law had been given, of which he had been zealous to the point of persecuting the Church. Now he was arrested, and he had to go away and think in quietness.

Then, returning to Damascus, as Luke has told us, he went into the synagogues and preached Jesus is the Christ, the result of thinking things out in Arabia. People were perturbed, the disciples were afraid. They said, Is not this the man who made havoc of the church, and has come here to hale us to prison? And he left. I do not know how long he stayed then; it may not have been long. Where did he go? Undoubtedly to Jerusalem, and ultimately to Tarsus. Barnabas met him in Jerusalem, and introduced him, and Jerusalem was suspicious of him, and so he went away to Tarsus. How long did he remain in Tarsus before Barnabas found him and called him to be his assistant? Without any question ten years. Then he became Barnabas' assistant, and they worked together, and then came the larger call.

Why stay with all these details? Because it dates this story which Paul now tells in this letter to the Corinthians in this twelfth chapter. He writes "fourteen years ago." Working that out, it places this experience in Tarsus in that ten years' sojourn "fourteen years ago." He was looking back now over this distance of fourteen years. There are many things explicable by time's passing. Looking back fourteen years ago, now he is boasting once more.

It is very interesting to notice his method. He had said in the previous chapter, and again now he says at the beginning of this, "I must needs glory, though it is not expedient; but I will come to visions and revelations of the Lord." Then, as though he was writing of someone else, "I knew a man in Christ fourteen years ago." I knew such a man, and we never find out by reading, until we reach the seventh verse, that he is writing of himself. "By reason of the exceeding greatness of the revelations, wherefore that I should not be exalted overmuch." Oh, then, Paul, you are the man; we have found you out! Yes, he attempted to be impersonal, but was not able to carry that through. He gives his secret away in that seventh verse.

What is the story he tells? It is that of a double experience, one of high exaltation, followed closely by one of deep desolation. Paul is boasting. He was caught up into the third heaven. He was caught up into Paradise. He was caught up, and "heard unspeakable words." The vision was such that he describes it as "the exceeding greatness of the revelation."

Someone says, Do you believe that story? I remember very well someone asking me that in the States, Does that mean he was caught up in bodily form, or that his spirit passed on? Of course my reply was obvious. My dear friend, how do you suppose I know, when Paul tells us twice over he did not know himself? "Whether in the body, I know not; or whether out of the body, I know not; God knoweth." But it was a time of strange exaltation. He was caught up to the third heaven. That is a Hebrew expression, equivalent to the sentence that follows, "caught up into Paradise." The third heaven to the Hebrew was the place where the saints and angels are, what we mean when we speak of Heaven. The first heaven was that of the atmosphere, the second that of the stellar spaces, and the third was a region somewhere, if the preposition be correct, beyond, outside; the third heaven, where is the manifestation and presence of God, the third heaven to which the Son of God ascended; the third heaven which is the abode of the saints made perfect, where are the angels and archangels, cherubim and seraphim—Paradise. Paul calls them "the exceeding greatness of the revelations." He says he "heard unspeakable words, which it is not lawful for a man to utter," and he never did utter them. Someone may ask me, Did you ever have an experience like that? Never. Do you think other people have had it? Undoubtedly. I am certain that experiences like that have been granted under certain conditions to certain persons, and always with a certain definite purpose. It is an interesting experience. How often people have wanted to tell me about their visions! I am always suspicious. I want to know what they had for supper the night before! If people have visions of this sort they are silent about them. Fourteen years had passed, and Paul had never told about them; and even now he could not tell. They were inexplicable, unspeakable words, words not lawful for a man to utter. It was a high experience.

But it was followed by an experience of darkness of the deepest kind. There are three movements here. "A thorn in the flesh." Thorn is a poor word. It is a stake in the flesh. That is the real word. It is a word that is equivalent to crucifixion, but it was in the flesh. That was physical. There was no doubt about that. Then "a messenger of Satan to buffet me." That is mental. Then unanswered prayer, apparently. That is spiritual. A great realm of darkness and desolation came to him, following upon this period of high exaltation. A stake in the flesh, a crucifixion. There can be no more powerful description of physical suffering than that. Then a messenger of Satan to buffet him. We understand that, in a measure. It is when we are down and suffering physically that the devil comes to buffet the mind. I can tell you some of the things he says, If God were good, would He permit this? The buffeting messenger of Satan. Then the third thing, "Concerning this thing I besought the Lord thrice." That does not mean three times. It is the Hebrew figure of ceaselessly, continuously, over and over again. "I besought the *Lord* thrice," and the stake remained, and the buffeting messenger of Satan did not go, and apparently his prayer was unanswered. I will put it in another way. His prayer was answered by denial of that which was sought, freedom from the stake in the flesh, freedom from the buffeting of Satan—No!

Then comes the next statement, and here there is a change in the Revised Version. The Old Version had it, "He said unto me," as though the thing was said then and there. I do not so read it. "He hath said unto me," through the process of the years, through that period of suffering, continued, from which he sought escape, which escape was not granted unto him, "He hath said unto me, My grace is sufficient for thee." He understood the purpose of the affliction. What was it? "That I should not be exalted overmuch." He repeats that twice.

The peril of any high spiritual experience is that of braggadocio, that of the uplifted chin. I have known people who have gone to Keswick and have received great blessing; but the trouble was that they came home and strutted round among their fellow members of their church with damnable pride. Paul saw the purpose of the affliction. "That I should not be exalted above measure."

Again he saw the method of it. "There was given unto me." Given to him? The stake in the flesh a gift? The messenger of Satan to buffet, a gift? The denial of the request in prayer, a gift? These things were given to him. He used that word about the first two, the stake and the messenger of Satan. I wonder if he would have looked upon those as gifts at the moment? Certainly not, because he begged to have them taken away from him. But fourteen years have passed, and he has had time to understand. Fourteen years ago these things happened, and the Lord has now said unto him, "He has said unto me," by the process of the years, I have no doubt: "My grace is sufficient for thee."

Notice his changed attitude toward the afflictions. One almost trembles to read it. "Most gladly therefore will I rather glory in my weakness, that the power of Christ may rest upon me. Wherefore I take pleasure in weaknesses, in injuries, in necessities, in persecutions, in distresses, for Christ's sake; for when I am weak, then am I strong." Now that is neither stoicism nor submission to a dispensation of God which is not understood. It is the language of a man who realizes that the things he desired to escape from were allies of the soul. "That I might not be exalted overmuch," above measure. Does that look a weak reason? It is not. There is nothing more hindering the work of God than the uplifted and proud Christian. "That I might not be exalted above measure." He has come to thank God that He denied his request. He has come to find out that that denial was a denial of love.

Here is a little poem written by an old friend of mine, Oliver Huckell:

"I thank Thee, Lord, for mine unanswered prayers—
Unanswered, save Thy quiet, kindly 'Nay,'
Yet it seemed hard among my heavy cares,
That bitter day.

"I wanted joy; but Thou didst know for me
That sorrow was the gift I needed most,
And in its mystic depths I learned to see
The Holy Ghost.

"I wanted health; but Thou didst bid me sound
The secret treasuries of pain,
And in the moans and groans my heart oft found
The Christ again.

"I wanted wealth; 'twas not the better part;
There is a wealth with poverty oft given,
And Thou didst teach me of the gold of heart,
Best gift of heaven.

"I thank Thee, Lord, for those unanswered prayers,
And for Thy word, the quiet, kindly 'Nay.'
'Twas Thy withholding lightened all my cares
That blessed day."

That is what Paul meant when he said, "There was given unto me."

Tarry for a moment with the word itself, that great word, "He hath said unto me, My grace is sufficient for thee." Fourteen years had passed. Was not this word slowly spelt out to him? I think it was. What does it mean? "My grace," the region of the Divine complacency is the region of power, proceeding to fulfilment of purpose. That which satisfies, God is sufficient. The word "sufficient" means "lifts," "bears," "carries." "My grace is sufficient for thee." The word spelled out to Paul was this: It is enough for you to know that you are in My grace. There is a meaning in all your life. There are some wonderful illustrations of this in the Scriptures. In Nehemiah's time, when the people were sadly mourning, he said to them, "The joy of the Lord is your strength." That simply means, What pleases God is your strength.

In that most remarkable word of Isaiah, "It pleased the Lord to bruise Him," all the afflictions and sufferings of the Christ are there set in the place of the Divine grace. It was the Divine intention, the Divine purpose. Ask God why, and we know why in His case. It was for us men, and for our salvation, that "it pleased the Lord to bruise Him," and He was content.

Now Paul says that thorn is God's "grace." It is the inner secret of power. It is that which makes the revelations of value in experience. "My grace is sufficient for thee." Of course there is more in that than we have often seen. I think it is a greater word than we have often understood. We have taken it meant, It is all right. I know you are in trouble, but I will uphold you. It is not that at all. It is that the trouble itself is part of the process. Before our Lord left His disciples He said to them one day, "Your sorrow shall be turned into joy." Not, You shall have joy in place of sorrow, but the sorrow shall be transmuted into joy. In sorrow is the making of joy. In suffering is the working of power. That is what Paul meant when he said, "It hath been said unto me." I have received an interpretation of all these things that troubled me at the time, some of which I sought to escape, the most poignant of which came in the fact that I was not allowed to escape. But in the process of time I have learned that all these things were in God's will; and the one place of safety is the place that pleases God, whether it be suffering, or whether it be joy; whether it be exultation or desolation. Is it in the will of God? If so, we are to rejoice in it. As Paul says in another of his letters, "Let us rejoice also in tribulation, for tribulation worketh patience."

This is a wonderful chapter, a wonderful story. Paul goes back in the concluding verses to claim his parity with all the apostles, not a whit behind any of them. Signs and wonders and powers having yielded themselves through him, he knows the authority of his apostleship, and argues for it, and if boasting is necessary, he boasts in his weakness, and glories in his weakness.

III. *His Programme*	xii. 14–xiii. 10
i. The Subject Approached	xii. 14–18
a. The Intention	14, 15
b. The Backward Look	16–18
ii. The Purpose of His Writing	19–21
a. Their False View	19a
b. The Truth	19b
c. His Fear	20, 21
iii. The Procedure at His Coming	xiii. 1–4
a. Investigation	1, 2
b. Proof	3, 4
iv. The Last Appeal	5–10
a. Made	5, 6
b. Argued	7–10
CONCLUSION	xiii. 11–14
I. *Exhortations*	11
II. *Salutations*	12, 13
III. *Benediction*	14

II CORINTHIANS xii. 14–xiii

NOTICE first that the apostle here says, "Behold, this is the third time I am ready to come to you," and then at the commencement of the thirteenth chapter he seems to have made up his mind. "This is the third time I am coming to you." I am ready to come, and I am coming. There are different interpretations of what he meant. There are those who imagine he meant, This is the third attempt at coming. I do not so read it, because presently he refers to "as when I was present the second time." I believe he is referring to an actual visit that he is intending to make. Contemplating a visit, he draws his letter to a conclusion by being very careful to make clear what his attitude in writing has been. He cared little for their approval of his conduct, but very much for their being approved before God. That had been the purpose lying behind this letter, and the first letter undoubtedly. Out of such desire he had delivered a message under a sense of responsibility to God, and with a consciousness of its authority. Finally he announced the method of his third coming to them to be that of severe investigation.

The subject is approached with that statement:

"Behold, this is the third time I am ready to come to you; and I will not be a burden to you; for I seek not yours; but you; for the children ought not to lay up for the parents, but the parents for the children. And I will most gladly spend and be spent for your souls. If I love you more abundantly, am I loved the less? But be it so, I did not myself burden you; but, being crafty, I caught you with guile. Did I take advantage of you by any one of them whom

I have sent unto you? I exhorted Titus, and I sent the brother with him. Did Titus take any advantage of you? walked we not by the same Spirit? walked we not in the same steps?"

There he was introducing and approaching final things. He clearly showed his intention not to be a burden to them. In his coming again he would follow his previous method. That will be remembered, that he was no burden to them; there was no financial relationship between them. He had wrought without fee or reward. He was coming like that again. "But be it so, I did not myself burden you; but, being crafty, I caught you with guile." That is open to many interpretations. What did he mean? Did he mean to say, you are crafty, and I employed the same method? Or did he mean being crafty himself? Was he speaking facetiously? I do not think so for a moment, and I was interested to read the Basic New Testament at that point. They have introduced a little sentence there. So far as I have read this Basic Testament, this is the only case in which they have put in words which are words of interpretation and not translation. In brackets they have inserted three words, "But [someone will say] being false, I took you with deceit." I think that is a most illuminative parenthesis. The translators evidently felt it was important that they should be understood, and so they suggest that Paul is saying what someone will say about him. They are not part of the text, and have been put in brackets. Someone will say, being crafty, I caught you with guile; and immediately he contradicts that particular view by the next words, "Did I take advantage of you?"

As we have seen, the letter was written with certain people in view who were opposed to Paul, critical of him, and denied his authority. Someone now seemed to suggest he was crafty towards them. He had not received any support from them directly, but he had done so indirectly. That is the thought that lies behind that; and Paul repudiates that charge, denies it as he says, "Be it so, I did not myself burden you. . . . Did I take advantage of you?" They suggested he derived pecuniary value, or remuneration through those whom he sent. That seems to me to be the whole point there, and he denies it entirely. By the form of questions he suggests that neither he nor those he sent, Titus or the other brother, had taken advantage of them. "Did Titus take any advantage of you? walked we not by the same Spirit? walked we not in the same steps?" He is claiming guidance by the Spirit, and there can be no craft, no deceit, no guile when men are doing that.

The purpose of his writing is seen in verses 19 to 21. It was their false view that he had been excusing himself. In that they were entirely wrong. He told them the truth. He had spoken "in the sight of God," "in Christ," and the purpose had been their edifying, their building up. So he vindicated his letters, his first and second, claiming that he had been speaking "in the sight of God," that he had been speaking "in Christ," claiming that he had been writing for their edifying. Here we get another revelation of the true attitude of the Christian minister. It should always be in the sight of God, in Christ, Christ-circumferenced; and it should always aim at the building up, the edifying of those to whom the message is sent.

There are two things here twice repeated, "lest by any means," and "lest when I come again," they would not be what he desired. That was why he had been writing. I think there is a suggestion in that of his intended severity. "Lest there should be strife, jealousy, wraths, factions, backbitings, whisperings, swellings, tumults." Lest there should be all these things. We must go back to the first letter to find out what he really meant. There was a divided state in the church, and he had written to show that they were all one in Christ, and that they should live and act as of one mind. On the contrary, he gives a list of terrible things that may happen if that is not so. Lest there should be these things obtaining, "lest when I come again, my God should humble me before you, and I should mourn for many of them that have sinned heretofore, and repented not"; lest they, divided, be quarrelling; he be mourning. For their edification and their disobedience and the absence of repentance, that is why he is writing.

In the first four verses of the thirteenth chapter he tells them the procedure at his coming. When he comes again there shall be strict investigation. Two or three witnesses shall be summoned, and their testimony shall be received, and he "will not spare" them.

Therefore he made his last appeal to them (5–10). He urged them to immediate activity before he came to them, in order that he might come not with severity, but in gentleness. He was quite careless how he might appear, though they might look upon him as reprobate. He was praying they might not be reprobate, but might be right.

Then comes this remarkable sentence, "For we can do nothing against the truth, but for the truth." Was there ever anything written more remarkable than that as to the final victory of truth? We can do nothing against it. It will run its way. It will triumph eventually. There is a sense in which it is well for us to remember that even to-day. You can do nothing against the truth, but for the truth. "For we rejoice when we are weak, and ye are strong; this we also pray for, even your perfecting. For this cause I write these things while absent, that I may not when present deal sharply, according to the authority which the Lord gave me for building up and not for casting down." What is he doing? As he draws this letter to a close, he is appealing to them to examine themselves, to try themselves, and to get right themselves, in order that he may not deal with them sharply, in order that he may spare them, in order that when he comes to exercise authority, he may do it with gentleness and not harshness. He is quite prepared, if the necessity occurs, to deal with them severely, to deal with them so as not to spare them.

So we come to the last paragraph of the letter. " Finally, brethren, farewell." And the word farewell there does not mean Good-bye. It means, Rejoice. " Finally, brethren, rejoice. Be perfected, be comforted." That takes us back to the opening of the letter in which Paul wrote to the comfort of God, and the comforting of others. " Be of the same mind." That takes us back to the first letter. " Live in peace," and that can only be as there is purity. The Divine order is always, " first, pure " and " then peaceable." " And the God of love and peace shall be with you."

Then follow two local salutations. " Salute one another with a holy kiss. All the saints salute you."

This letter, perhaps with the exception of that to the Galatians, the severest letter we have from the pen of Paul in many ways, ends with the benediction in its fulness. Here is an occasion when we have the full apostolic benediction. " The grace of the Lord Jesus Christ, and the love of God, and the communion of the Holy Ghost, be with you all." The grace of the Lord Jesus Christ. The Lord, that is the word that marks His Divinity; Jesus, that is the word that evidently marks His humanity; Christ, that is the word of His Messiahship. The grace of the Lord Jesus Christ, the One through Whom grace had its epiphany. Paul, when writing to Titus, says, " The grace of God hath appeared," has had its epiphany. I like to transliterate the Greek word. I have said if I had to build a church and name it, I would call it the Church of the Epiphanies, not the Epiphany; and I would base it on that passage in Paul's letter to Titus. The grace of God has had its epiphany, bringing salvation to all men, teaching us, and looking for the epiphany of the glory, the appearing of the glory. It is the same word. The grace of our Lord Jesus Christ through Whom grace had its epiphany, glory will have its epiphany, its outshining, its full manifestation. The grace of our Lord Jesus Christ.

" And the love of God," that deep fountain-head, of which grace is the outward working and manifestation; the God Who so loved the world that He gave His only begotten Son.

" And the communion of the Holy Ghost." The communion and fellowship of the Holy Ghost " be with you all," that through which we enter into relationship with Christ and with God, through Whose activity there is interpreted to us for evermore the things of Christ, and consequently the things of God. That is the great apostolic benediction. It is a marvellous benediction. I am always sorry when anyone changes it in any form or fashion. My reason for objecting to a vesper being sung after the benediction is that I like the benediction to be the last thing in the service. I do not mind a vesper being sung before the benediction. That great apostolic benediction is a wonderful thing. Paul ends his letter with it. It is in the threefold power of the grace of the Lord Jesus Christ, and the love of God, and the fellowship of the Holy Spirit that communion of saints is possible and is perfected. It is through all that is resident within that great benediction that purity is possible and perfected.

So the letter ends. It is not the easiest letter for detailed consideration, but it is a great letter, a sequel to another, the letter that was called forth because some people were disobedient to the first letter; and some were critical of Paul's authority. Not that he cared about himself personally, but that he cared very much about the sacredness of his authority, and its meaning to his children in the faith.

www.ingramcontent.com/pod-product-compliance
Lightning Source LLC
Chambersburg PA
CBHW050434240426
43661CB00055B/2383